MULTIPLE FORMS
OF LITERACY
Teaching Literacy and the Arts

CAROLYN L. PIAZZA
Florida State University

Merrill,
an imprint of Prentice Hall
Upper Saddle River, New Jersey   Columbus, Ohio

Library of Congress Cataloging-in-Publication Data
Piazza, Carolyn L.
     Multiple forms of literacy : teaching literacy and the arts /Carolyn L. Piazza.
         p.   cm.
     Includes bibliographical references and index.
     ISBN 0-13-095503-5
     1. Language arts.   2. Arts—Study and teaching.   3. Literacy.
I. Title.
LB1576.P577   1999
372.6′044—dc21
                                                       98-33602
                                                          CIP

Cover photo: © Wayne Aldridge, International Stock
Editor: Bradley J. Potthoff
Production Editor: Mary M. Irvin
Design Coordinator: Diane C. Lorenzo
Production Coordination and Text Design: Tally Morgan, WordCrafters Editorial
Services Inc.
Cover Designer: Dan Eckel
Production Manager: Pamela D. Bennett
Director of Marketing: Kevin Flanagan
Marketing Manager: Suzanne Stanton
Advertising/Marketing Coordinator: Krista Groshong

This book was set in Bookman by Carlisle Communications, Ltd., and was printed
and bound by R. R. Donnelley & Sons Company. The cover was printed by Phoenix
Color Corp.

© 1999 by Prentice-Hall, Inc.
Simon & Schuster/A Viacom Company
Upper Saddle River, New Jersey 07458

Printed in the United States of America

10 9 8 7 6 5 4 3 2 1

ISBN: 0-13-095503-5

Prentice-Hall International (UK) Limited, *London*
Prentice-Hall of Australia Pty. Limited, *Sydney*
Prentice-Hall of Canada, Inc., *Toronto*
Prentice-Hall Hispanoamericana, S. A., *Mexico*
Prentice-Hall of India Private Limited, *New Delhi*
Prentice-Hall of Japan, Inc., *Tokyo*
Simon & Schuster Asia Pte. Ltd., *Singapore*
Editora Prentice-Hall do Brasil, Ltda., *Rio de Janeiro*

Preface

Since the dawn of recorded history, the visual arts and literacy have gone hand in hand. Early engravings etched on rocks and bones marked the presence of humankind, while drawings and symbols in caves, on pottery, tree bark, animal hides, and stones told stories of battle and warfare, ceremonies, and daily rituals. Using symbols and signs that often blurred the distinction between art and writing, our ancestors documented a visual and phonetic language that unraveled the mysteries of their lives and opened up new texts for future generations to read. Along with the legacy of the visual arts, the human tradition manifested itself in the performing arts as well. Dance enactments of magic rituals and sacrifice, war and peace, and celebrations of harvests and seasons represented the primal beginnings of cross-cultural communication. On cuneiform tablets were some of the first lines of ancient Mesopotamian songs and hymns. Ancient storytellers chanted their tales, making way for the preservation and recording of a rich folklore shaped and handed down through oral tradition.

Fast forwarding in time to the eighteenth and nineteenth centuries, literacy and the arts decidedly manifested themselves as inspirations for one another. Musicians and artists alike were fascinated by European folklore, medieval legends, and heroic or mythical characters. Goethe's *Faust*, for example, a literary and lyrical masterpiece, represented the quintessential hero of Western civilization and became the source of numerous dramas (e.g., the tragedy by playwright Christopher Marlowe), works of art (e.g., Delacroix's "Mephistopheles Appearing to Faust in His Study"), and music (e.g., Schubert's "Gretchen at the Spinning Wheel"). Literature, too, found its counterpart in the arts. Wagner's music-dramas, represented by his monumental opera *The Ring*, a synthesis of sound and story, is a testimony to the intrigue and unbounded imagination that literary sources provide.

In the postmodern world, literacy and the arts continue to provide inspiration and the means by which popular culture takes shape. Contemporary ballets reinterpret some of the traditional fairytales of Perrault and the classics of Beatrix Potter. Novels such as Hugo's *Hunchback of Notre Dame* are made into films. The fluid intermingling of the arts and literacy earmark the twenty-first century with accelerated fervor as the advance of new technologies promises to make even greater demands on our ingenuity for expressing, communicating, representing, and interpreting meanings. It is not enough to be content with motivating students to learn to read a book; they must learn to read the world. Moreover, given the myriad meanings for literacy, it is probably more accurate to speak of "multiple" literacies rather than "a" literacy. This book is for people who recognize that art, music, dance, drama, and film are forms of literacy that play an important role in the development of children's lives, especially in the information age, where more than ever the need exists to shape and express the world in meaningful ways. In short, this book demonstrates how teachers can pay special tribute to the arts as communicative forms that embellish and extend language systems and cast reflected light on the artful features naturally inherent in language and literacy.

Purpose and Content of This Book

The purpose of this book is to extend communicative choices available to students by going beyond language symbols to that of multiple symbol systems offered by "the arts" (visual arts, music, dance, drama, and film, including video, TV, and computer technology). By defining literacy broadly, the possibility exists for specifying a wider range of curricular options that highlight the *arts* in *language arts.* While creative "arts" activities often appear in teachers' magazines or pop up as topics at conferences, they are usually not given thorough coverage in standard language arts texts. This book provides a sound way to integrate the literacies, not as tack-ons but as relevant options for producing and representing meanings. A related, reciprocal outcome of this book is to have children practice and use a wider variety of literacies to enhance and reinforce the traditional language arts: reading, writing, speaking, and listening.

The presentation of *multiple forms of literacy* centers on holistic tasks that include literacy products, process strategies, procedures, and resources. The text unites typical language arts forms (e.g., stories, poetry, and reports) with other expressive or communicative forms of representation (e.g., the arts) to produce a set of hybrid discourses that are mutually dependent on one another for creating meaning. For example, in the chapter on visual literacy you will find a discussion of cartooning, because the humor of cartoons often relies heavily on the combined effectiveness of the picture and the verbal message. Similarly, in the chapter on music literacy you will find a task on songwriting, because the appeal of a popular song relies on the symbiotic relationship between the lyrics and the music.

After the hybrid discourse products are introduced, you are offered a broad range of *inquiry* strategies for shaping and responding to multimedia messages. Each strategy brings with it a fresh and original language for giving advice or asking aesthetic questions about the array of shared *conceptual and stylistic elements* across various literacy forms. For example, shape and movement, or theme and mood, although defined differently for each discipline, are fundamental building blocks in art, music, dance, poetry, and story. This means that students get repeated exposure to the same overlapping concepts or stylistic elements reworked and practiced in a variety of contexts. In addition to strategies for producing and representing ideas, educators also develop their students' abilities to engage in aesthetic response by going beyond the pragmatic function of language to a deeper, expressive function of communication. An aesthetic response brings an artistic stance to experience that arouses the person's intellect and sensibilities and cultivates a fuller and richer transaction with literacy.

Throughout the book, the products and process strategies are embedded in tasks that recognize children's different abilities, talents, needs, learning styles, interests, and cultural background. You will find that the tasks fit nicely into Howard Gardner's framework of multiple intelligences and also address the National Arts Standards (1994) and NCTE/IRA Standards (1996). If instructors of language arts methods courses wish to conceptualize their literacy programs along either of these lines, Appendices A and B will help in getting started. In this book, however, we consider a communicative perspective as the governing gaze with which to account for multiple literacies (see Chapter 1). The way in which this book is organized for your use is discussed next.

Organization of This Book

The first chapter presents a classroom vignette, defines multiple literacies, and outlines the theoretical framework that substantiates the approach taken in the book. After the first chapter, the others follow a similar format. Each begins with a classroom vignette that shows how teachers and students integrate literacies and apply them in ways that enrich understandings of communication. Following the vignette are five major strands that organize the multiple literacy tasks. The tasks in the first two strands, the inquiry and languaging strands, are fluid and easily woven into the others. The last three strands represent specific genres that are recognizable in both text and talk (e.g., the story, poetry, or information strands).

◆ Inquiry strand: In this strand we focus on process strategies for helping children form ideas in pictures, images, rhythms, gestures, and movement. Cumulatively, these strategies underscore the importance of diverse "ways of knowing and responding" to the world.

◆ Languaging strand: In this strand we interpret a myriad of symbol systems for expressing ideas. Whether used alone or in combination, pictures, sounds, rhythms, movement, nonverbal actions, camera angles, or electronic images convey information and point of view.

◆ Poetry strand: In this strand we consider multiple ways of producing, performing, representing, and interpreting poetic verse. We discuss sample questions and aesthetic elements that emphasize the artistry in poems.

◆ Story strand: In this strand we experiment with multiple ways of producing, performing, representing, and interpreting stories.

Included in this strand are arts-inspired tasks and narrative strategies for exploring various kinds of stories.

◆ Information strand: In this strand we consider multiple ways of producing, performing, representing, and interpreting information from a creative and critical perspective. We also study important auxilliary information for enhancing and extending literacy lessons.

The section on school–community links that appears near the end of each chapter makes a strong case for moving learning experiences outward to the community. Teachers and students have much to gain by working with arts experts. Although school and community organizations may have their own distinct philosophies and aims, they also have overlapping goals and outcomes. Collaborative partnerships provide opportunities for children to participate in a variety of educational and community affairs with the help of role models and volunteers.

Each chapter concludes with professional development activities that inspire the creative teaching of multiple literacies in the classroom. The act of creation engages all of us. Teachers who weave the arts into their own experiences will gain firsthand insight into the communicative power of the literacies. At the end of the book is a postscript that extends our discussion of multiple literacies by offering sample thematic units to try out in the elementary classroom.

Suggestions for Using This Book

Because teachers are always looking for new ways to engage students in the communicative process, this book places traditional language arts content within a broad communicative framework that includes the arts as alternative forms of meaning making. Each chapter is comprised of literacy tasks, arranged in strands that unite language with one or more of the arts. Within each task are descriptions of literacy products that guide the process strategies (and response techniques) that children select and use. The classroom activities that embrace these products and process strategies are not prescriptions per se but illustrative examples or choices for augmenting the traditional reading and language arts methods course. With minimal adaptation, the tasks are suitable for students of any age. Each chapter can stand independently, allowing instructors to present the content in a manner that matches their preferences and classroom needs. Arrangement by art form makes it easy to pick and choose sections at will to incorporate into the overall course organization and planned syllabus. One way to use this book is to cut across each of the chapters *horizontally* to locate a single literacy strand and develop it using all the arts. For example, let's suppose you are doing a unit on stories. You might want to select tasks from the story strand of each chapter. Students would interpret stories through artwork and picture cues (art literacy chapter), select mood music to accompany story action and conflict (music literacy chapter), perform movement phrases to interpret the story (dance literacy chapter), enact and dramatize the story (theater literacy chapter), and translate the story into a movie (film literacy chapter). Going across the chapters horizontally would not only provide a well-rounded view of story but also a medley of inquiry options and symbolic forms (inquiry and languaging strands) to incorporate into these strands.

Another way to use the book is in a *vertical* fashion, skimming down a single chapter to select a particular conceptual or stylistic element that students might practice within each strand. For example, let's say that you are introducing the concepts of rhythm and beat. Since the music literacy chapter seems like an obvious place to start, you might go to it, select tasks from each strand—language beats and sound play from the language strand, a rap from the poetry strand, and advertising jingles from the information strand—and have students practice rhythm and beat as they appear in different discourse forms. In this way, as students shift their skills across genres, they engage in a kind of flexible thinking to define and redefine concepts.

You might also consider combining and assembling literacy tasks within and across chapters to develop themes that integrate multiple literacies across the curriculum. In Chapter 1, Mrs. Smith's fifth-graders study medieval times by reading the Bayeux tapestry (visual literacy), by writing a troubadour's ballad about courtly love and chivalry (music literacy), by interpreting the commoners' life through peasant dances (dance literacy), and by performing and filming the dramas of Robin Hood (theater and film literacy). These multiple literacy tasks summon the use of visual thinking, composing, aesthetic response, story interpretations, and critical viewing using students' diverse talents and predilections for learning. If you are interested in organizing literacy tasks in this way, you might turn to the postscript at the end of the book for examples of thematic units that pull it all together.

All of the tasks included in the book are inspired by an appreciation for our rich communicative heritage in all its marvelous forms. Whether using the tasks alone or in combination, imaginative teachers will find many clever ways to engage students in exploring their own visions and creative landscapes.

Audiences for This Book

Designed as a supplementary resource, this book is appropriate for a diverse audience. Undergraduates can use it to accompany a core language arts text. Graduates and practicing teachers will find it a valuable resource for an in-service course, upper-level language arts course, or graduate seminar (such as the integrated curriculum). The book challenges classroom teachers to seriously address the new standards on viewing and representing literacy by collaborating with arts specialists in the schools and community. Similarly, arts specialists will find this book a good starting place for building partnerships with the classroom teacher. When the book is used as a bridge for exchanging ideas and working on shared goals, it has the potential to provide a higher level of pedagogical mastery for everyone involved. Finally, I hope people who love language and the arts and who enjoy working artfully will find this book a useful resource to add to their personal libraries.

Acknowledgments

I want to acknowledge my appreciation to my family for their constant support and encouragement along the way. I especially want to express gratitude to my mother, who inspired a love of language and the arts in all her children. Thanks also to my colleague, Cynthia Wallat, whose advice and guidance I cherish, and to my editor, Brad Potthoff, and his assistant, Mary Evangelista, whose editorial guidance and counsel were invaluable during the progress of this book. Finally, special thanks to the reviewers who read the manuscript and offered valuable suggestions: Thomas W. Bean, University of Nevada Las Vegas; Ruth Beeker, University of Arizona; Susan M. Blair-Larsen, The College of New Jersey; Ward A. Cockrum, Northern Arizona University; Laurie Elish-Piper, Northern Illinois University; Sheila Fitzgerald, Michigan State University, Retired; Barbara Illig-Aviles, Duquesne University; Donna J. Merkley, Iowa State University; William J. Oehlkers, Rhode Island College; and David G. Petkosh, Cabrini College.

Contents

Chapter 5   **Theater Literacy: Performing Language**   **145**

Introduction: The Literacies

Vignette: Medieval Magic

In Mrs. Smith's fifth-grade class, children are studying the medieval period. The teacher plans to use multiple literacies as tools for discovering the rich history, culture, and social customs of the period and for showing the class how to construct meaning from a wide array of communicative possibilities.

The first group of students read pictures of the Bayeux tapestry, an embroidered linen that chronicles the bitter war between King Harold of England and the Duke of Normandy in 1066. In visually attractive panels, which in the original stretch 230 feet long and 20 inches wide, the tapestry documents visual details of weapons (arches and arrows), protective clothing (metal helmets and mail shorts), battles and armies, travel routes, chivalry, and daily life. Viewing key panels projected overhead and replicated from the book The Bayeux Tapestry *(Denny and Filmer-Sankey, 1966), children compile lists of what they see and classify the items into categories (e.g., clothing, foreign words, animals, symbols, feelings, etc.). They ask and respond to questions about the tapestry to form hypotheses about its story, which subsequently guide the search for information that will confirm or refute their hunches. Based on the findings, they refine or reinterpret the story before sharing it with the rest of the class.*

The second group of students write and sing troubadour ballads. The troubadour's ballad was a short narrative folk story sung orally by minstrels and bards of Europe in the Middle Ages. Usually, the bards were simple folk who told of legends or history in song accompanied by a lute, a stringed instrument with a delicate sound. The most famous of the ballads of the Middle Ages dealt with courtly love. To find out about the rules of courtly love, children search the Internet for information. At the music center, some children listen to Anonymous 4, an international music group that sings medieval ballads. The lyrics translated from French to English help them understand the relationship between the troubadour and the maiden to whom he is singing. The music, which conveys feelings of love through tones and simple melodies, communicates poetic messages that transcend language and the limits of consciousness. The children decide to write their own ballads, which they put to familiar music and sing to the class.

The third group of students interpret and present the daily life of medieval peasants and commoners through movement and dance. The children consider typical chores and duties of medieval townsfolk and try out movement sequences to portray them (e.g., working in the fields, sewing and mending, building and repairing). The village peasants enjoyed merrymaking in the streets to celebrate life's important events: marriages, new friends, religious holidays, and the like. After consulting books about medieval times, the children decide to interpret A Medieval Feast *(Aliki, 1983a) and* A Medieval Wedding *(Aliki, 1983b) in dance and movement.*

The fourth group of students performs a morality play to portray the values of the commoners and royalty. The morality play, often performed by guilds in the town square and produced on pageants (rolled wagon-stages), dramatized moral themes such as the conflict between good and evil (Fiero, 1995). Children decide that The Adventures of Robin Hood and His Merry Outlaws *(McSpadden, 1984) makes good play material for revealing and enacting the conscience, ideals, and ethics of common folk in medieval Europe. To get ideas for developing the play, they view* Robin Hood *movies (e.g.,* Robin Hood: Men in Tights, *1993;* Robin Hood: Prince of Thieves, *1991;* Robin Hood, *1991).*

These group projects, designed as part of the medieval unit, utilize multiple forms of literacy to hypothesize and confirm predictions about pictures, music and its lyrics, movement interpretations, dramatic actions, and film images. Multiple channels or mediums of communication serve not only as a springboard for constructing knowledge, but also as a resource for acquiring communication skills and presenting information in forms for public scrutiny.

Placing language arts within a wider communicative context is an idea endorsed by professional organizations such as the National Council of Teachers of English (NCTE, 1996). A modern-day literacy program, they argue, should offer students many opportunities to develop and represent ideas and messages in many different forms by going beyond oral and written language.

In the chapters that follow, you will examine in further detail how multiple literacy tasks can reinforce new standards and augment traditional competencies in reading, writing, listening, and speaking. These tasks emphasize the dynamic interplay of literacy and the arts and draw on strategies and resources that include many different symbol systems (alphabetic, pictorial, gestural) and communicative channels (aural, kinesthetic, visual) for carrying meaning. Throughout the book we refer to this array of communicative possibilities as multiple literacies.

WHAT ARE MULTIPLE LITERACIES?

The term *multiple literacies* refers to the complex amalgam of communicative channels, symbols, forms, and meanings inherent in oral and written language (verbal and nonverbal) as well as the arts—visual arts, music, dance, theater, and film (including television, video, and technology). One way to think about multiple literacies is to consider language and the arts as *inquiry*, the systematic process of forming ideas. Although linguistic inquiry is an important starting point in this book, the visual arts offer ways to ask questions and respond to ideas and feelings in terms of colors, lines, movements, rhythms, textures, or perspectives. Music and dance suggest ways to hear and express ideas in tones, sounds, rhythms, distance, and space. Drama, film, and modern technology chart ways to invent and represent meanings in terms of images and point of view.

Another way to think about multiple literacies is to consider them as *multimodal forms of representation* or mixed varieties of meaning-making, shaped and presented in different ways. Eisner (1981), a well-known educator and supporter of the arts, reminds us that "the realm of meaning has many mansions" (p. 52). He maintains that people possess a dynamic range of communicative and expressive talents for meaning-making and expression. While each communicative form illuminates its own particular means for conveying a message, there are unlimited possibilities for joining language with the arts to create a hybrid or combined product that is more than the sum of its parts. A good example of this is producing a TV commercial. Advertising is often a thoughtful mix of words, music, art, dramatic props, and nonverbal messages, all effectively presented in a film composition that imprints a particular perspective and message on the consumer's mind.

Finally, we can think about multiple literacies as an array of *conceptual and stylistic elements* that people use to create powerful products and aesthetic messages. Not surprisingly, multiple forms of literacy share features with one another. For example, music and poetry share rhythm, texture, and beat just as some paintings and picture books share themes, portraits, plots, and conflict. Alliteration and onomatopoeia bring sounds to words in poetry just as volume and timing bring life to musical notes or costumes and design bring flair to dance. The conceptual and stylistic elements that each "artist" chooses allows us to view, question, and respond to our subjective knowing, personal preferences and values, emotional pleasures, and ideals of beauty and truth. Unveiling the various ways that the arts and literacy concepts overlap expands their creative utility and demonstrates their unique relevance to one another. Thinking about multiple literacies in all these ways is fundamental to conceptualizing a theoretical framework for the book.

A COMMUNICATIVE PERSPECTIVE

Based on our definitions of multiple literacies, the tasks in this book require an expansive set of communicative choices dependent on the kind of product or form of representation being created by whom and for what purpose. Given a particular product and aim, a person will determine what stylistic choices to make and what inquiry processes to follow. For example, let's suppose that an artist, musician, and linguist are studying a tree. The artist, who wants to paint a picture, is likely to see and observe the tree, attending to stylistic elements of color, lines, texture, and shape. The musician, composing a musical score, might engage the aural senses to hear the motion and rhythms of the tree, and the linguist, creating a nature poem, is likely to brainstorm words and phrases to structure ideas in print. Although all of the artists involve themselves in a creative process and develop unique products, each has his or her own preferred means and symbols for doing so. A governing gaze that entertains the notion of multiple literacies must therefore be broader than language and account for many different sounds, signs (gestures), and symbols for constructing and interpreting meaning (Barthes, 1967; Bruner, 1966; Gardner, 1993; Greene, 1991; Vygotsky, 1962, 1978). It should frame *conceptual and stylistic elements* that overlap, defining them in context specific ways. Above all, it should take into account a repertoire of inquiry strategies for inventing ideas and extending communicative possibilities. A communicative perspective (Kinneavy, 1980; Moffett, 1987) that takes all of these into consideration can be summarized as:

Who
says what to whom,
for what purposes,
where, and
in what channel?

This means that the communicative perspective can be said to consist of five communicative elements, including sender (who), receiver (to whom), message (what and for what purpose), context (where), and medium (in what channel). A *sender* (whether a speaker, writer, artist, musician, dancer, actor, or actress) is one who produces a *message* (artwork, text, speech, gestures, musical score, play, composition, or electronic image with a particular purpose for a *receiver* (audience, viewer, listener, or implied reader). The *receiver* looks for signs and signals in the *message* that they can interpret. Often, this interpretive frame connects to previous experiences or is tied to conventions shared by a sender and receiver. The *medium,* or channel of expression—ranging from words and print symbols (language) to paints and sculpture (art) to musical notes and instruments (music) to gestures and movement (dance) to props (drama) to images (film)—provides symbolic meanings, while the *context* frames meaning and provides cues to interpretations (Cazden, 1988; Erickson and Shultz, 1981; Green and Weade, 1987; Mishler, 1979). The context can be as conspicuous as a place or situation (e.g., museum, rock concert) or as transparent as the moment-to-moment interactions that emerge between people and symbols (e.g., conversations, moods, impressions, or responses). Table 1-1 summarizes these elements using the literacies discussed in the opening vignette.

TABLE 1–1   Elements of a Communicative Event

Who (Sender)	What (Message or Purpose)	In Which Channel (Medium)	To Whom (Receiver or Audience)	Where (Context)
Anonymous artist	Battle of Hastings story	Woven linen tapestry 230 feet long and 20 inches wide	Unknown; viewers today	England; today's classroom; art gallery
Troubadours	Ballads; songs of courtly love and chivalry	Music played on lute	Kings and queens; maidens; peasants; listeners today	Royal courts; streets; hamlets; villages; today's concert halls; outdoor festivals
Dancers; peasants	Folk dances	Music; clothing; movements; gestures	Townsfolk; today's students	Hamlets; streets; villages; today's theaters
Actors and actresses	Filmed drama; adventures of Robin Hood	Camera angles; dialogue; props; costumes; movements	Class; movie buffs; theater goers	Today's stage and movie theaters; school assemblies

As we proceed through each chapter you may wish to consider these communicative elements as they pertain to the multiple literacy tasks that are introduced. However, in actual practice, the elements are not explicitly stated in theoretical terms but are embedded in the questions and practices that are used by teachers and children. Let's consider the visual arts example (Figure 1-1) to show how observation and questioning implicitly tap into the communicative framework. As you view and construct meanings for the painting by Winslow Homer, note the communicative elements (in parentheses) which guide the content of the questions.

◆ What do you see? How does this work make you feel? *(receiver)*
◆ What features make you feel this way? *(medium; context)*
◆ What is the theme or content of Homer's work? *(message)*
◆ What artistic elements contribute to the theme? *(medium; message)*

- What is the impact of this work? What does it mean to you? *(purpose; receiver)*
- What do you know about the artist and his or her work from external sources? *(context)*

Homer's *Country School*

Winslow Homer's painting *The Country School* (Figure 1-1), is being exhibited at a museum near your home. You attend the opening and observe the way the curators have arranged the works of art. The space around the paintings, the filtered lighting in the room with spotlights on the artwork, the classical music being played in the background, and the quiet hum of voices are all part of the situational *context*. As you approach Homer's painting, you enter into yet another *context*, that of a country classroom with rows of benches and unpainted wooden floors. The schoolroom seems simple and austere, yet warmed by sunlight. The subject of the painting is a young female school teacher, whose body posture and position suggests a sense of authority and control. Dressed in a simple black frock covered with an apron, her hair pulled up in a chignon, the teacher stands before a handful of children who seem comfortably engaged in reading: everyone, that is, except for a whimpering child, whose tears don't seem to be attracting much attention from the others.

Figure 1–1 *The Country School. Winslow Homer (1871).* Reproduced by permission of the Saint Louis Art Museum.

While Winslow Homer's *message* confers a quiet, contemplative classroom, it is not just a mood story that the scene portrays but rather a glimpse into Homer's relationship with his own society and institutions. It tells us about the way in which teachers and students might have interacted, the norms of society, and a particular moment in history. If a viewer knows about Homer's life and work, they bring even more contextual background to the painting. Knowing that Homer was born and raised in Cambridge, Massachusetts, the birthplace of the common school, suggests that Homer may have had intimate knowledge of the one-room schoolhouse. During this time period (the late nineteenth century), Protestant values and morals pervaded the common school, where teaching was considered respectable employment for women. Knowing also that Winslow Homer did freelance illustrations for *Harper's Weekly* helps us to understand the crisp detail of portraits, the light, and the shadows, and the realism recorded in his subject matter. It was also about this time that the camera was invented. Contemporary social conditions could now be recorded easily; painting could appear almost like photographs. This, too, is reflected in Homer's work.

The *medium* is a set of signals or a communicative channel that delivers meaning and provides cues to interpretation. In Homer's painting, the medium—oil on canvas—contrasts light and dark in two or three tones to achieve an air of simplicity. Perhaps the size of the painting (21 3\8 by 38 3\8 inches) also signifies a certain amount of constraint and concentrated silence. The *viewer/receiver* reads all these messages and constructs meanings from them. The key to reading or interpreting a communicative event, then, is to understand the relationships and interactions among its basic elements. Table 1-2 summarizes these interpretations. The elements of this perspective, implicit in all the tasks outlined in this book, are like a kaleidoscope: They are shaped in different ways and have different interpretations based on the elements that are assembled.

A communicative perspective will be the implicit departure point for the creative teaching of multiple literacies. Such a perspective will help the teacher recognize similarities and overlapping questions across the literacies and attend to multiple communicative channels for building and representing meanings.

LOOKING AHEAD

In the chapters ahead you will see how multiple literacy tasks bring together the artful nature of language with the creative inspiration and expression of the arts (visual art, music, dance, drama, and film, including television, video, and technology). These chapters, designed to extend and reinforce the language arts, build on Gardner's multiple intelligences and address the national standards of literacy and the arts (see Appendices A and B). In the postscript you will find thematic units that illustrate how to assemble the literacy tasks to address content across the curricula.

TABLE 1–2 Communicative Elements of Homer's Work

Who (Sender)	What (Message or Purpose)	In Which Channel (Medium)	To Whom (Receiver or Audience)	Where (Context)
Winslow Homer	*Content of Painting:* presents schooldays in the late nineteenth century; reflects the life of the artist; suggests social norms and conditions	*Nature of Painting:* size of artwork; oil painting; portraitures	*Viewers:* children; teacher; art critic	*Places:* museum; country schoolroom *Environment:* music; filtered light; spacing; spotlights; arrangement of pictures

The remaining chapters in this book follow a singular format. Each chapter highlights one particular form of literacy (art, music, dance, theater, or film) for you to practice and build into the traditional language arts curriculum (see the Preface). A vignette opens the chapter and offers a glimpse into a classroom where a teacher uses a product–process approach for teaching literacy tasks. A product–process approach suggests that you consider the necessary features of a task and written product (including purpose and audience) and then select strategies and resources accordingly. In other words, a product–process approach gives equal attention to the product that is being produced and the process strategies and resources necessary to produce it.

Following the vignette are multiple literacy tasks (consisting of literacy products, strategies, and resources) that can easily be adapted for children of all ages. The literacy tasks are organized into five strands. The first strand, inquiry, emphasizes a variety of process strategies for forming ideas and responding critically to various literacy products. The second strand, languaging, introduces the many symbolic forms that communication takes: words, sentences, and paragraphs; the language of movement, camera talk and messages in pictures, rhythms, colors, and patterns. Although these two strands can be used as literacy tasks in and of themselves, their main function is to help the literacy learner invent ideas and use different symbols (alphabetic, pictorial, gestural) for communication. The remaining strands—poetry, story, and information—apply the inquiry and languaging strands to create products that use special conceptual and stylistic elements to serve particular purposes and audiences.

Each chapter ends with a section on school–community links and activities for professional development. Through partnerships and apprenticeships with experts in the community, teachers widen and complete the circle of learning for themselves and their students.

◆ *Works Cited*

Professional References

Barthes, R. (1967). *Elements of semiology* (trans. A. Lavers and C. Smith). New York: Hill & Wang.

Bruner, J. (1966). *Toward a theory of instruction.* Cambridge, MA: Harvard University Press.

Cazden, C. B. (1988). *Classroom discourse.* Portsmouth, NH: Heinemann.

Eisner, E. (1981). *The role of discipline-based art education in America's schools.* Santa Monica, CA: Getty Trust Publications.

Erickson, F., and Shultz, J. (1981). When is a context? Some issues and methods in the analysis of social competence. In J. Green and C. Wallat (Eds.), *Ethnography and language in educational settings* (pp. 147–160). Norwood, NJ: Ablex Publishing.

Fiero, G. (1995). *Medieval Europe and the world beyond.* Madison, WI: Brown & Benchmark.

Gardner, H. (1993). *Frames of mind: The theory of multiple intelligences,* 10th anniv. ed. New York: Basic Books.

Green, J., and Weade, R. (1987). In search of meaning: A sociolinguistic perspective on lesson construction and reading. In D. Bloome (Ed.), *Literacy and schooling* (pp. 3–34). Norwood, NJ: Ablex Publishing.

Greene, M. (1991). Texts and margins. *Harvard Educational Review, 61,* 27–39.

Kinneavy, J. (1980). *A theory of discourse: The aims of discourse.* New York: W. W. Norton (original work published in 1971).

Mishler, E. (1979). Meaning in context: Is there any other kind? *Harvard Educational Review, 49,* 1–19.

Moffett, J. (1987). *Teaching the universe of discourse.* Portsmouth, NH: Boynton/Cook.

National Council of Teachers of English (1996). *Standards for the English language arts.* Urbana, IL: NCTE.

Vygotsky, L. (1962). *Thought and language.* Cambridge, MA: MIT Press.

Vygotsky, L. (1978). *Mind in society.* Cambridge, MA: Harvard University Press.

Children's References

Aliki (1983a). *A medieval feast.* New York: HarperCollins.

Aliki (1983b). *A medieval wedding.* New York: HarperCollins.

Denny, N., and Filmer-Sankey, J. (1966). *The Bayeux tapestry.* New York: Atheneum Books.

McSpadden, J. W. (1984). *The adventures of Robin Hood and his merry outlaws.* New York: Greenwich House.

Art Literacy: Visualizing Language

Vignette: *Tar Beach*

The children in Mr. Jones' second-grade class are getting ready to study storywriting using narrative texts of prose and art. Mr. Jones begins by showing children a large art reproduction of Faith Ringgold's story quilt Tar Beach (which is housed and displayed at the Guggenheim Museum in New York). The quilt (Figure 2-1) shows adults and children up on top of an apartment roof with a tar floor. It is summertime and the children are lying on a mattress with pillows looking up into the sky while a little girl is flying over the George Washington Bridge of New York. At another place on the quilt are four adults playing cards. Nearby is a table covered with a blue polka-dot tablecloth, and on it is watermelon, fried chicken, and drinks. Stitched around the border of the quilt are the words of the story, Tar Beach.

Mr. Jones asks children to describe what they see in the visual reproduction of the work. How does this work make you feel? What do the colors, shapes, borders, textures, and repetitions communicate to you? Explain whether or not you think Ringgold is a storyteller. Children read the words stitched around the border of the quilt. Mr. Jones asks: How do the words fit together with the picture?

Next, Mr. Jones reads the picture book Tar Beach (Ringgold, 1991). Children compare the art print with the picture-book version. "Do you like seeing the story all at once, or do you prefer reading it in parts as sequenced in the book?" asks Mr. Jones. "How does the author illustrate her work in the book?" When the discussion ends, Mr. Jones tells the children about the author and artist, Faith Ringgold, who grew up in Harlem in the 1930s. In her biography, Ringgold reveals the prejudices that existed toward African-Americans during this time. The child in her art symbolizes a little girl's dream of flying and changing things for her family. It is a message of joy and hope.

The children learn that Ringgold is a major American artist and that she creates not only quilts but murals, paintings, abstract works, masks, and soft sculptures. Ringgold introduced the "art performance," in which she displayed and enacted her work. This personal history prompts the children to go back to the quilt to read it again, this time focusing on the interplay of words and art as they reflect the details and meanings of Ringgold's life and work.

Figure 2-1 *Tar Beach*. Faith Ringgold. Reproduced by permission of Faith Ringgold Inc.

At this point the children want to create their own story quilt. They begin by visualizing ideas, brainstorming, and sketching their own story line: What will happen? Who will be there? What will the characters be doing? What colors, textures, lines, and gestures will help convey this information? How will borders be used to communicate? What word, symbol, phrase, or story will be added to their quilts? Children sketch a design or picture on individual oaktag quilt blocks made from a predrawn square template. They lay out the quilt blocks on a storyboard, number the blocks on the back in the order desired, and then write their stories across the blocks, along the borders, or in any other decorative outline or direction. The blocks are hole-punched. Before sewing the blocks together with yarn, children laminate the quilt blocks, bringing out the colors and designs and providing durability. When the paper story quilts are completed, Mr. Jones invites parents and the community to attend a showing of the children's story quilts.

Story quilts are only one of many art forms that can be used in the literacy classroom. Ringgold's work is particularly noteworthy because she combines narrative text with fabric to weave a rich story to be read both visually and verbally. The children in Mr. Jones' class are learning to "read" the story quilt, a unique kind of text that uses language and other symbol systems of color, texture, words, and fabric to form pictures and communicate meanings. Background information about the artist, Faith Ringgold, offers children a context in which to make inferences and interpretations about the artwork. Whether reading graphic designs, images, ancient pictographs, or tapestries such as the Bayeux tapestry discussed in Chapter 1, children should be given opportunities to critically interpret various forms of visual expression. In this chapter you will learn more about how to help children become producers and interpreters of aesthetic "texts." For our purposes, we define aesthetic texts as artistic literacy forms that bring appreciation, beauty, and richness to the human experience.

The chapter begins with ways of thinking in pictures and language. It then goes on to introduce several combined art and literacy forms that can be added to the language arts curriculum.

INQUIRY STRAND: SEEING IDEAS

Marcel Proust, a French novelist of the twentieth century, once said that "the voyage of discovery lies not in finding new landscapes, but in having new eyes." Observing with an open eye and "seeing" and thinking along different paths prepare students for the array of literacy forms they can discover and enjoy. In this strand, children rely on the visual channel to think beyond the word to that of colors, shapes, lines, movement, balance, and textures. To see an idea stretches children's imagination and stimulates new ways of knowing and responding to the world (Berger, 1985; Gardner, 1993). As an aesthetic choice that children make, the visual channel complements linguistic thinking and provides a flexible option for creating and presenting ideas. Although you can use any of the tasks in this section independently, here they are employed as strategies to be included in any number of literacy tasks in this chapter and throughout the book.

The Writer's Scrapbook

Students keep a writer's scrapbook of special events to document a stream of memories that combine visual and verbal images. They place "clippings," postcards, photos, and other memorabilia in these books and sketch thoughts and brief statements about the images and artifacts. Using these scrapbooks to heighten the meanings of events in their lives helps them observe and take stock of their social interests and personal growth. When children need ideas for writing, they share the scrapbooks with peers, query the authors about their collections, and make observations about the contents and arrangements. The teacher introduces the idea of a scrapbook by sharing family albums, artist sketchbooks, and other keepsakes of writers, such as *The Writer's Drawing Book* (Pullinger and Rothenstein, 1995), an amusing collection of art completed by some of the world's best writers. The children's book *Mouse's Scrapbook* (Carlidge, 1995) sparks interest in keeping a scrapbook and shows what kinds of articles to place in it. Table 2-1 offers additional suggestions for collecting items to begin a writer's scrapbook.

As the collections are being put together, the students can respond to one another by asking questions such as:

◆ How did you get interested in this?

◆ What memories come to mind as you look at this?

◆ Tell me a story about one of your objects. How did you come to acquire it?

◆ Where were you when you located it? Who was with you?

Dream Diaries

Day- and nighttime dreams are a way to recognize the importance of imagination, fantasy, and "what if's." A dreaming mind moves from association to association, some in color, some in sound or smell, and some in visual images. With a little coaching, children can learn to capture the details of a dream or learn to quiet the mind so that ideas flow and wander. The dream diary is a repository for ideas that capture fleeting thoughts, free associations, partial ideas, and picture images. Collecting and remembering bits of dreams or ideas (whether a symbol, picture, color, perception, or action) may be an ideal way to create an interesting new twist to ordinary

TABLE 2–1   Scrapbook Memorabilia

◆ Collect favorite things. Include sketches and drawings, photos, art prints, and magazine pictures. Save tokens from places visited and enjoyed (a menu from a place you like to eat, ticket stubs from a great movie, or advertisements of your favorite toys).

◆ Collect sensory words and colorful reminiscences. Capture bits and pieces of conversation, create word images of travel or faraway places, write descriptions of objects, and collect sensory words: soft words, color words, texture words, or any other tactile impressions.

◆ Collect small artistic objects. Keep samples of ribbon, glitter dust, confetti, or swatches of fabric to show colors you like. Tack on pretty buttons or seashells, dried flowers, or colorful beads. Decorate with rubber stamps and stickers.

◆ Collect decorative stationary or greeting cards (e.g., valentines). Find samples of designs or letterheads to add a visual impact to invitations, personal letters, poetry, name tags, place cards, or any other festive type of writing.

◆ Collect computer clip art. Make a "sampler" of favorite emblems, pictures, or letter fonts. Find logos on letterheads, address labels, or other personalized correspondence.

◆ Collect worldwide stamps related to favorite books. For instance, the British, Swiss, and Australians have a collection specifically for children's book classics. In Switzerland, for example, you find *Heidi* and *Pippi Longstocking,* among others. In Sweden, you find *Pelle's New Suit.* Italy has stamps of *Pinocchio,* and Canada has stamps of Lucy Maud Montgomery's *Anne of Green Gables.* There are also stamps that honor children's book authors or illustrators. Go to your post office and find out more.

events or to adorn a piece of writing with added excitement or mystery (Armstrong, 1993; Bradbury, 1990; Dee, 1984). For example, witness how a recorded set of images, written in the first person, can be changed easily to third-person story narrative.

Diary Entry

A rush of waters crash and flow. Watching from a log above the falls. Below, white water coursing in all directions, pushing through rocks for an outlet. I'm noticing the rise and fall of my chest, a fly darting about, the heat of the sun on my arms. The sun is just atop the overhanging foliage—green leaves in motion against blue sky. The foaming river rushes up against a large brown boulder. . . .

Narrative

A rush of waters crashed and flowed. Jenny watched from a log above the falls. Below, white water coursed in all directions, pushing through rocks for an outlet. Jenny, too, was testing for direction. As she watched the foaming river rush up against a large boulder, she thought of Peter. Could she wear away his resistance?

Shaw (1980, pp. 5–6)

As these selections illustrate, thinking in images and vivid details stirs the senses and encourages use of narrative techniques. Teachers might introduce the dream diary as a source of inspiration by reading the collection of poems called *The Morgans' Dream* (Singer, 1995), in which the reader travels through the world of sleep and private dreams of the Morgan family. James (1990) tells about a little girl's dreams and hopes for the future in *The Dream Stair,* and Garrison (1986) explores the Japanese folktale *The Dream Eater,* in which a child meets a creature who eats bad dreams. Children can share their ideas about the books and then discuss them from a writer's perspective:

◆ How does the author show the dream and make it seem real?

◆ What language devices does the author use to show a character moving in and out of dreams?

◆ What are some characteristics of dreams? (illogical? distorted? exaggerated?)

As a way to begin writing, students explore their own dreams and free associations. They ask questions that capture the dynamic imagery, magic, and action of dreams, such as:

◆ What did the dream remind me of?

◆ If my dream were something else, what would it be? (an animal? a poem?)

◆ Would it speak in colors? sentences? music?

◆ In my dream, are there details I should notice? (e.g., a water stain on the ceiling?)

◆ How was I feeling during this dream? What was I doing?

Doodling Print Forms

Doodles are a kind of visual note-taking that incorporate writing and artful scribbles to create a versatility in writing and art (Dyson, 1989; Gardner, 1980; Goodnow, 1983; Kellogg, 1970; Zalusky, 1983). Children experiment and play using space to move physically on paper (of various sizes, shapes, colors, and textures). They also select different writing implements (pencils, pen, magic markers, charcoal, pen and ink, crayons) to make their marks. As Figure 2-2 illustrates, doodling can lead to creative discovery.

◆ What comes to your mind when you look at your doodles?

◆ What would you consider to be happy lines, angry lines, crazy lines, peaceful lines?

◆ Which of your lines are diagonal, vertical, horizontal, circular, or have other recognizable shapes?

Figure 2-2 *Ideas in Doodles*

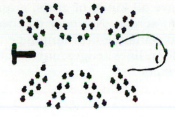

Porcupine

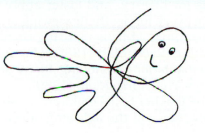

Happy lines

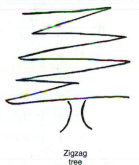

Zigzag
tree

- ◆ Which of your doodles show patterns, designs, contrast (tall/short), texture (smooth/jagged), or overlap?
- ◆ What pictures, images, feelings, or stories are evident in your doodles?

These questions lead children to speculate about the way that lines and patterns create images and emotions. For those who are not doodlers, yet anxious to play with design visually, the computer's graphic tool bars come in handy. Special computer art packages such as Broderbund's "The

Print Shop Deluxe" have all kinds of grids, graphics, and letter fonts for children to "doodle" on screen. Not only do these activities foster visual thinking but they also reinforce oral language as children describe patterns, alignments, colors, lines, edges, intersections, frames, sequences, or pictures they have made.

Aesthetic Viewing

Aesthetic viewing is a way of seeing and attending based on what we choose to see, what assumptions we make, what experiences we have encountered previously, and where we are situated in time and space. Viewing and responding to visual images can make children better observers, inspire ideas for literacy, and foster appreciation for many styles of artwork. Using artwork for aesthetic viewing and response helps children identify cues to meaning, while sensitizing them to what they are seeing, feeling, and thinking (Rosenblatt, 1985). Have children view and interpret works of art as a basis for developing literacy. Figure 2-3 is a reproduction of van Gogh's *The Starry Night* (1889).

The teacher helps children construct an interpretation of the painting by asking some of the following questions:

- ◆ What do you see? (e.g., swirls, stars, village, trees?)
- ◆ What kinds of lines create the sky? Are these lines quiet or active? Are they thick or thin? (e.g., long, thick brush strokes?)
- ◆ How would you describe the colors of the painting? (e.g., vibrant, cool, cheerful, melancholy?)
- ◆ What do you think about this place?
- ◆ What do the cypress trees remind you of? (e.g., flames?)
- ◆ Is this a calm painting or a dynamic one?
- ◆ If this were a piece of music, what would it be?
- ◆ Is this painting real or imaginary? both?

The children discuss these and other visual graphic questions. Then they pursue their study of van Gogh and his works, returning to the painting with new insights and comments. A popular videodisk by Voyager Company and a CD by Educational Resources ("Vincent van Gogh") focus on the artist. Also available are books such as the Metropolitan Museum's *What Makes a van Gogh . . . a van Gogh?* (Muhlberger, 1993b), and the World's Greatest Art Series, *van Gogh* (Venezia, 1988).

Paintings such as *The Starry Night* provide a powerful impetus for writing stories or poems. They also offer literacy contexts for practicing techniques such as point of view, description, or metaphor. For example, to practice these literacy techniques in van Gogh's *Starry Night,* children might imagine themselves standing at some place in the picture (consider-

Figure 2-3 *The Starry Night.* Vincent van Gogh, (1889). Reproduced by permission of The Museum of Modern Art.

ing what is in front of them, behind them, to their sides, or in the distance). They might imagine what it feels like in van Gogh's setting or what they might be doing if they were "in" this picture. When they look at the colors of the landscape, they might associate moods (blues for melancholy) or discover metaphors (the cypress trees as flames). Table 2-2 shows how different art forms can invite situated uses of language for literacy learning.

Creative Visualizations

Creative visualization, sometimes referred to as *guided imagery,* is an invention technique that allows readers and writers to form impressions, conceptions, or feelings by creating images played out as motion pictures of the mind (Ghiselin, 1952; John-Steiner, 1997; Rohman, 1965). These

TABLE 2–2   Art Forms and Literacy Uses

Art Form	Literacy Use
Portraiture	Writing a dialogue or monologue; describing character appearances and moods
Abstracts	Describing feelings and emotions; discovering ideas in movement; creating poetic images
Landscapes	Writing descriptive settings; creating poetic metaphors

mental pictures might originate from highly descriptive passages such as a short verse in a poem or a rich character description. For example, in Figure 2-4, a third-grader creates an elaborate dragon picture based on the poem "The Dragon of Death" (Prelutsky, 1976).

Thinking in visual images can lead writers beyond semantic understandings to explore Gardner's spatial and kinesthetic intelligences as well. In the next example, the teacher helps children image the search for a treasure map.

> Picture yourself as an explorer in a forest looking for a treasure map. You are wearing a large, felt black hat with a big, pink feathery plume jutting out. You have on long, colorful dungarees with gold borders and brass buttons. The sleeves of your billowing satin blouse are blowing in the wind. The sun is beaming in your eyes as you squint to read a dusty yellow map. The first place on the map leads to a rabbit hole that is next to a big oak tree. Sticking out from the hole is a folded sheet of paper that tells you to go to the brook, where you will find a bottle with a message in it. You stumble over a rock, pick yourself up, and meander down to the brook. There lying in the sand is a distorted glass bottle. At the bottom of it you see a note. . . .

The children finish the story and see if they can draw the story sequence and locations as they imagined it. The teacher asks:

◆ Did the passage create moving pictures that you could *see? What pictures did it imprint on your mind?*

◆ How did the passage "show" you an image rather than "tell" you information?

◆ What forms of description did the passage use to create action, sensory images, and settings (comparisons, dialogue, concrete nouns, and adjectives)?

Creative visualizations can be a great starting point for helping children write descriptive vocabulary based on a simple character trait (e.g., he was stocky and stylish) or an action sentence from a story (e.g., the basketball

The Dragon of Death

In a faraway, faraway forest
lies a treasure of infinite worth,
but guarding it closely forever
looms a being as old as the earth.

Its body is big as a boulder
and armored with shimmering scales,
even the mountaintops tremble
when it thrashes its seven great tails.

Its eyes tell a story of terror,
they gleam with an angry red flame
as it timelessly watches its riches,
and the dragon of death is its name.

Its teeth are far sharper than daggers,
they can tear hardest metal to shreds.
It has seven mouths filled with these weapons,
for its neck swells to seven great heads.

Each head is as fierce as the other,
Each head breathes a fiery breath,
and any it touches must perish,
set ablaze by the dragon of death.

All who have foolishly stumbled
on the dragon of death's golden cache
remain evermore in that forest,
nothing left of their bodies but ash.

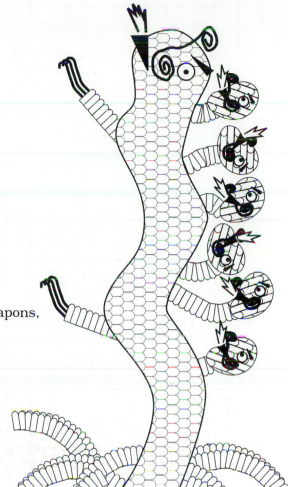

Figure 2-4 *The Dragon of Death. Jack Prelutsky (1976). In Nightmares: Poems to Trouble your sleep.* Reprinted by permission of W. W. Morrow.

player bounded up to the platform like an exuberant golden retriever). Now is also a good time to introduce stylistic elements that have inherent picturesque qualities such as personification (the star winked at me), hyperbole (it rained buckets), metaphor (creeping footsteps are silent snow), and similes (legs like a crane).

A slightly different interpretation of creative visualization is offered by Olshansky (1994, 1995). She describes an image-making program that integrates children's visual imagery at every stage of the creative process. Children are asked to make colorful collage images from handpainted textured papers, bubble paintings, salt on watercolors, or marbelized papers and to read the designs, pictures, rhythms, and ideas that they spark, a kind of self-administered Rorschach (Olshansky, 1994). This process of image finding and free association stretches the imagination and starts ideas flowing. Olshansky recommends providing children with high-quality art materials capable of producing grand ideas. Hot Off the Press makes some interesting abstract and decorative papers, called "Paper Pizazz," that can be found at most craft shops.

Graphic Organizers

Graphic organizers are ways of communicating and illustrating ideas in visual form. These visual maps are excellent planning tools to show concepts, classifications, structures, and meaning relationships. There are many ways of presenting information visually (e.g., webbing, clustering, time lines, mazes, crosswords, and other pictures or diagrams). Children can collect these graphic organizers and use them to display ideas. A few of the most common organizers are listed in Table 2-3. Transparencies such as *Graphic Organizers for Reading and Writing* (Macmillan/McGraw-Hill, 1997) or visual software programs such as *Inspiration* or *Timeliner* offer additional resources for organizing.

LANGUAGING STRAND: THE VISIBLE WORD

The visual arts have a strong relationship to the power and beauty of words, jointly collecting for us a moment, a memorable image, a heightened awareness of what is. An imprint on a T-shirt, a bumper sticker, an advertisement, or a menu design can all reflect the combined force of art and words. In this strand we define the visible word as a symbolic message that draws attention to words in an artful way. Becoming aware of "visible words" and the thoughts, intentions, force, and creativity behind them offers children a set of meaningful symbols to unwrap the power of hidden messages. Combined visual and verbal messages release creative energies by focusing attention on associations and visual effects. The forms introduced here can be used as informal writing, as prewriting and prereading strategies, or as messages in and of themselves.

The Visual Dictionary

One special type of dictionary used by students of all ages is the visual dictionary, which consists solely of pictures with detailed labels that define various parts. For example, Figure 2-5 shows the parts of a camera. Several publishers put out lovely visual dictionaries for older children either in book form (e.g., *Dorling Kindersley's Ultimate Visual Dictionary* [1994]) or as computer CDs (e.g., *Macmillan's Visual Dictionary: Multimedia Edition CD*, which has over 3500 color images).

TABLE 2–3 Graphic Organizers

◆ The hierarchical organizer categorizes information by level of importance.

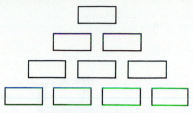

◆ The flowchart is a kind of sequential pattern that places events in a chronological order with a specified beginning and end.

◆ Time lines are another type of sequential pattern that place events in a temporal realm.

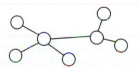

◆ A compare/contrast list is an effective visual for showing similarities and differences, likes or dislikes, pros or cons.

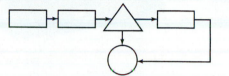

◆ A web is a visual display of categories of related information that center on a core concept or idea.

◆ A cyclical organizer can visually build a continuous circle of process events or illustrate a central concept embedded in concentric circles of influence.

Viewfinders

Back door

Film counter window

Shutter button

Wrist strap

Lens   Film advance wheel

Figure 2-5   *Camera in a Visual Dictionary*

Children of all ages should be encouraged to create their own visual dictionaries. In preparation, children trace or cut out pictures from magazines draw freehand, or list words of objects they would like to collect (e.g., airplane, tree). When adequate collections are available, the teacher helps students discover themes for classifying: objects that move, items of clothing, foods, favorite illustrator pictures, or ABC order. As they are putting the visual dictionary together, they should examine objects and their features in detail.

◆ What do I see?
◆ How is it put together?
◆ How does it work?
◆ What is each part called, and what does it do?

Figure 2-6 *Logos*

A common class book can be duplicated and placed in the school library. Children use these dictionaries for expanding vocabulary, learning sight words, and demonstrating alphabetical order.

Logos

Logos are a part of graphic arts and include a very specialized symbol, name, or trademark that signifies a larger set of meanings. The meaning of a logo depends on the associations that are made with it and the context in which it appears. Calvin Klein's "CK" on T-shirts, and Nike's monogram on athletic shoes might symbolize "class," "youth," or "solidarity in peer groups." Labels on wearable art or treasured objects can make them soar beyond their original value, depending on shared societal and cultural values and meanings. Logos are the signatures of many corporations and private businesses, which use them for name identification and advertising (see Figure 2-6).

A successful logo is simplistic but demands attention. Often we see them on packages, mailing envelopes, business cards, greeting cards, shopping bags, and other products (e.g., pizza boxes, fast-food wrappers, toys). The key to creating a successful logo is to persuade or affect the viewer through a clear message conveyed in a letter, word, or image (Place, 1995). Sometimes this single message is expressed through artistic features such as color, texture of paper, shape, or typeface; at other times it is elicited through a shared symbol or metaphor (e.g., a flag meaning patriotism, or FTD, meaning swiftness). Asking and responding to questions about logos help children think critically about the ordinary, everyday images that surround them.

Figure 2-7 *Alpine Logo*

Alpine

♦ What is the impact of the logo in terms of its design, color, size, shape, and placement on the object?

♦ What effect does the logo have on the consumer? What happens if the logo is changed in any way (e.g., copied in black and white instead of color?) How is the meaning changed?

Now consider the logo "Alpine" in Figure 2-7. What associations and ideas does this simple statement convey? Although reproduced in black and white, its special hue of wintergreen gives the sensation of fresh, cool air, and the image of a mountain covered with scented pine trees. The sunset shadow evokes a feeling of vastness, and the word "Alpine" indicates something fresh or outdoors. The logo provides a clean, inviting feeling and a sensation of openness, vastness, and beauty.

♦ Where might such a logo appear?

♦ What kind of product or service might use this kind of image?

These questions open up a discussion of advertising, ethics, and persuasion. For example, can a tobacco company deceive consumers by advertising cigarettes using the Alpine logo? How? Would the Alpine logo be good for marketing a toothpaste?

Students can create name tag or business card logos to say something about themselves or their interests. For example, someone with musical ability makes musical notes out of the letters in his or her name, or someone who loves poetry and art creates an acrostic using their favorite colors and words.

Silly
Understanding
Energetic

Computer clip art such as *Graphics Express* from Tiger Software offers whole sets of logos to choose from as a way to decorate or publicize. The key is to select and combine artistic elements and linguistic features to send a message or meaning to the recipient or consumer.

Literacy Prints

Graphic artists tell us that they use the "look of words" to create meanings and influence feelings (Brier, 1992). English words have distinct shapes and graphic characteristics, such as length, width, form, spacing, and line quality (e.g., ascenders such as *h, l,* and *t,* or descenders such as *g* in the word "highlight").

h i g h l i g h t

Words can be made to shout, dribble, or dance:

[**SHOUT**, *DRIBBLE*, Dance]

Sentences can carry a message by their particular font or typeset (e.g., the dripping, dribbling look of the statement "I love to play on rainy days"):

[I LOVE TO PLAY ON RAINY DAYS]

The visual positioning and representation of words in certain contexts can create emphatic meanings, contrast, and even metaphors for ideas. For example, consider a sign posted on a gate that says

BEWARE OF DOG

Or a letter superimposed on a drawing such as the one in Figure 2-8 symbolizing strength, freedom, and power.

Good illustrators know how to build meanings using the images of alphabet letters and word configurations. They experiment with scripts by writing on a curve, outlining, shadowing, using different colors, adding dots, lines, swirls, or objects (e.g., stars, flowers). They make lines heavy, light, staggered, narrow, or wide for special effects. A good example of this are humorous children's books such as *Walking, Talking Words* (Sherman,

Figure 2-8   *Superman Logo.*

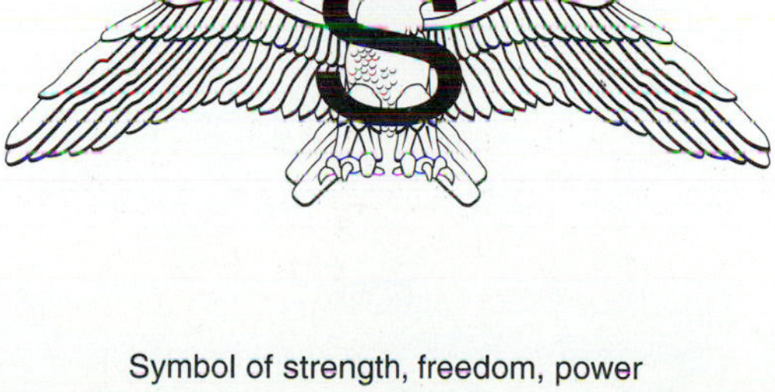

Symbol of strength, freedom, power

1980) and *Anno's Alphabet* (Anno, 1975), where letters as pieces of textured wood are placed at unusual angles to create optical illusions. As shown in Figure 2-9, graphic features can convey ideas by decorating and drawing letters (Ostrom, 1997).

One way to bring this to children's awareness is to ask questions about the look of words.

Figure 2-9 *Lettering*

Synonyms

Lettering styles and words
that show similar meanings

Homonyms

Lettering styles and words that show differences in spelling and meanings, even though the words sound alike

Homographs

Letter styles and words that show differences in meanings and pronunciation even though the words are spelled the same

Antonyms

soft

HARD

Lettering styles and words that show opposite meanings

Homographic Homophones

Lettering styles and words that show differences in meaning even though the words are spelled alike and sound the same

Figure 2-9 *Continued*

Figure 2-10 *Brushscript Fonts.*

Morgan Omega Type
OLD ENGLISH CAPS
Old Style *Old Spirit*
Paint Stroke Plato Font

◆ What meaning or rule is suggested by the size, slant, proportion, or shape of the letters? What associations do you make?

◆ What do you think of when you see TALL letters (slender, stiff, big, trees, sticks)? Or short, **wide** letters (girth)? What about letters with **shadows** (mystery)? Or *slant* letters (movement)?

◆ What associations do you make when you see certain font styles? When you see Gothic lettering do you think of churches, gargoyles, cold, or gray? When you see Italic lettering, what do you think of?

These and other questions can make children aware of how graphic art conveys very important symbolic meanings that imprint indelible associations in readers' minds.

Have children collect and examine slogan buttons, bookmarks, bumper stickers, magazine and music cassette covers, or other available consumer items. Desktop publishing offers ways of dressing up words to communicate a message in a special way. Decorative, ornamental, and script fonts such as those shown in Figure 2-10 are available on most computer word-processing programs.

In the language arts classroom, using different fonts for poetry and advertising can invest words with special meanings or carry important subliminal messages. The artistic qualities of these literacy forms are discussed later in the chapter.

Calligraphy

Calligraphy comes from two separate Greek words: *kallos,* meaning "beautiful," and *graphos,* meaning "writing." Calligraphy refers not only to well-made letters but also to their decorative arrangement. Unlike handwriting, where legibility is primary, calligraphy is a deliberate attempt to create something beautiful. The Chinese bestowed respect on calligraphy by considering it fine art, on a par with paintings. The art of calligraphy was also central to Islamic art and Hebrew biblical writings. Hebrew writing, to this day, includes a special script that is written from right to left. Acquainting children with these beautiful scripts (Figure 2-11), introduces them to the

אבגדהוזחטיכלמנ **Hebrew**

ظ ض ش ش ز ذ خ ج ث ت ا **Arabic**

Chinese

Figure 2-11 *Calligraphy*

symbols, meanings, and values of other cultures and, again, exemplifies how lettering itself may constitute an aesthetic text.

Two lovely examples of calligraphy in children's books are the *Book of Kells* (Cirker, 1982) and *Illuminations* (Hunt, 1989). Children interpret "grotesque" figures, animals, people, and other fanciful borders in the miniature detailed paintings that enshrine the first letter of a word in ancient manuscripts. An example of such picture writing is shown in Figure 2-12.

In a time when technology makes available beautiful fonts and scripts for displaying prose, children should become aware of the way in which words can have an impact on us just by the way they look. If children do freehand calligraphy, they will pick up a terminology for handwriting practice as well. Chinese hand scrolls (horizontal) and hanging scrolls (vertical) using Chinese calligraphy and landscape drawings can be worked on as murals. Attaching dowel rods at the ends will make the scrolls easy to roll up for storing and transporting. Available at crafts stores are books on the basics of learning to do calligraphy and ways to use it [e.g., *A Beginner's Guide to Calligraphy* (Galate, 1980), *Do It Yourself Calligraphy* (Weinberg, 1996), or *Calligraphy for Kids* (Bostick, 1991)]. The teacher might place these children's books at an activity center.

Figure 2-12 *Illuminated Manuscript.* Reproduced by permission of Art Resources.

Graffiti

Graffiti is derived from the Italian word for "scratch." These are word draw-ings, images, or epithets, scratched on walls or painted with aerosol spray paint, that leave a record of one's self in a public place. Graffiti became popular with streetwise teenagers in the mid-1970s and 1980s in the Bronx and Brooklyn, in New York subway trains, and on urban walls. In the late 1980s graffiti moved from the street to the gallery as urban folk art. Although the distinction between graffiti and urban folk art remains controversial, there is no denying that Keith Haring's chalk figures on New York subway posters received well-deserved acclaim by the modern art world (Atkins, 1990). Today's graffiti is part of hip-hop culture, a kind of performance art that grew out of jazz, reggae, and rap. It is communal, in-teractive, and physical. Often, one colorful voice feeds off the other to make political statements, show group pride, delineate territory, or exhibit cre-ative prowess. Children will want to determine for themselves what they consider art or graffiti. *Mother Goose Comes to Cable Street* (Stones, 1982) is a good book for children to discuss. These stories "for the eye" show the visible signs of childhood, including a hopscotch grid on sidewalks, hand-prints in cement, or carvings of initials on trees and park benches. Teach-ers ask:

- How does graffiti make you feel?
- Is all graffiti art? What makes it art?
- What makes one design superior to another?
- Why is it done?
- What are the differences between art, graffiti, and vandalism?

Children can be asked to look for places in their communities where graffiti appears. In many cities one can find graffiti painted on storefronts or concrete walls. In the classroom, children might want to turn a bulletin board into a graffiti wall. Covering the board with butcher paper, children take felt-tipped pens and add words or phrases, statements, or free reflec-tions. A graffiti board gives children a public voice and makes them aware of how free speech is tested in the community. Since graffiti artists make stunning visual images out of their names, or what they refer to as "tag-ging," children might start there.

In addition to bulletin board graffiti, have children create murals on a pa-per table cloth covering their desks to provide an on-going project for use during free time. You might want to divide children into groups to prepare this mural around a common theme, such as *The Children's Supermarket*. Groups would work on sections such as the bakery, the dairy, and fruits and vegetables. Many graffiti magazines, such as *Airbrush Action,* are available for children to thumb through. These magazines not only offer visuals of graffiti but provide articles, "how to" tips, and interviews with graffiti artists.

POETRY STRAND: LOOKING AT POETRY

Although most poetry is enjoyed when read aloud for its rhythm and rhyme, its capacity to express ideas and feelings through visual elements is equally important. According to Spender (in Ghiselin, 1952, p. 112), "the poet should be able to think in images; he should have as great a mastery of language as a painter has over his palate." Of course, visual and auditory qualities are intimately intertwined and cannot be separated. However, for purposes of this chapter, we concentrate on the visual and artistic aspects of poems, leaving the sonorous effects and rhythm to the chapter on music.

Poetic Still Life

Poetic still life is "painting" and positioning an object or idea with words or decorative letters. *Shape poetry* is a picture painted with words and looks

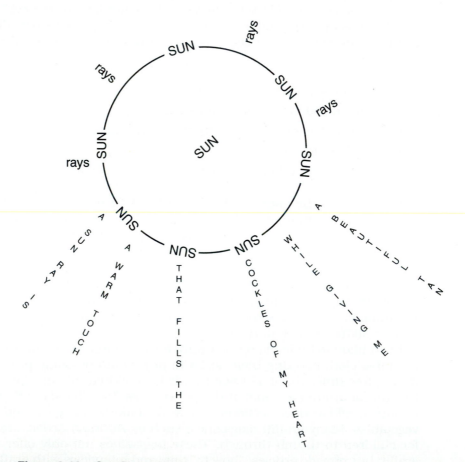

Figure 2-13 *Sun Shape Poem*

like the thing it represents. Its meaning comes from the arrangement of letters and words as well as the words themselves. For example, consider the shape poems in Figures 2-13 and 2-14.

To write a shape poem, it is helpful to have a common object or picture in hand (e.g., a seashell, an apple, or a magnifying glass). Using this visual image, brainstorm words, phrases or sentences about it.

Next make a shape of the image, drawing it freehand, tracing with stencils, or copying it. Coloring-book pictures are especially good for copying because of their dark outlines. A transparent sheet of paper placed over the outline serves as an overlay to write the words along the lines forming the picture. When the top sheet of paper is removed, a picture shaped out of words will appear. Children can use the word paintings for an art exhibit or place them in a class book.

Figure 2-14   *Pig Shape Poem*

Concrete poetry also exploits the visual plan or "look" of the poem, but instead of creating a picture, its meaning is accomplished by stanza groupings, line breaks, varying lengths of lines, or other typographical arrangements of words or letters on the page. In particular, it pays special homage to the use of *white space,* the empty areas around words that create the visual and aural pause in poetry. It may present itself at the end of a line, between words, between stanzas, or along any special contour or shape. White space is a lot like *negative space* in painting, where the "emptiness" around and within the objects or shapes is essential to the unity, variety, and balance of the work. Writers should be encouraged to think about the purposeful use of white space as it affects the visual look, rhythm, and meaning of poetry.

The poem below makes use of symbols, upper- and lowercase letters, unusual word breaks, white space, and compressed length to create double meanings and images for the words "sticks" (lanky and long like the poem; permanence, as in growing old) and "signs" (Keep Off; Don't; Stop) as the poem "yanks" the reader's eye down the page to convey the unstoppable cycle of growing old.

old age sticks
up Keep
Off
signs)&

youth yanks them
down(old
age
cries No

Tres)&(pas)
youth laughs
(sing
old age
scolds Forbid
den Stop
Must
n't Don't

&) youth goes
right on
gr
owing old

"Old Age Sticks" by e. e. cummings (Firmage, 1991)

Figure 2-15 *Grandfather Clock*
(Courtesy of Sandra Clary)

TICK TOCK
TICK
TOCK
TICK
TOCK

TWELVE
ELEVEN　ONE
TEN　　　　TWO
NINE　　　THREE
EIGHT　　FOUR
SEVEN　FIVE
SIX
SECOND
MINUTE
HOUR
DAY
WEEK
MONTH
YEAR
DECADE
CENTURY
MILLENIUM
EON
ETERNITY

TICK TOCK
TICK
TOCK
TICK
TOCK

GONG!

Cumming's poem makes a visual impact on the reader by showing the perpetual dialectic between adults and youth, viewed in a nonconventional way. Another example designed with different fonts, lettering styles, and use of white space is shown in Figure 2-15. For special occasions, the students can transfer poems like this onto transparencies or slides and have a slide show accompanied by music.

Finally, formula poems, with their prescribed syllable patterns and word counts, have both a visual or graphic form and create a picture in the mind's eye. Examples of poems that look like diamonds and convey various visual images through words are shown in Figure 2-16. Cinquain has

Cinquain Pattern

1st line, one word: title
2nd line, two words: describe title
3rd line, three words: show action
4th line, four words: show feelings
5th line, one word: another word for title

> *Book*
> *treasured friendship*
> *mysteries to explore*
> *chapters laughing and echoing*
> *Sanctuary*

Diamante Pattern

1st line, one word: subject noun
2nd line, two words: adjectives
3rd line, three words: participles
4th line, four words: related to the subject
5th line, three words: participles
6th line, two words: adjectives
7th line, one word: opposite of subject noun

> *Music*
> *inspiring flowing*
> *ringing of bells*
> *notes and strong chords*
> *filling my head*
> *lingering whispering*
> *Poetry*

Figure 2-16 *Formula Poems*

a five-line syllabic form and diamante has seven lines. The formula provides the visual shape while the words evoke a picture image. To evoke images in formula poems or other poetic still life, have children ask unusual questions about ordinary objects: For example, "wonder why" questions such as *why is the sky blue?* or "hypotheticals" *(How might an artist hear the sound of birds?)* or creative questions that juxtapose ordinary ideas with the unfamiliar or strange *(What does happiness look like? How heavy is the ocean?)*. As children begin their poetic still life, they ask themselves some additional questions.

♦ How can I shape or arrange the poem so that it will appeal to the eye?

♦ What colorful verbs and vivid adjectives will I use?

♦ What mind picture do I want the reader to form?

♦ How might the title, sequence, and development of the poem create a special visual effect and meaning?

♦ Will I use sentence structure, diction, and conventions as a conscious strategy to construct a visual effect?

Concrete, shape, and formula poems are naturals with children. Collections of children's concrete poems on a variety of subjects include *If Dragonflies Made Honey* (Kherdian, 1977), *Eats Poems* (Adoff, 1988), and *A Moon in Your Lunch Box* (Spooner, 1993). These books show an artful arrangement that dazzles and bestows beauty on words. Some other favorites are the multilingual collection *Concrete Poetry: A World View* (Solt,

1980), *Concrete Is Not Always Hard* (Pilon, 1972), and *In the Eyes of the Cat: Japanese Poetry for All Seasons* (Demi, 1994), a useful resource for introducing haiku and other Japanese poems to children.

Poems about Art and Art-Inspired Poems

Many poets write in response to a piece of art, and vice versa. For example, William Carlos Williams', "The Dance" was inspired by Brueghel's painting "The Kermess." Conversely, nature poets such as Wordsworth and Shelley inspired many of the landscape paintings of nineteenth-century Romantic painters. Many books are available where poetry and art work independently. Consider the famous poem of Robert Frost (1988) called *Birches*, recreated in soft, impressionistic watercolors that convey images of nature and the beauty of words. Or consider the deep emotional realism worked by an inference of the color red in the following haiku:

Dead bird on the road
I nearly passed it by—oh
one small splotch of blood

Courtesy of Katya Sabaroff Taylor

Art images, too, can be inspired by words. The haiku below might be likened to a Picasso abstract:

A broken mirror
we see the image severed
is the seer slit?

Courtesy of Tom Taylor

To generate ideas for visual poetry, use beautiful pictures from calendars, posters, postcards, or magazines. Scanning photographs onto the computer or using a digital camera that records a "photo" on a disk can project pictures electronically to achieve similar results.

STORY STRAND: ART THAT TELLS STORIES

"Words and pictures are like two voices," says Steven Kellogg, a well-known illustrator of children's books. "They are like singing different melodies of a duet." The pictures tell stories and educate the eye while the words artfully activate the message. In this section we look at the visual aspects of storytelling through picture books and comic books. We also consider some of the story narratives found in ancient script, buffalo hides, and fabrics and textiles.

Picture Books

The picture book is "a unique art object, a combination of an image and an idea that allows the reader to come away with more than the sum of the parts" (Kiefer, 1995, p. 6). This dual story line of concrete images arranged in a narrative sequence creates an interplay between text and media, complementing one another in a synchronous whole. Picture books are not literature but rather a form of visual art, says well-known educator Sylvia Marantz (1992). The pictorial content, with its dazzling colors, lines, textures, designs (arrangements like repetition, balance, patterns), backdrops (a fabric collage, color), and technical choices (layout and size of pictures, borders and ornamental features, media used, typeface, endpapers, and paper type) bring life to memorable characters [e.g., *Curious George* (Rey, 1994)], create feelings and moods [e.g., *Flamboyan* (Adoff, 1988)], present a particular point of view [like that of the ants in *Two Bad Ants* (Allsburg, 1988)], acquaint us with cultural information [e.g., *Seven Candles for Kwanzaa* (Pinkney, 1993), the American holiday inspired by African traditions], or take us back in time [e.g., *Book of Kells* (Cirker, 1982), which shows reproductions of the illuminated manuscripts of the medieval age].

Since a picture book's depth of information cannot be dismissed by focusing solely on the words, the teacher should prepare to talk about art elements in picture books. Table 2-4 outlines some art elements that can be discussed using literature. In addition to emphasizing these elements, call attention to the type of medium and its effects (collage, watercolor, pastel drawing, paint, oils, pencil drawing, etc.), the genre of art (abstract, drawings, portraits, still life, sculpture), or the style of art (cubism, impressionism). As children read and interpret pictures, they will discover the effects and functions of art on written stories. They may associate softness with rounded shapes and rigidity with angular ones. They might feel the intensity of black outlines, the cheerfulness of pastel colors or the detachment of strictly defined boundaries and borders (Nodelman, 1992). Picture books enrich a child's visual verbal literacy (Stewig, 1995) because the child must decode visual messages in pictures and encode these into oral language. As such, they offer a visual context for the development of reading, writing, and oral language.

Research suggests that picture books are a framework for response and storytelling (Manzo and Legenza, 1975; Morrow, 1987). Some questions children can discuss about picture books in reader and writer workshops include:

◆ What do you see? (Is it a picture, action, movement, people, etc.?)
◆ How many different things do you see in the picture?
◆ In what way do the words and pictures complement one another?
◆ How do characters come alive through description? What do their clothes, jewelry, possessions, and homes say about them?
◆ What in the setting activates the reader's imagination and contributes visually to the audience's understanding of the scene?

TABLE 2-4   Elements of Art

Art Element	Children's Book
Color: What colors do you see? Which predominate? Why were they chosen? Do the colors suggest certain emotions, feelings, or moods? the passing of time (season)? cultural symbolism, or history? Do the colors imply relationships between objects?	*Flamboyan* (Adoff, 1988) Gauguin-type portraits; summer print dresses; calypso colors; tropical Caribbean island; flame flowers and high blue skies
Lines: What effect do the lines have? Do they show movement like water? Are they tall like trees? Are they jagged and chaotic? Are they curved and fluid? Do the lines lead the eye somewhere? Do the lines create a recognizable object?	*Harold and the Purple Crayon* (Johnson, 1990) A continuous purple line meanders here and there, builds objects for Harold to inhabit and tells a story
Shape and size: Are there recognizable geometric shapes (circles, squares, ovals, rectangles, cylinders)? What effect does the shape or size have? (How might a gnarled tree make you feel? a tall pine? a weeping willow?)	*Baboushka and the Three Kings* (Robbins, 1961) Geometric shapes, figures, and contours along with the simplicity of three bright colors (blue, orange, and yellow); creates the folk culture and symbolic traditions of simple peasants in Russia; ornamental elaboration of the architecture using detailed black outlines fills in the geometric shapes and intricate carvings; objects suggest opulence, humble surroundings, or horror and frivolity
Texture: Do the objects seem visually real? Have you felt these objects before? How dominant a role do the objects play in this story? Do the textures enhance your understanding of the text? your enjoyment?	*Snowballs* (Ehlert, 1995) Creates an irresistible impulse to touch; gives the illusion of something real; uses cut-and-paste papers; arranges objects like a collage; tactile imagery

◆ What is in the context that helps us feel or see an event or action, empathize with characters, or develop a point of view?

Picture books are no longer just for younger readers. In the 1970s picture books with highly symbolic meanings and adolescent story lines were created (see Kiefer, 1995, App. D). Older students can also write picture books for younger children or peers. Removable stick-on-paper allows the student to place paper beneath a picture on each page and write a story to go with the illustrations. Kiefer (1995) suggests holding a mock Caldecott Award to select favorite illustrators or illustrations. Children also have their own art exhibits for displaying favorite pictures they have created in their picture books.

Comic Books

Comic books are a kind of childhood lore that opens up worlds filled with robots and vampires, superheroes and warriors, or aliens and space creatures. For many children comic books are the single most important entry to reading. The comic book blends art and writing in a way that makes maximum use of visual and verbal language, especially pithy and familiar forms of communication, actions, situations, or interests that create humor, retell history, or explode with adventure. The visual story usually depicts human actions, habits, fads, historical or political events, personalities, or contemporary themes that have been turned on their heads for broad audience appeal. The graphic artist enhances meanings by the placement, size, and colors of the pictures, the camera angles, silhouettes, and perspectives, the position of the eyes and where the face is directed, and the shape, posture, gestures, and direction of the character's body (Gerberg, 1989).

Children who enjoy reading humorous comic books such as the Archie series or Disney characters might enjoy writing their own comic stories.

Cartoon character   Thaddeus Turtle
Location   Hawaii
Profession   Private Eye
Active verb   Drinks

Thaddeus Turtle, private eye, drinks coffee in Hawaii.

Figure 2-17 *Spot Drawing*

Figure 2-17 suggest a startup activity for writing cartoons. Write down the name of a cartoon character, location, profession, and some active verbs and put them together to go with a "spot drawing." (Koch, 1980).

Children also keep a file box of ideas, complete with pictures and words, on recipe cards to help them generate a story line. They look at the pictures and ask themselves:

- ◆ Who or what is doing the talking (a person or an object)?
- ◆ What message is communicated by the character's body shape or pose?
- ◆ What do the character's facial expressions suggest?
- ◆ What kinds of symbols are used to convey information (a heart, teardrop, thunderbolt)?
- ◆ What would happen if the pictures were cleverly mixed and matched or arranged as a collage of pictures?
- ◆ Do the pictures extend the text, enhance it, or explain it?
- ◆ What words are used to add color or mood?
- ◆ What makes the cartoon funny (something unexpected; an animal personified; clever dialogue)?

After this warm-up, children create or select pictures that represent the story they wish to tell, deleting features they wish to leave out and adding those they wish to include. Introduce the children to *Cartooning for Kids* (Lightfoot, 1993) to make simple expressions (Figure 2-18) and simple movements (Figure 2-19). Those who feel uncomfortable drawing can trace silhouettes of cartoons, create computer illustrations, or cut and paste

Suspicious　　　*Worried*　　　*Happy*　　　*Tired*

Figure 2-18　*Simple Expressions*

Figure 2-19 *Simple Movements*

with computer clip art. Children assemble casts of characters in notebooks or envelopes so that they can copy these later. Some characters represent archetypes such as the good guy, bully, or cheapskate. Others might be juxtaposed to illustrate complementary personalities such as Charlie Brown, who is usually seen as a loser, and Lucy, who is usually pushy and bullying Charlie Brown. Still others might introduce a cast of characters or superheros, as part of a series such as Marvel's Spiderman or Brenda Starr. The teacher should point out special stylistic elements used in comic books, such as onomotapoeia (POW, WHAM, WHEW), idioms (a frog in one's throat), double meanings (stamp the envelopes), and clichés (a wild goose chase). Also to be noted are unexpected phrasing, fresh wording, rhyme, or rhythm to create incongruity or absurdity. The words of a comic book usually take the form of dialogue, titles, or captions. Often, these words are highlighted in balloons or displayed as a caption at the bottom of a frame. Although a comic book has all the elements of a story sequenced in frames, the writing is usually very short: a word, phrase, or one or two sentences to accompany the pictures. In the beginning the scene and character are introduced; in the middle, the action continues; and in the end the joke or puzzle is delivered.

It is usually good practice to have children write collaboratively before writing alone. The teacher might suggest that children work together on a comic book. They pick a theme (e.g., family, play, pets, or other topics of interest to them), and "audition a cast of characters" by writing short dialogues for each. If they want three or more characters in a frame, they must decide who will speak first and place the character to the left side of the frame. Children have to decide how many frames they will need to give the most effective punch. When the comic books are finished, they are placed in the classroom library to share. Role-playing and dressing up like comic book characters to enact the storyline can be an enjoyable option for sharing.

Older children especially like comic books. They can also explore political cartoons or "editorial cartooning" as vehicles for studying opinions and uncovering social, political, and economic issues. Recognizing caricatures of well-known people, historical references, historical symbols (e.g., the Republican elephant or Democratic donkey), and the use of stereotypes stimulates some of the following questions:

- ◆ What is happening in the cartoon? What is the issue?
- ◆ What is the cartoonist for or against? What is his or her bias?
- ◆ What special-interest group might the artist be trying to reach?
- ◆ What is the historical background or current social situation that prompted this drawing?
- ◆ What controversial issue is identified?
- ◆ What gross generalization is being used to create humor?
- ◆ If the cartoon shows a caricature of an important public figure, how does it compare to a realistic image or photograph of that person?

Comic books are sold in bookstores, supermarkets, and newsstands, and often may be found at garage sales. Teachers can use comic books to broaden children's reading and writing interests and reinforce the tight connection between the picture and the word.

Ancient Story Art

Egyptians made their marks on cave walls in 3800 B.C. using picture writing and hieroglyphics. The word *hieroglyph* comes from the words *hiero,* meaning "holy," and *glyph* meaning "writing." The "symbols and words of the gods," painted on the walls of Egyptian tombs, temples, pyramids, and statues, added beauty and imposed magical power. Hieroglyphics are fun to write and to interpret. Children can study phonetic and pictorial messages such as those in Figure 2-20 and create some of their own. A good reference book is *Egyptian Hieroglyphics: How to Read and Write Them* (Rossini, 1989).

The remnants of early picture writing and decorations span the globe from India to North America, from Turkey to Russia. Children will enjoy exploring their own heritage by examining the early narrative artwork of Native Americans. Have them assume the role of archeologists making educated guesses about early art represented on pottery, buffalo and bison skins, birchbark, rocks, sand, and story robes. Recorded stories of battles, horse raids, and other important events of history are discovered through symbols and pictographs. Children piece history together through the indigenous sign language that allowed nomadic tribes to communicate with one another, or hypothesize about the symbols on steep cliffs, stone walls, and the ceilings of caves. The teacher can ask some of the following questions:

◆ How many people do you think lived in the caves? How do you know?

◆ What did the Indians eat? How do you know?

◆ What other symbols helped you know more about the Indians' daily life?

◆ What clues will future historians find out about your life?

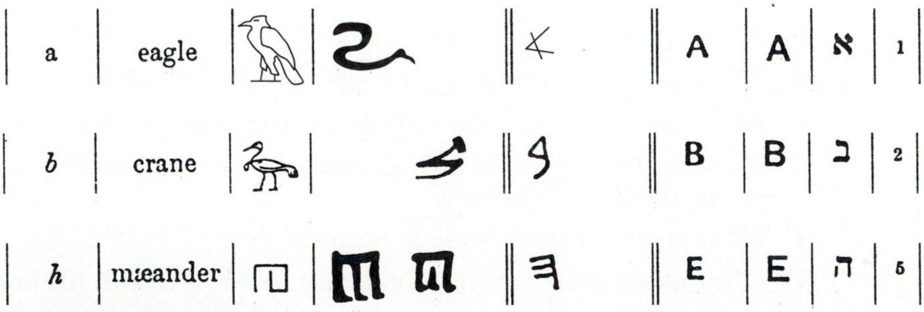

Figure 2-20 Hieroglyphics

Several books on the topic are available for children to explore, including *Native American Rock Art: Messages from the Past* (La Pierre, 1994) and *Signs, Letters, Words: Archeology Discovers Writing* (Hackwell, 1987). To learn more about Native American symbols and designs, refer to an article by Wardle (1990) that discusses the various meanings for color, materials, and symbols, such as *water, corn, sun, deer,* and *lightning.*

Stories in Fabrics and Textiles

In Chapter 1 the fifth-graders studied the Bayeux tapestry as part of a unit on Medieval times. The children used this fabric art to identify and make hypotheses about the Battle of Hastings. As they problem-solved about the meaning of the tapestry, they were learning new vocabulary words for the objects and ideas presented in the visual designs. Since ancient times, many cultures have created stories out of cloth (e.g., Amish quilts, West African story cloths, or Plains Indian ledger paintings, to name a few). The story of the Pándau (*pah Now*), an embroidered tapestry cloth made among the Hmong people in the mountains of southwest China, is told in Mai's story *The Whispering Cloth* (Shea, 1995). Mai tells the compelling events of her personal hardships and circumstances as a refugee in a time of war and confinement.

Another dark time of history is recorded in some of the earliest story quilts created by African-American women slaves for the mistress of the plantation. Although they had to work within the guidelines and rules of the owner, sometimes they disguised symbols, escape routes, and messages in the quilts. Early American public documents and archives show that quilt designs told stories of pioneer life, revolutionary and civil wars, arrival of immigrants, superstitions, and the daily life events of the early settlements (Anderson, 1991). [If children want to know more about how quilting patterns got their names, share a few stories with them, such as *Eight Hands Round—A Patchwork Alphabet* (Paul, 1991) or *The Quilt-Block History of Pioneer Days* (Cobb, 1995)].

The language arts instructor can also use fabric art to help children write. Have children cut out different shapes from swatches of cloth and paste them on construction paper. Children must use their imaginations to build animals or characters from the fabric and write stories to go with them (Figure 2-21). Finding stories in pictures is not limited to fabric art and textiles. The teacher will also want to call children's attention to stories told in stained glass, in mosaics and on pottery.

Stories about Art and Artists

Reading children's stories with art as a theme is an excellent way to teach literacy and the visual arts at the same time. These books are usually about fictional characters with a propensity toward creativity and a resistance to "fitting the mold." The themes teach children to cherish their

Figure 2-21 *Animal Print Art*

uniqueness and creativity and at the same time help them to appreciate beauty and the arts. There are a vast number of books on the market with art as a theme. Two of my favorites are *Camille and the Sunflowers* (Anholt, 1994), a fictional story of Van Gogh's stay in the south of France as seen through the eyes of a young boy, and *Bonjour, Mr. Satie* (de Paola, 1991), which tells of a feud between two Parisian artists. Biographies about artists and illustrators and books like those in the Masters of Art series by Raboff or the Metropolitan Museum books discuss the lives of individual artists and their unique works in color, subject matter, and composition (e.g., Monet, Raphael, Degas, Rembrandt, Da Vinci, Picasso, and Cassatt). Individual titles can introduce sculptors [e.g., *Alexander Calder and His Magic Mobiles* (Lipman and Aspenwall, 1981)], photographers [e.g., *Dorothea Lange: Life through the Camera* (Meltzer, 1985)], and many famous painters [e.g., *Monet* (Wright, 1993) or *Diego* (Winter, 1991)]. The books *Lives of the Artists* (Krull, 1995), and *Talking with the Artists* (Cummings, 1992) offer interesting details and anecdotal accounts of artists. The teacher can question children about biographies.

- How does reading a biography of an artist or illustrator change how we see their work?

- What can be learned from reading about the artist and the creative process?

Having information about the creator of artwork, although not always necessary for a response by the viewer, does allow children background that might provide new insights and meanings.

INFORMATION STRAND: PICTURE THIS . . . INFORMATION

Seeing is often believing, and one trick of persuasive marketing is to imprint on the consumer's mind an idea so unforgettable that the viewer is moved to take action or endorse a product. In this section we consider those texts whose purpose is to get things done or appeal to the consumer by relying heavily on conveying information through images and pictures (Britton, et al., 1975). Advertising, greeting cards, and travel brochures are good examples of how writers and media specialists sell images and words.

Advertising

Advertising and marketing are big business. Advertising's function is to sell goods or services and make consumers believe that it is in their best interest to buy. Advertising appears in the Yellow Pages of the phone book, in junk mail, in catalogs, in magazines, on discount coupons, on highway billboards, on radio and the Internet, and on TV ads for toys, games, and foods. Helping children create their own advertisements shows how words and pictures capture the consumer's attention and motivate desire or action. Before writing, have students collect advertisement flyers and talk about propaganda devices and effective advertising techniques.

- What is being advertised? What connotations are being evoked by the words and pictures?

- What picture or logo accompanies the ad? What effect does it have? (For example, the Lucky Charms cereal box uses a leprechaun as the logo and includes a game.) What associations do you make?

- How is the product viewed? What can it do for you? Why should you want it? (e.g., Suzuki, "makes us free")

- What are the reader's values, hopes, needs? How will this product fulfill these?

- How is the ad arranged? What colors are used? What kind of typeface is used?

◆ What words are printed with pictures? (e.g., Frosted Flakes: boys are compared to tigers) How is persuasion created visually and verbally?

◆ Who might be the audience for this product, and how might it appeal to them?

◆ What techniques are used to help you remember this work? Are there repetitive motifs? Are the ideas centered? flat? Do the pictures recede? stand out?

This systematic line of questioning involves children in thought that demands analysis and prepares them to write an advertisement of their own. To get started they bring in something they would like to sell—clothes, games, or other personal objects—brainstorm the uses and details of their object, and look for catchy slogans, words, and pictures to feature the object (refer back to the section on the visible word and shape poetry). After designing their ads, the class assembles them by category into a general catalog and distributes it to other classes for mail orders.

Greeting Cards

Greeting cards are big business in this country, perhaps because they show and say what we often cannot say ourselves. Greeting cards present a good opportunity to talk with children about contemporary society.

◆ What do cards say about a society?

◆ What themes seem to be shared information in a culture?

◆ What counts as acceptable humor? and to whom?

The students begin by arranging the cards by genre (birthday cards, anniversary, get well, sympathy, thank you, wedding) by types of pictures (e.g., all the cards with "bears" on them), by medium (photographs, drawing, torn paper), or other categories. Once the cards are categorized, students discuss the range of themes, appeals, and meanings within categories. They do a "market analysis" by trying to predict what types of people might buy particular types of cards, or they interview consumers to talk about features of cards that attract them.

The children also create greeting cards of their own. They can draw freehand or use *The Print Shop Deluxe* for the Apple computer. *Make Cards!* (Solga, 1992) and *Making Cards* (King, 1996) provide art activities to help children make greeting cards. The students share the strategies they use to create different types of greeting cards. For example, many greeting cards today use visual and verbal humor, twists of logic, double meaning, backhanded compliments, or other techniques. More serious cards (telling someone we care, saying we are sorry, or congratulating someone on an accomplishment) may include a poem, a wise proverb or saying, or a verse that is short but heartfelt. The children can find cards that exemplify these and share them with others.

Travel Writing

"It's Just Like You're There" when you read a travel brochure or poster that shows a special place through anecdotes, inspiring words, and colorful photographs. Travel writers are observers with a keen eye and an awareness of the sensory nature of words. Children can create an imaginative journey through pictures, photographs, and language (e.g., metaphors, special vocabulary, and imagery). Have them begin by reading through travel brochures, guidebooks, or magazine ads to get a feeling for this kind of writing and art. Next, they can select a destination that they would like to write about. Literary trips based on books they are reading stir up interest. After reading *Anne of Green Gables* (Montgomery, 1983), they can create a travel brochure to Green Gable House in the Haunted Forest on Prince Edward Island, or map out the journey and quest of *Jason and the Golden Fleece* (Fisher, 1990). Other travel brochures might include the Enchanted Forest of Snow White and the Seven Dwarfs, Never Never Land of Peter Pan, or Pooh Corner. Consider having older children make travel maps based on books that include journey themes, such as *The Ballad of Lucy Whipple* (Cushman, 1996).

Once the writers select a destination, they make notes about key words, special souvenirs, taped interviews, or dated slides of a place that brings back memories. Since brochures make use of colorful language and exaggeration, children brainstorm a list of phrases that persuade by appealing to the senses (e.g., warm summer breezes, opulent surroundings, a tropical paradise, or timeless natural splendor). Children can plan their own imaginative trips (e.g., caravans, around-the-world adventures) selecting pictures, type styles, borders, and graphics to make the brochure come alive in visual form. The brochures can be placed in a classroom "tourism" agency for others to read.

A more extended form of writing, and another way that students can experience travel writing, is through *itineraries*. Itineraries often detail the places to visit, number of days to spend at a particular place, and attractions to explore. For example, consider day 1 of an itinerary brochure advertising "3 Days/2 Nights at Disney World":

Friday: Depart for Orlando at Disney World. Upon arrival, check in at the hotel and pick up Disney's three-day passes. Board the hotel shuttle to the park and go off on your own for an afternoon in the Magic Kingdom. Stroll down Main Street USA, and enjoy some of the attractions at Liberty Square, Tomorrowland, and Frontierland. Wonderful surprises are in store for you at the Haunted Mansion and Country Bear Jamboree. Opt to take a ride on Space Mountain or visit the Hall of the Presidents. Later, enjoy a complimentary snack at the Plaza Ice-Cream Parlor on Main Street and do some shopping for

souvenirs. Board the bus back to the hotel. The evening is free for you to relax, go for a swim, or try your skills at the video arcade.

Children can practice writing itineraries by starting with the events of
their own day. Have children keep itineraries for the weekend. What did
they do on Friday evening? Saturday afternoon? Sunday?

◆ *School-Community Links*

Museums and galleries are experiencing profound shifts in their relationship with communities as public funding dries up and diverse community interest groups seek greater involvement in the identification and
preservation of culture. Teachers and administrators have an obligation
to establish meaningful relationships between schools and community to
advance the arts. An artist-in-residence program allows the teacher to invite a practicing artist to work at the school for a specified period of time.
In many schools, the art instructor may be available to do this, or perhaps parents with a special talent in the arts are willing to share their
craft with children. Young people observe artists in their work setting and
experience the flow of their typical workday. By observing and interacting with the artist, they gain practical firsthand knowledge of the craft.
Once a semester, the artist in residence, the teacher, and the student
review writing and art portfolios to select "best work" to exhibit in store
windows, businesses such as McDonald's and Pizza Hut, local banks, or
shopping malls.

Children should also be their own curators, planning exhibits and displaying artwork at the school. During the year, they collect, sort, and
mount drawings and story art. They think of titles for their paintings and
write that title and their name on a card to place next to the artwork. The
local art director discusses the exhibition with them and children begin doing the publicity and invitations for the exhibit.

Another way in which children can reach out to the community is by visiting local galleries and museums. For example, say that you plan a visit
to the art gallery to view the animal sculptures of a local artist. Inviting this
sculptor into the class to talk about the work ahead of time can generate
a discussion of what to look for and what questions to ask about the objects. Children also learn how the artist gets ideas and how much time he
or she spends working on a piece. When children arrive at the gallery, they
walk together at first as you tell stories that stimulate interest about some
of the sculptures. Later children can sit and relax in front of a sculpture
that is especially intriguing to them. They are told not to worry about taking everything in all at once. Galleries and museums are to savor and enjoy over and over again. A stop at a gallery bookshop at the end of a visit
allows students to bring home pamphlets and reproductions of the works
in books or on postcards.

Visiting artists' studios and going to hands-on museums, outdoor museums, fine arts galleries, and folk festivals are an important part of educating children. With the popularity of the Internet, children can travel vicariously to the world's renowned museums and galleries both abroad (e.g., the Louvre in Paris, France) and in the United States (the Metropolitan Museum of Art or the Guggenheim Museum in New York City) without leaving home. There are also some excellent children's books about museums, such as *Art Dog* (Hurd, 1996), *Visiting the Art Museum* (Brown and Brown, 1990), or *ABC: Museum of Fine Arts* and *ABC: Museum of Modern Art* (Mayer, 1986a,b).

◆ *Activities for Professional Development*

1. Invite your colleagues to a Monet breakfast at school. To prepare for it, research all you can about the life and work of Monet (e.g., he lived between 1840 and 1926; he was a French artist who pioneered the impressionist movement; his art exhibits visual sensations of nature through color and light; his subjects include picnics, café life, street scenes, boating parties, and fashionable tourist resorts). One of his most famous subjects was the water lilies at his summer home in Giverny. Fresh lilies might be a perfect centerpiece for your breakfast table. Next find art reproductions of Monet's work, such as his seascape named "Impression: Sunrise" or the "Rouen Cathedral, West Facade, Sunlight." (Monet's work can be found on the Internet, in calendars, and in stores that sell reproductions of art prints.) These images can be placed on easels or used to decorate the invitations, place cards, tablecloth, and tableware. Gather children's books about Monet to display at the table and around the room. For example, *Linnea in Monet's Garden* (Bjork, 1995) or *What Makes a Monet . . . a Monet?* (Muhlberger, 1993a). Finally, treat your colleagues to a French breakfast: croissants, "croutes au fromage" (cheese on toast—baguettes with gruyere cheese), juices, café, "tarte" (tarts or shortcrust pastries), and beautiful colored fruits of the season. The Monet breakfast will be a special occasion for everyone and a nice way to introduce the importance of art and literacy. Bon appétit!

2. Learn to play and experiment with art. Take any art medium such as watercolor and get yourself a medium-sized brush and special watercolors at any Wal-Mart or arts and crafts store. A wonderful resource for the beginner is *Watercolor for the Artistically Undiscovered* (Hurd and Cassidy, 1992). It comes with 48 pages of watercolor paper, a set of paints, and a brush. Play with brush strokes such as making wiggles, lines, and splotches. Dip the brush in water and splatter it on the page. Drop a spot of paint on paper and then smear or blot it with a paper towel. Drop water on a paint stroke to watch it run. Let one

color dry and then add in another. Combine colors or leave spaces of white paper to show through. Just muck around and experiment. Learn to play all over again as children do when they are learning something new.

3. Use questions to elicit a creative visualization. Start with an ordinary place such as an ice cream parlor and model a set of probing questions that paint visual images. Have others write a narrative and draw a picture of what they see based on your set of questions.

Is it empty or lively? Who eats here? Does it have decorations, colors, pictures on the walls? Would you come here to watch people? stare out the window and relax? What kinds of ice cream flavors do they sell? Any interesting names? What else can you buy here? What does it smell like here? What would be a good photograph to capture this place? What else goes on here? What happens and when? Who is selling the ice cream? What are they wearing? Are there buildings around the ice cream parlor? Is it in a mall? near a hotel? How do you get to the ice cream parlor?

◆ *Works Cited*

Professional References

Anderson, S. M. (1991). *Collector's guide to quilts.* Radnor, PA: Wallace Homestead Books.

Armstrong, T. (1993). *7 Kinds of smart: Identifying and developing your many intelligences.* New York: Plume.

Atkins, R. (1990). *Artspeak: A guide to contemporary ideas, movements, and buzz words.* New York: Abbeyville Press.

Berger, J. (1985). *Ways of seeing.* New York: Penguin.

Bradbury, R. (1990). *Zen in the art of writing.* Santa Barbara, CA: Joshua Odell Editions.

Brier, D. (1992). *Great type and lettering designs.* Cincinnati, OH: North Light Books.

Britton, J., Burgess, T., Martin, N., McLeod, A., and Rosen, H. (1975). *The development of writing abilities.* Schools Council Research Studies. London: Macmillan Education Ltd.

Dee, N. (1984). *Your dreams and what they mean: How to understand the secret language of sleep.* New York: Bell Publishing.

Dorling Kindersley's ultimate visual dictionary (1994). Kent, WA: Pacific Pipeline.

Dyson, A. H.(1989). *Multiple worlds of child writers.* New York: Teachers College Press.

Firmage, G. G. (1991). *e. e. cummings complete poems: 1904–1962.* New York: Liverlight Publishing Co.

Gardner, H. (1980). *Artful scribbles: The significance of children's drawings.* New York: Basic Books.

Gardner, H. (1993). *Frames of mind: The theory of multiple intelligences.* New York: Basic Books.

Gerberg, M. (1989). *Cartooning: The art and the business.* New York: William Morrow.

Ghiselin, B. (1952). *The creative process.* New York: Mentor Books.

Goodnow, J. (1983). *Children's drawing.* London: Fontana.

Hurd, T., and Cassidy, J. (1992). *Watercolor for the artistically undiscovered.* Palo Alto, CA: Klutz Press.

John-Steiner, V. (1997). *Notebooks of the mind: Explorations of thinking.* New York: Oxford University Press.

Kellogg, R. (1970). *Analyzing children's art.* Palo Alto, CA: National Press Books.

Kiefer, B. Z. (1995). *The potential of picturebooks: From visual literacy to aesthetic understanding.* Upper Saddle River, NJ: Merrill.

Koch, K. (1980). *Wishes, lies, and dreams.* New York: Perennial.

Macmillan/McGraw-Hill (1997). *Graphic organizers for reading and writing.* New York: Macmillan/McGraw-Hill.

Manzo, A. V., and Legenza, A. (1975). A method for assessing the language stimulation value of pictures. *Language Arts, 52*(8), 1085–1089.

Marantz, S. S. (1992). *Picture books for looking and learning: Awakening visual perceptions through the art of children's books.* Phoenix, AZ: Oryx Press.

Morrow, L. M. (1987). The effects of one to one story readings on children's questions and comments. In S. Baldwin and J. Readance (Eds.), *Thirty-Sixth yearbook of the national reading conference.* Rochester, NY: The National Reading Conference.

Nodelman, P. (1992) *The pleasures of children's literature.* New York: Longman.

Olshansky, B. (1994). Making writing a work of art: Image-making within the writing process. *Language Arts, 71,* 350–356.

Olshansky, B. (1995). Picture this: An arts-based literacy program. *Educational Leadership, 53,* 44–47.

Ostrom, L. (1997). *The ABC's of creative lettering.* Carlstadt, NJ: EK Success.

Place, J. (1995). *Creating logos and letterheads.* Cincinnati, OH: North Light Books.

Pullinger, K., and Rothenstein, J. (1995). *The writer's drawing book.* Boston: Shambhala Publications.

Rohman, D. G. (1965). Prewriting: The stage of discovery in the writing process. *College Composition and Communication, 16,* 106–112.

Rosenblatt, L. (1985). Language, literature, and values. In S. N. Tchudi (Ed.), *Language, schooling, and society* (pp. 64–80). Portsmouth, NH: Boynton/Cook.

Shaw, F. W. (1980). *30 Ways to help you write.* New York: Bantam Books.

Solt, M. E. (1980). *Concrete poetry: A world view.* Bloomington, IN: Indiana University Press.

Stewig, J. (1995). *Looking at picture books.* Fort Atkinson, WI: Highsmith Press.

Wardle, B. L. (1990). Native American symbolism in the classroom. *Art Education,* 43, 13–25.

Zalusky, V. (1983). Relationships: What did I write? What did I draw? In W. Frawley (Ed.), *Linguistics and literacy* (pp. 91–124). New York: Plenum Press.

Children's References

Adoff, A. (1979). *Eats Poems* (illus. S. Russo). New York: Lothrop, Lee, & Shepard.

Adoff, A. (1988). *Flamboyan* (illus. K. Barbour). New York: Harcourt Brace Jovanovich.

Allsburg, C. V. (1988). *Two bad ants.* Boston: Houghton Mifflin.

Anholt, L. (1994). *Camille and the sunflowers.* Hauppage, NY: Barron's Educational Series.

Anno, M. (1975). *Anno's alphabet: An adventure in imagination.* New York: Thomas Y. Crowell.

Bjork, C. (1995). *Linnea in Monet's garden* (illus. L. Anderson). New York: Farrar, Straus & Giroux.

Bostick, W. A. (1991). *Calligraphy for kids.* Franklin, MN: La Stampa Calligrafa.

Brown, L. K., and Brown, M. (1990). *Visiting the art museum.* New York: E. P. Dutton.

Carlidge, M. (1995). *Mouse's scrapbook.* New York: Dutton.

Cirker, B. (1982). *Book of kells: Selected plates in full color.* Mineola, NY: Dover Publications.

Cobb, M. (1995). *The quilt-block history of pioneer days* (illus. J. D. Ellis). Brookfield, CT: Millbrook Press.

Cummings, P. (Ed.) (1992). *Talking with the artists.* New York: Bradbury Press.

Cushman, K. (1996). *The ballad of Lucy Whipple.* Boston: Houghton Mifflin.

Demi (1994). *In the eyes of the cat: Japanese poetry for all seasons* (trans. H. Tzesi). New York: Henry Holt.

de Paolo, T. (1991). *Bonjour, Mr. Satie.* New York: Putnam.

Ehlert, L. (1995). *Snowballs.* Orlando, FL: Harcourt Brace.

Fisher, L. E. (1990). *Jason and the golden fleece.* New York: Holiday House.

Frost, R. (1988). *Birches* (illus. E. Young). New York: Henry Holt.

Galate, L. (1980). *A beginner's guide to calligraphy.* New York: Dell Publishing.

Garrison, C. (1986). *The dream eater.* New York: Aladdin Books.

Hackwell, J. W. (1987). *Signs, letters, words: Archeology discovers writing.* New York: Simon & Schuster.

Hunt, J. (1989). *Illuminations.* New York: Bradbury Press.

Hurd, T. (1996). *Art dog.* New York: HarperCollins.

James, B. (1990). *The dream stair.* New York: Harper & Row.

Johnson, C. (1990). *Harold and the purple crayon.* New York: Harper & Row.

Kherdian, D. (1977). *If dragonflies made honey* (illus. J. Aruego and A. Dewey). New York: Greenwillow Books.

King, P. (1996). *Making cards.* London: Collins Children.

Krull, K. (1995). *Lives of the artists* (illus. K. Hewitt). New York: Harcourt Brace & World.

La Pierre, Y. (1994). *Native American rock art: Messages from the past* (illus. L. Sloan). Charlottesville, VA: Thomasson-Grant.

Lightfoot, M. (1993). *Cartooning for kids.* New York: Firefly Books.

Lipman, J., and Aspenwall, M. (1981). *Alexander Calder and his magic mobiles.* New York: Hudson Hills Press.

Mayer, F. C. (1986a). *ABC: Museum of fine arts, Boston.* New York: Harry N. Abrams.

Mayer, F. C. (1986b). *ABC: Museum of modern art.* New York: Harry N. Abrams.

Meltzer, M. (1985). *Dorothea Lange: Life through the camera.* New York: Viking Press.

Montgomery, L. M. (1983). *Anne of Green Gables* (illus. J. Lee). New York: Grosset & Dunlap.

Muhlberger, R. (1993a). *What makes a Monet . . . a Monet?* New York: Metropolitan Museum of Art.

Muhlberger, R. (1993b). *What makes a van Gogh . . . a van Gogh?* New York: Metropolitan Museum of Art.

Paul, A. W. (1991). *Eight hands round—A patchwork alphabet.* New York: HarperCollins.

Pilon, A. B. (1972). *Concrete is not always hard.* Middletown, CT: Xerox Education Publication.

Pinkney, A. D. (1993). *Seven candles for Kwanzaa* (illus. B. Pinkney). New York: Dial Books.

Prelutsky, J. (1976). The dragon of death. In J. Prelutsky (Ed.), *Nightmares: Poems to trouble your sleep* (illus. A. Lobel). New York: Greenwillow Books.

Rey, M. (1994). *The complete adventures of curious George.* Boston: Houghton Mifflin.

Ringgold, F. (1991). *Tar Beach.* New York: Crown Publishing.

Robbins, R. (1961). *Baboushka and the three kings* (illus. N. Sidjakov). Hyannis, MA: Parnassus.

Rossini, S. (1989). *Egyptian hieroglyphics: How to read and write them.* Mineola, NY: Dover Publications.

Shea, P. D. (1995). *The whispering cloth: A refugee's story* (illus. A. Riggio, stitch. Y. Yang). Honesdale, PA: Boyds Mills Press.

Sherman, I. (1980). *Walking, talking words.* New York: Harcourt Brace Jovanovich.

Singer, M. (1995). *The Morgans' dream.* New York: Henry Holt.

Solga, K. (1992). *Make cards!* Cincinnati, OH: North Light Books.

Spooner, M. (1993). *A moon in your lunch box* (illus. Ohlsson). New York: Henry Holt.

Stones, R. (1982). *Mother goose comes to cable street: Nursery rhymes for today.* London: Children's Rights Workshop of London.

Venezia, M. (1988). *Van Gogh.* Chicago: Children's Press.

Weinberg, S. (1996). *Do-it-yourself calligraphy.* Mahwah, NJ: Watermill Press.

Winter, J. (1991). *Diego* (trans. A. Prince, illus. J. Winter). New York: Alfred A. Knopf.

Wright, P. (1993). *Monet.* London: National Gallery.

◆ *Additional Resources*

Note: Asterisks indicate resources that are cited in the chapter.

Videotapes and Catalogs

A & E Home Video Catalog
Arts and Entertainment
P.O. Box 2284
South Burlington, VT 05407-2284

Art Education in Action
Getty Trust Publications
1200 Getty Center Drive, Suite 500
Los Angeles, CA 90049-1682

Faith Ringgold: The Last Story Quilt
Homevision
4411 N. Ravenswood Ave.
Chicago, IL 60640
800-262-8600
(28 min. VHS part of the *Portrait of an Artist* series, 1991)

Linnea in Monet's Garden
First Run Features
153 Waverly Place
New York, NY 10014
800-229-8575
(30 minutes, color, 1993)

National Gallery of Art Videotape Catalog
National Gallery of Art
Department of Educational Resources
Fourth and Constitution Avenues, N.W.
Washington, DC 20565

The PBS Home Video Catalog
1320 Braddock Place
Alexandria, VA 22314
800-645-4PBS

Teaching in and through the Arts
Getty Trust Publications
1200 Getty Center Drive, Suite 500
Los Angeles, CA 90049-1682
(30 minutes, VHS, 1992)

Slides

National Gallery of Art
Department of Education Resources
Fourth and Constitution Avenues, N.W.
Washington, DC 20565

Art Prints, Postcards, Posters, and Other Visuals

Airbrush Action
Cliff Stieglitz Publisher
P.O. Box 3000
Denville, NJ 07834-9680
800-232-8998

CP Graphic Organizers
Continental Press
520 East Bainbridge St.
Elizabethtown, PA 17022

Fine Art Posters, Multicultural Art Prints, Folk Art Prints
Dale Seymour Publications
P.O. Box 10888
Palo Alto, CA 94303

Graphics Express
TigerDirect Inc.
8700 West Flagler St.
Miami, Florida 33174

Multicultural Art Print Series
Getty Trust Publications
1200 Getty Center Drive, Suite 500
Los Angeles, CA 90049-1682

National Gallery of Art Teaching Packets
National Gallery of Art
Department of Educational Resources
Fourth and Constitution Avenues, N.W.
Washington, DC 20565

Paper Pizazz
Hot Off the Press
1250 N.W. Third Street
Department B
Conby, OR 97013
503-266-9102

Postcard Books
Running Press
125 South 22nd Street
Philadelphia, PA 19103

Abbeville Press
488 Madison Avenue
New York, NY 10022

Miscellaneous Art Kits

Fun with Hieroglyphs (1990).
New York: Metropolitan Museum of
Art and Viking.

Schories, P. (1995). *Native American
Designs: A Dutton Sand-Painting Kit.*
New York: Dutton.

Schories, P. (1996). *Circus: A Dutton
Sand-Painting Kit.* New York: Dutton.

Computer Software and Technology

Inspiration and *Timeliner*
Educational Resources
1550 Executive Drive
P.O. Box 1900
Elgin, IL 60121-1900
800-624-2926

Kid Pix
Broderbund Software
Dept. 15, P.O. Box 6125
Novato, CA 94948
(MAC or IBM)

Macmillan's Visual Dictionary:
Multimedia Edition CD
Educational Resources
1550 Executive Drive
P.O. Box 1900
Elgin, IL 60121-1900
800-624-2926

Pop-up Greetings Kit (1996)
Printpaks Inc.
(Windows and Mac 1.0)
513 N.W. 13th Ave. Suite 202
Portland, OR 97209

The Print Shop Deluxe
Broderbund Software
Dept. 15, P.O. Box 6125
Novato, CA 94948
(MAC)

Vincent van Gogh CD
Educational Resources
1550 Executive Drive
P.O. Box 1900
Elgin, IL 60121-1900
800-624-2926

The Vincent van Gogh Laserguide
(1991)
Voyager Company
The Chicago Art Institute
1351 Pacific Coast Highway
Santa Monica, CA 90401

Internet Addresses

ArtsEdNet
http://www.artsednet@getty.edu
(Getty Internet Service for Educators)

Fine Art Pictures
Usenet
Newsgroup:alt.binaries.pictures.fine-
art.digitized
(digitized fine art pictures for
downloading)

KidArt
Gopher
Name: KIDLINK Gopher
Address: kids.ccit.duq.edu
Choose: KIDART Computer Art
Gallery
(a gallery of works by kids)

School–Community Arts Partnerships

Art Museum/School Collaborations
The North Texas Institute for
Education on the Visual Arts
University of North Texas
Denton, TX 76201

Association of Waldorf Schools of
North America
3911 Bannister Road
Fair Oaks, CA 95628

Getty Center for Education in the Arts
401 Wilshire Boulevard, Suite 850
Santa Monica, CA 90401

John F. Kennedy Center for the
Performing Arts
Washington, DC 20566
(Program Department: Very Special
Arts)

National Gallery of Art
Fourth and Constitution Avenues, N.W.
Washington, DC 20565
(*Guide to Resources and Programs*)

Smithsonian Office of Elementary and
Secondary Education
Arts and Industries Building
1163 MRC 402
Smithsonian Institution
Washington, DC 20560

Music Literacy: Listening to Language

Vignette: Cowboy Songs

In Mrs. Rodriquez's literacy class, the third-graders are studying the American cowboy by singing songs from Songs of the Wild West (Axelrod, 1991). Through song, the children discover the life and legend of the cowboy and the mood and spirit of the Old West. The class sings "Home on the Range," the cowboy's national anthem, which originated as a poem back in 1873. Mrs. Rodriquez has the children recite the words of the song, then she plays a few lines that have been prerecorded on audiotape. The children sing the melody, line by line and verse by verse. Two of the four verses are printed here.

VERSE 1
Home on the Range
Oh give me a home
Where the buffalo roam
Where the deer and the antelope
play
Where seldom is heard
a discouraging word
and the skies are not cloudy all day.

VERSE 3
Where the air is so pure
The zephyrs so free
The breezes so balmy and light
That I would not exchange
my home on the range
For all of the cities so bright.

After all four verses are sung, Mrs. Rodriquez asks the following questions: What is a range? What words of the song describe the range? How does the melody help to suggest the mood of the plains and the cowboy? What words in the song were new for you? (e.g., zephyr was a god of the west wind and refers to a breeze from the west; balmy means soothing) Why do you think this song was written?

Now the class turns to other songs, such as "Git Along, Little Dogies," "Cowboy Jack," and "The Cowboy." These songs give the children a sense of the cowboy's work: tending to the cattle, branding, herding, and rounding them up. To give children an image of the west as portrayed by artists of the time, Mrs. Rodriquez uses the artwork of some of the best known western artists, such as Frederic Remington, Thomas Eakins, and George Catlin.

Finally, the class sings "Buffalo Gals" and "Sweet Betsy from Pike" to initiate a discussion about the role of women in the Wild West. They consider the special bravado of cowgirls such as Annie Oakley and learn more *about the women who braved months of heat, dust storms, and dangers of the wilderness to fulfill their dreams and future expectations.*

BUFFALO GALS
As I was walking down the street, down the street, down the street
A pretty little girl I chanced to meet
Oh she was fair to see.
Buffalo Gals won't you come out tonight? Come out tonight? Come out tonight?
Buffalo Gals won't you come out tonight?
and dance by the light of the moon?

SWEET BETSY FROM PIKE
Oh, do you remember sweet Betsy from Pike
Who crossed the high mountains with her husband Ike
With two yoke of oxen, an old spotted hog,
A proud Shanghai rooster, and one great big dog?

After all the verses of the songs have been sung, the teacher concludes with a series of questions: Who were buffalo gals? In what way were cowboys and buffalo gals storytellers? Poets? Why are we fascinated by stories of cowboys and cowgirls? Why do you think historians refer to "Home on the Range" as the cowboy's national anthem? Why do you think these songs were written? What did you learn about the early west through songs? Did you get a portrait of the cowboy and the cowgirl? What was this portrait? What was the special bond between people and nature? Why was being a cowboy considered a "manly profession"? What work did he do to earn this title? How is the cowboy portrayed in art and the movies? Why were so few songs written about the cowgirl?

After discussing these questions, the children sing the songs again. As they sing the legends and folklore of the cowboy and cowgirl, history comes alive in a manner different from reading a history book. Because the spirit of the times is embedded in melody and narrative, children seem to enjoy, and perhaps remember better, the stories that history has to tell. At the same time, children experience the poetry of music by discovering the rhythms of words, rhymes, and verse.

Some of the children in Mrs. Rodriquez's class are second-language learners, exploring American culture and the English language for the first time. The words and the music provide instructional support for them as they develop word fluency and acquire new word meanings. When these children sing in unison, they practice words and expressive features of print without drawing attention to their limited English. Second-language educators have long extolled the benefits of using music for teaching English to nonnative speakers and for enhancing all childrens' cultural awareness (Failoni, 1993; Jolly, 1975).

Music is part of our history, but it is also a major part of our everyday lives. It organizes our work, religious ceremonies, and our memorable events (e.g., weddings, football games, political rallies, parades, and memorial services). It also influences our ideas and values (as in advertising) and fulfills our desires for pleasure and entertainment (whether attending a symphony or a rock concert). As we explore this chapter, we discover the many forms of music that live in literacy. It is hoped that the ideas suggested here will create a desire to learn more about the music of the written word and its uses in the literacy classroom.

INQUIRY STRAND: HEARING IDEAS

The melodic and rhythmical features of language are a valuable means of creative thinking. According to Gardner (1993), "the aural imagination is simply the working of the composer's ear" (p. 101)—the tools for working with sound: its tones, rhythms, forms, and movement. Some believe that a sensitivity to sound and rhythm helps develop abstract reasoning along the lines of Piagetian cognitive stages (Bamberger, 1982); others believe that we are endowed with an inborn musical grammar like that of Chomsky's language theory (Jackendoff, 1995; Lerdah, 1996). Notwithstanding music's origin and acknowledged learning impact, language users can build on the power of music and the euphony of words for generating ideas. As an aesthetic choice music offers another available form of inquiry to be used by the literacy learner.

Creative Listening (with Music)

Creative listening is using what you hear to construct novel ideas and meanings. Burns (1988) suggests that music can enhance creativity in writing or other forms of literacy. Listening to music supports a mindset that nurtures free association (Glenn, 1992), especially new connections or memories of special events, places, people, and times in our lives (e.g., accordion music and a family reunion, or John Denver's music and a trip to the mountains). Random associations allow thoughts to meander and emotions and sensory perceptions to surface. Since music gives birth to ideas and aural strategies, the teacher should offer authentic listening activities in the literacy classroom. One possibility is for the teacher to prepare an audiotape with five different listening selections of about 1 minute in length, each representing a different kind of music (e.g., chant, classical, opera, rock and folk.) As the children listen to each selection, they are asked to respond in any way they like (pictures, scribbles, words, symbols, mappings). During sharing time the teacher notes the source of children's associations (personal experiences, something read, a movie, a visual image) and the

TABLE 3-1   Ideas for the Musical Notebook

- Write down all the different kinds of music heard in a seven-hour day.
- Write down thought ramblings while listening to music you like.
- Make a note of what you are doing when you listen to music, where you usually are, and how you feel when you hear certain kinds of music.
- Note instances where music creates associations with products, words, feelings, and other actions, such as the national anthem marking the opening of a sports event or an advertising jingle that accompanies a soft-drink commercial.
- Collect old song lyrics and talk about how they reflect the human experience.

form it takes. This activity helps generate ideas for writing and offers the teacher insights into children's preferred learning styles.

Another musical task for inspiring ideas is to have students listen to musical selections (e.g., Tchaikovsky's "Waltz of the Flowers" or Confrey's "Kitten on the Keys") to design a collage of words and pictures based on the melodies. Children share their designs and brainstorm words and phrases associated with the images they see. Encouraging children to keep notebooks of these images stimulates the mind's imagination and moves the writer emotionally. Some musical experiences to record in their notebooks are suggested in Table 3-1.

Critical Listening (with Music)

Critical listening involves evaluating and judging what you hear. When children listen critically to the musicality of language and musical elements, they begin to understand and respond to music's influence on attitudes and behavior. Film music, advertising jingles, and patriotic songs are particularly suited for eliciting responses or creating an altered state of mind. These music forms are often used as a medium to shape beliefs and feelings, create emotional appeal, direct or capture attention, stimulate desire, suggest a mood, or promote certain personal or social behavior. Since an important aim of the language arts class is to develop discriminating listeners, children need direct interaction with music. Here are some of the overlapping elements that music and language share and manifest in communicative compositions.

Rhythm

Rhythm comprises the accent patterns ordered in groupings or measures; the visceral life of music. Have children clap loudly on the upbeat ($^-$) and softly on the downbeat ($_$) to the poem in Figure 3-1, which is marked by two different rhythm patterns. The teacher can have children listen to words and sounds linked to rhythms containing steady beats, strong beats, weak beats, or long beats. Alternating intensities of a beat or repeating and varying words prepares children for writing poetic verse and

First Rhythm Pattern					Second Rhythm Pattern			
MELLOW	song	MELLOW			mellow	SONG		mellow
SONG	mellow	SONG			song	MELLOW		song
WHY	oh	WHY			why	OH		why
make	tunes	that	CRY		MAKE	TUNES	THAT	cry

Figure 3-1   *Rhythm Patterns*

performing choral readings. Start with the familiar stress and meter patterns associated with a poem such as a limerick. Have children clap and sing the rhythm pattern using nonsense words.

Duh DAH duh duh DAH duh duh DAH

(There ONCE was a FEL-la named JIM)

Duh DAH duh duh DAH duh duh DAH.

(who JOGGED ev-ery DAY to stay TRIM)

Duh DAH duh duh DEE,

(he DID-n't eat MUCH)

Duh DAH duh duh DEE,

(lots of VEG-gies and SUCH)

Duh DAH duh duh DAH duh duh DAH.

(said it GAVE him his VIG-gor and VIM)

Timbre

Timbre (pronounced "tamber") is the quality of sound made by an instrument or voice. To focus children's attention on the ornamentation and color of musical instruments, record the sounds of instruments (e.g., violin, flute, timpani) and have children identify them alone or in combination (Copland, 1988). Ask the children such questions as: Why is the flute associated with birds, the bassoon with comic figures, and the trumpet with ceremonial events? Then use words and phrases like those of famed musician Aaron Copland to develop a vocabulary that expresses the tone color of each musical instrument.

Piccolo	Thin and shrill
Violin	Light and lyrical
Cello	Sober and serious
Flute	Soft, feathery, cool, fluid, agile
Trumpet	Brilliant, sharp, commanding
Oboe	Nasal, pastoral
Trombone	Noble, majestic
Clarinet	Smooth, open, hollow
English horn	Plaintive
Kettle drum	Rumbling

Children will discover that the timbre and vocabulary of sounds can add mood and suspense to story scenes or poetic verse. You can use almost any household item as a sound instrument. *Making Musical Things* (Wiseman, 1979) offers over 50 ingenious ways to make instruments, from bottle-cap castanets to keys on strings.

Melody

Melody is a series of tones that form a complete musical idea. A musical subject, like a dramatic plot, moves from beginning to end. One way to help children identify a melody direction is to follow the rising and falling of word inflections in a familiar song using modulating lines or melodic contours. For example, children listen to the first line of "Old Folks at Home" and make a visual map using circles, dashes, dots, or lines that move up and down an imaginary baseline:

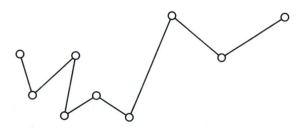

Then they compare their diagram with the actual musical notes printed in Figure 3-2.

Having children represent visually what they hear will help the teacher assess whether or not students understand the thematic material.

Figure 3-2 *"Old Folks at Home"*

Harmony

Harmony consists of two or more notes heard together. Texturing music through overlapping melodies and words is a strategy that embellishes literacy performances. Have children work in groups reading a pattern book such as *Traveling to Tondo* (Aardema, 1991). The narrator reads the story while others repeat the chorus or refrain that describes the sound that each animal makes as it joins the caravan to Tondo (e.g., cat: ika-o; pigeon: bwa-wa; python: swe-o; tortoise: ta-ka). When the repetitive parts of the story are read, children try different harmonies with voice and music. They layer the reading by substituting the xylophone for the cat in the two-part harmony, the resonator bells for the pigeon in the three-part harmony, and the sticks for the python in the four-part harmony:

Solo	Two-Part Harmony	Three-Part Harmony	Four-Part Harmony
◆ ika-o, ika-o, ika-o	◆ Xylophone ◆ bwa-wa, bwa-wa, bwa-wa	◆ Xylophone ◆ Resonator bells ◆ swe-o, swe-o, swe-o	◆ Xylophone ◆ Resonator bells ◆ Sticks ◆ ta-ka, ta-ka, ta-ka

Tempo

Tempo is the timing or speed at which music is played. In prose and poetry we often refer to this concept as *pacing*, knowing when to summarize information to speed up passages and when to elaborate passages to slow them down. Children can perform musical rhythms and beats at various speeds (slow like an elephant, fast like a gazelle) using homemade instruments. Identify nonsense words that match the sound of the instrument you are using (e.g., scrapers, swish; sticks or spoons, clackity clack; pots and pans, boom boom; or keys, ding-a-ling). Then have a group repeat the sounds and clap to different tempos.

Once students have been exposed to some of these elements of music, they are ready to listen with increased accuracy and greater refinement. To find out more about any of these elements, have children view videos from *The Music Box*, Children's Video Collection.

Appreciative Listening (with Music)

Appreciative or aesthetic listening is listening to music for enjoyment and pleasure. Literacy and musical experiences can evoke new appreciation for the richness of meanings produced by symbols and sounds. A worthwhile goal of the literacy program is to acquaint children with a broad musical repertoire. Scheduling a musical moment each day develops children's sensibilities and personal connections to aesthetic work. As shown in Table 3-2, musical moments are followed up by reading a book that coincides in mood and theme.

Teachers use this music not only to show similar dramatic effects with literature but also with art and poetry. Selecting a Gauguin painting with exotic images of the South Sea Islands, coupled with reggae music and colorful poetry from the book *Coconut Kind of Day: Island Poems* (Joseph, 1992), helps children see similarities with regard to moods, topics, images, and rhythms. Children begin to ask new kinds of questions: How does this poem or painting resemble the music of Mozart? How do artists, composers, and painters show energy or loneliness? Which painting looks like jazz? Which looks like a sonata? To expose children to many varieties of music, they might start a music-lending library to exchange favorite music on cassettes or CDs.

LANGUAGING STRAND: SOUNDS AND RHYTHMS OF LANGUAGE

Listening to the musicality of the voice and spoken word is part of language learning. From the endless stream of undifferentiated sounds, infants discriminate language from background noise. Dialogue duets between adults and children help teach them the rhythm of conversations and the various ways in which speech conveys human emotions and feelings (Heath, 1982; Snow, 1977). In this section we exploit the musical quality of our language to underscore its effects on prose and speech. The sounds and rhythms (or prosody) of language are defined as the intermingling of music and words. Together they offer a set of symbols (words, notes) and stylistic elements (sounds, tempo, volumes, rhythms) that children use to create meanings and interpretations.

TABLE 3-2   Listening to Music and Language

Listening Selections	Language and Literacy Uses	Children's Prose or Poetry
Western classical music selections		
"Wiegenlied" (the famous "Brahm's Lullaby"), by Johannes Brahms	Rhythms, mood	*Moonsong Lullaby* (Highwater, 1981)
"Symphony of Fanfares" by John Joseph Moray	Pomp and ceremony	*Singing America: Poems That Define a Nation* (Philip, 1995)
"The Four Seasons" by Antonio Vivaldi	Setting moods: poetry, story writing	"Seasonal Poetry" in *Random House Book of Poetry for Children* (Prelutsky, 1983)
"Carnival of the Animals" by Camille Saint-Saens (for imagining animal movements; 14 pieces, each representing a different animal)	Humor and animals	*Selected Poetry of Ogden Nash* (Nash, 1989).
World music selections		
African music	Chants, call and response, rhythmical beats	*Talking Drums of Africa* (Price, 1973)
Music from Zambabwe (Tracey Recording, Pacific Palisades, CA)	Color, timbre, vocabulary, pronunciations	*Baby-O* (Carlstrom, 1992)
Caribbean music	Rhythms, syncopation, play and games	*I Have a News: Rhymes from the Caribbean* (Jekyll, 1994)
Caribbean Carnival: Songs of the West Indies (songbook)		
American music selection	Improvisation	*Charlie-Parker Played Be-Bop* (Raschka, 1992)
"Maple Leaf Rag" by Scott Joplin		

Earobics

Earobics are listening exercises that focus children's attention on sounds. Sounds are everywhere: birds singing, motors humming, crickets chirping, and fires crackling. Attending to sounds produced by living things and objects sets the stage for encoding and decoding language and shows the many forms that communication takes. Have the children listen to a sequence of five recorded sounds (e.g., dog barking, footsteps, door bell, scream, laughing children). Next, ask them to make up a short episode to explain what is happening in the order that the sounds are heard.

Mother left me home alone one night. She went to visit Mrs. Smith next door. Suddenly I heard Rusty bark. Then I heard footsteps coming up the walk. The door bell rang and I screamed. When I calmed down I went to the door and kept the chain across the door as I opened it only about 3 inches. I saw the man who wrote out Mother's insurance policy. He knew I was afraid, so he

TABLE 3-3   Sounds

Type of Sound	Cause of the Sound
Annoying	Fingernails skidding down a chalkboard
Endearing	A little dog snoring
Adventurous	Crash of waves or river rapids
Serene	Rain falling, ocean rhythms
Frenzied	Campfire sizzling and crackling

gave me a paper through the crack in the door. When he left, I laughed at myself but felt smart for having done what I did.

After they do this, they reread the passage and substitute sounds for words (e.g., for dog, bow-wow, or for doorbell, ding-dong). Specific behaviors and actions can stimulate sound associations (Table 3-3).

Older children can experiment with sound effects for setting moods in storytelling, drama, or film (see Chapters 5 and 6). For example, thunder conveys an ominous night, and laughter suggests gaiety among friends. Words and phrases that create images based on sounds (e.g., a "blustery day," "clashing opinions," or a "whining story") are placed in notebooks for later use in writing.

Literary Sounds

Sounds that comprise some written words and speech are known as literary sounds. The sound system (phonology) of language, when combined and composed in several ways, creates different functions and articulated effects. Consider how your mouth must be formed to say *snort, snit, snarl,* and *sneer* or *flicker, flutter,* and *flurry*. Words characterized by "sn" sounds produce repeated hissing sounds while those beginning with "fl" produce a rapid flapping sound. Understanding literary sounds makes it possible for children to acquire some of the stylistic elements that writers use. Table 3-4 shows a few of these.

Nonnative speakers can share some foreign words and phrases that carry melodious sounds, such as the French *c'est la vie* (pronounced "SAY la vee"), meaning to celebrate fancy and throw caution to the wind, or humorous sounds such as the German guttural "r" and "ch" in *übermensch* (pronounced "OO ber mensh"), meaning Superman. The lively movement of the Spanish word *cucaracha* (pronounced "coo ca RA cha") or the songlike quality of the Italian word *bellissima* (pronounced "bay LEE see ma") are other examples. Some poets write in English *and* in a foreign language

TABLE 3-4   Literary Stylistic Elements

Literary Device	Examples
Alliteration: the relationship between words and identical consonants which precede the first accented vowel (slip, slide). This poetic device creates sound and rhythm. It is the repetitive use of the same initial consonant in words used in succession. Often, it gives movement to a poem or prose (e.g., vitamins for vim and vigor). Sounds in poetry offer cadence and beat; in prose they offer rhythm and pacing.	Take a simple purple pansy In a perfect pewter pot Sit it on a painted porch Where the sun pours down a lot. Pamper the posey with patience Add poetic words of praise Now watch this pompous perennial Makes its way to the patio stage.
Assonance and consonance: the repetition of vowel or consonant sounds as they appear in words that echo one another in the middle and end of lines. They are recurring vowel sounds in the presence of changing consonant sounds such as "hit" and "will" or "moment" and "loaded." Or they are recurring consonant sounds that often appear at the end of the word and resonate with the vowel sounds (e.g, "batch" and "botched" or batch and "catch").	A naughty sleezy weasel Stole a painting from an easel While a measley eager beagle Stole it back to please an eagle "Not for me, this is not regal" Said the cunning hawk-eyed eagle "I cannot seize a weasel's work Until this deal is legal."
Onomatopoeia: words that imitate the sound associated with a thing or action in a poem or story (kerplunk, twitter, wham). This device produces an effect of motion and sound. The use of onomatopoela helps to create the meaning of the word by its effect on the sentence.	Bump and bang Twist and turn Dents and scratches Tires burn Fast and furious Swing and sway It's a slam-dunk Bumper-car day
Rhyme: similar sounding words. If words sound exactly the same, they are full rhymes (e.g., could/would). If the rhyme is more fluid and draws on the sense of the poem but is only close in sound, it is called a half rhyme (e.g., silver/deliver). A half rhyme is sometimes referred to as "off rhyme" or "near rhyme" or "slant rhyme."	After the storm, we see a form An arc of red, green, and pink, A rainbow design blue, lemon, and lime, All gone in a blink of a wink.

Repetition: patterns that use words, phrases, lines, or questions over and over for cadence, pleasure, and structure. They are like the repeated sounds of windshield wipers, moving back and forth, or the steady pulse beats of a pendulum.	Oh where have you been, silly goose, silly goose?
	Oh where have you been, silly goose?
	      1st Verse
	—I've been to the lake, to bathe and sun-bake
	Make no mistake, father goose
	    (repeat first two lines)

TABLE 3-4   Literary Stylistic Elements *(continued)*

Literary Device	Examples
Repetition (continued)	2nd Verse —I've been to the barn, to cackle and charm No need for alarm, father goose. (repeat first two lines) 3rd Verse —I've been to the fair, to visit the mare No cause for a scare, father goose.

for musical effect. In the book *If I had a Paka: Poems in Eleven Languages* Pomerantz (1982), the author uses words from languages such as Swahili, Serbo-Croatian, Native American, English, Samoan, Dutch, Vietnamese, Japanese, Indonesian, Spanish, and Yiddish. Here is one in Vietnamese:

Toy Tik Ka

I like fish. Toy tik ka.
I like chicken. Toy tik ga.
I like duck. Toy tik veet.
I like meat. Toy tik teet.
But though I like ka, ga, veet, teet—
Fish and chicken, duck and meat—
Best of all I like to eat.

Pomerantz (1982)

A multicultural activity that is fun for children is to identify onomatopoeic sounds in different languages (e.g., *din don*—in Spanish, for ringing the bell; *chichicherichi-kee kee ker REE kee,* for the sound of a rooster in Italian; or *coo-coo-RI-co,* for crow in Jamaican).

The Language Beat

The beat of language refers to its repeated patterns of stress and timing. Writers often make conscious use of stylistic devices to accentuate these features. The rhythms give prose or poetry an aesthetic quality that matches that of music. Speech, too, with its prosodic or musical qualities, gives people a unique voice print that assists or impedes the natural flow of a conversational exchange. Some of these stylistic elements are shown in Table 3-5.

TABLE 3-5   Musical Stylistic Elements

Music Device	Examples
Rhythm: a pattern of sounds perceived as equal beats over and over in more-or-less equal intervals (Baldick, 1990). There are several kinds of rhythm:	Hippity, hippity hop Can't get my feet to stop They jiggle and wiggle Waggle and flop Till my shoestrings are ready to pop!
Rising rhythm, in which the voice moves upward in stress and tone. *Falling rhythm,* the opposite of rising rhythm.	My carnival favorite, the Ferris wheel, goes round and round and up and down And off we go first high, then low It swings and sways rocks to and fro It's coming down There goes my bow!
Running rhythm, in which a tripping of words over the tongue is felt.	A B C D Tell me what you think of me E F G H Say nice things or let it be I J K L Listen up or you will see M N O P I'll skip the rest and go to Z.
Rocking rhythm, which involves a stressed beat, followed by unstressed beats, leading up to the next stressed beat.	Hush, little baby, don't say a word Mama's going to buy you a mocking bird And if that mocking bird don't sing Mamma's going to buy you a diamond ring. *Traditional lullaby*
Cadence: the musical version of punctuation marks. Just as we use periods to mark off sentences and commas to set off phrases, so we use full and half closes with notes to end music pieces. In poetic verse, line breaks, white spaces, and punctuation help create a cadence.	ONE-two March beat ONE-two ONE-two-three Waltz beat ONE-two-three ONE-two-three-four Native American ONE-two-three-four drum beat

TABLE 3-5   Musical Stylistic Elements *(continued)*

Music Device	Examples
Meter: the cadence and syllable stress that gives rhythm to speech. The teacher should be familiar with the beat patterns. Children can substitute expressions such as "ta-tum" or "weak-strong" for iambic. Clapping to the beats or using rhythm sticks is an ideal way to involve the children in beat patterns. A metronome that measures tempo can also help children keep beat, clap to syllables, or accent words.	There once was a rabbit named Cy u / u u / u u / Who wanted to sing and to fly u / u u / u u / He could not think straight u / u u / But I must relate u / u u / He learned how to multiply. u / u u / u u
Iambic (iamb) u /	*Song:* Mexican hat dance (opening); *Word:* balLON
Trochaic (trochee) / u	*Song:* "Sing a Song of Sixpence"; *Word:* SiLly
Anapestic (anapest) u u /	*Song:* Brahm's lullaby; *Word:* unforeSEEN
Dactylic (dactyl) / u u	*Song:* Strauss waltz; *Word:* RECtangle
Spondaic (spondee) / /	*Song:* "California, Here I Come" (opening); *Word:* RAILROAD
Poetry is measured in feet, which are groups of syllables, stressed or unstressed, that combine to form the rhythmical units. Monometer 1 foot Dimeter 2 feet Trimeter 3 feet Tetrameter 4 feet Pentameter 5 feet Hexameter 6 feet Heptameter 7 feet Octameter 8 feet	Jack/and Jill/went up/the hill (4 feet— tetrameter)

Metrical Feet:

If you have trouble remembering the metrical feet, memorize this.

> Trochee trips from long to short.
> From long to long in solemn sort
> Slow Spondee stalks; strong foot! yet ill able
> Ever to come up with Dactyl trisyllable.
> Iambics march from short to long.
> With a leap and a bound the swift Anapests throng.

Samuel Taylor Coleridge [1772–1834]

Two special chapters in *Knock at a Star: A Child's Introduction to Poetry* (Kennedy and Kennedy, 1982) provide samples of poetry with a beat: "Word Music" and "Beats That Repeat."

POETRY STRAND: THE PULSE OF POETRY

Poetry is a metaphor for music. Writers often shape their work to create melody, language play, and sound. In Western culture, the first poems were sung by bards and troubadours (traveling poets), who knew that their listeners would remember information longer if they sang songs with catchy rhythms and simple plot lines. Like music, poetry expressed the feelings and ideas of the poet and gave continuity and pattern to the words heard. The pulse of poetry refers to the rhythmic beats and music that all of the literacy forms in this section contain.

Choral Poetry

Choral poetry is like a musical performance, the joining of speaking voices into a chorus to express and interpret poetry. Using paralinguistic cues or voice qualities such as inflections, pronunciation, volume, pitch, intonations, and phrasing, children recite poetry with the support of a group. Choral poetry helps to build fluency, a smooth flow, and easy pronunciation as they practice reading, listening, and speaking. When selecting materials for choral poetry, look for rhymes that are easy to memorize or have appealing characteristics. Humor, rhyme, and other literary features linked to pictures are particularly suitable for young children (Barclay and Walwer, 1992; Lamme, 1990). The teacher can copy the poem on an overhead or chart paper for easy viewing and identify the lines for single voice, two voices, or multiple voices. The next step is to focus on the rhythm and flow of the words. Clapping the beat, using rhythm sticks, or beating a drum offers practice with tempo and volume. Once children have a sense of the beat, they can help the teacher place musical marks or cues over the words. In this way they remember how to read the poem using music notation (see Table 3-6).

TABLE 3-6   Musical Notation

Dynamics	Tempo
< Crescendo (pronounced), "cruh SHEN dō"), meaning increasing or gradually growing louder	Presto (pronounced "PRESS toe"), meaning fast
> Decrescendo (pronounced "dee cra SHEN dō"), meaning growing softer	Adagio (pronounced "un DA jō), meaning slow; at ease
p Piano, meaning soft	Allegro (pronounced "uh LEG grō"), meaning spirited
pp Pianissimo (pronounced "pee a NEE see mō"), meaning very soft	Andante (pronounced "un DAWN tay"), meaning to walk or moderate speed
f Forte (pronounced "FOR tay"), meaning loud	
ff Fortissimo (pronounced "for TEE see mō"), meaning very loud	
m Mezzo (pronounced "MET tsō"), meaning medium	

To practice choral poetry with concepts such as loud, soft, fast, and slow, have children listen to the poem song *The Animal Fair* (anonymous) and have them sing along as they follow the musical and print cues.

I went to the animal fair,/

*   *

The birds and beasts were there./

*   *

The big baboon, by the light of the moon,

*   *

Was combing his auburn hair./

*   *

The monkey, he got drunk,/

*   p   *

And sat on the elephant's trunk./

*   *

The elephant sneezed and fell on his knees,

*   <   * f

An what became of the monk, ||: the monk :|| the monk?

*   ff   *   *   *

Anonymous

Key:

*	Stress	>	Grow louder
p	Soft	<	Grow softer
/	Slight pause	f	Loud;
||: :||	Repeat	ff	Very loud

Finally, as shown in Table 3-7, children should experiment with a variety of choral poem arrangements. Voices reflect variations, like the instruments of an orchestra. There are many books suitable for choral reading. A popular selection is *Joyful Noise: Poems for Two Voices* (Fleishman, 1992).

To judge the recitation of choral poems, children ask some of the following questions:

- Did the speakers read aloud with expression and phrasing?
- Did the speakers associate beats, syllables, and time values with the rhythm of poetry?
- Did the speakers use paralinguistic cues (speed, inflections, volume, pronunciation, pauses, and rhythm)?
- Did the speakers use nonverbal cues (gestures, facial expressions, movements, and eye gaze)?
- Did the speakers harmonize with others in the chorus?

TABLE 3-7   Choral Poem Arrangements

Unison: singing or speaking together.

Refrain: regular recurring phrase in songs and poems.

Antiphonal verse: a form of choral presentation performed by two alternating groups.

Expandable verse: a kind of chain where children use their imaginations to build a song. As each stanza is read, new voices are heard.

Call and response: poems with two parts. It is a basic request, question, or command followed by a second statement that suggests that the first statement should be answered.

Echoic verse: a line spoken by a reader which is then repeated by the audience.

Musical rounds: melodies performed by two or more voices entering at different times.

Rap

Rap is a running commentary on the social realities of urban and modern life. It isn't quite the spoken word or conventional singing, but instead, resembles a kind of speechifying whose layered effect (music overlapping talk) creates texture. Curt and sharp-witted, this verbal art performance emphasizes words over music. Although rap has had a recent resurgence, its verbal strategies have a long tradition in African American communications (Abrahams and Gay, 1975; Dandy, 1991, Kochman, 1981; Smitherman, 1977).

Children can begin studying raps using poetry with a beat. Have children find traditional poems that have a rap tempo or movement that can be performed. Younger children might read and perform rhyming raps such as *MC Turtle and the Hip Hop Hare: A Happenin' Rap* (Vozar, 1997) or *Yo Hungry Wolf? A Nursery Rap* (Vozar, 1995) and accompany these with drums, gourd shakers, tin cans, or rattles.

Children can create raps as book talks. The rap serves as a way to respond to a special book or to inspire others to read it. For example, here's a motivational talk rap, *The Watsons Go to Birmingham—1963* (Curtis, 1995).

This is a book you all should read,
it will have you laughin' and slappin' your knees.
Boom Boom . . . Chikaaaa.
Boom Boom . . . Chikaaa.

The story is of the Watson family,
a family of five you will see.
Young Kenny's growing up, Byron's being bad,
and Joey is the sweet girl
we all wish we had.
Boom Boom . . . Chikaaa
Boom Boom . . . Chikaaa

The family's on their way to Birmingham
From Michigan to Alabama they must span
Boom Boom . . . Chikaaa
Boom Boom . . . Chikaaa

In Alabama they'll learn a lesson
you will see
That the world isn't all that
they thought it would be
Boom Boom . . . Chikaaa
Boom Boom . . . Chikaaa

The story is a great one
you will see
If you read *The Watsons Go to Birmingham—1963.*
Boom Boom . . . Chikaaa
Boom Boom . . . Chikaaa

Raps not only summarize stories but tell original stories as well. *Nathaniel Talking* (Greenfield, 1988) is an example of several raps that collectively tell about a young boy's view of the world. Raps are enjoyable for children and provide another way to approach traditional forms of literacy. Several "pedagogical rap ideas" can be found in Macklis (1989) or Jeremiah (1992). For those interested in a description of rap and the history of this pop-music genre, see the book *Rap* (Greenberg, 1991).

Once children have read raps and used them in familiar ways, they may want to create their own original raps. Children are undoubtedly more familiar with raps than adults are, so now is a good time to let them be the experts and teach you what they already know. They can bring in contemporary rap music such as Puff Daddy, L L Cool J, or Big Willie Smith. Since many raps come in two different versions, the "clean version" and the one with the parental advisory label, be sure to check the CD covers. Children will enjoy teaching the class their favorite rhythms and lyrics. Of course, just about any subject matter can be turned into a rap. Older children can search newspapers and magazines for political and social topics, since rap often deals with urban life, societal problems, and youth culture. Have children brainstorm ideas for their topic. Meanwhile, the teacher inductively helps children identify the historical and contemporary characteristics of rap:

- ◆ Originally used as an introductory ritual between males and females, to impress, persuade, or to give information; today, it is used to entertain.
- ◆ Highly stylized and flamboyant; short, choppy speechifying.
- ◆ Uses voice effects (i.e., whines, growls), intonations, pitch, and sounds.
- ◆ Uses slang, exaggerations, wild comparisons, and active verbs.
- ◆ Spoken and delivered at a very fast speed.
- ◆ Accompanied by a performance (often, gestures and movements).
- ◆ Forces an overt response on the part of the listener and absorbs the audience (hand clapping, laughter, sing-along).

Once children have a topic and some guidelines, they are ready to develop and structure the content as a story, poem, biography, report, diary, or letter. Some may first prefer to create a musical beat with rhythm sticks, finger snapping, foot stomping, or other inventive sounds and then match them to the content; others may do the opposite; and still others may go back and forth between rhythm and words. You can show children some typical musical beats by referring back to the rhythm section. Have the children perform raps in different choral arrangements (e.g., over an audible beat or echoed as you read a poem).

Ballads

As introduced in the medieval unit of Chapter 1, the ballad is a simple verse or short narrative song that tells a story of love or adventure. Children in Mrs. Smith's class studied courtly love and then were asked to write their own ballads. Since one purpose of the ballad was to entertain, and because it had to be recited and remembered, the ballad embodied characteristics that the teacher felt important for the children to consider.

- ◆ Tells a story (topics involved love, adventure, intrigue and super-natural influences).

- ◆ Narrative usually focused on a single important episode; plot was the central element; began where the action was already in progress and heading toward calamity (for intensity and heightened emotional impact); emphasis was on action and dialogue rather than description and characterization.

- ◆ Used plain language that was often formulaic and used incremental repetition (as a mnemonic for reciting the story); often included re-frains.

- ◆ Was often written in Middle English (*thee, thou, knave,* or *fortnight*); used archaic words (*lass, lad,* or *yonder*).

- ◆ Usually consisted of the abcb rhyme pattern; question-answer exchanges were common.

- ◆ Was sung to a modal melody (musical scales with exotic Greek names that originated in medieval times).

- ◆ Was written as a quatrain (four lines per verse); was often eight syllables with four stresses per line (like the folk song pattern or singsong rhythm).

After reviewing the characteristics of the ballad, the children selected someone or something they loved and brainstormed ideas about the love relationship or episode. Since medieval romance involved stories of adventure in a chivalric sense, themes from romantic novels or grand adventures were suggested (star-crossed lovers, extraordinary feats for love, scorned love, mishaps at sea, and piracy). Once they had some ideas, they selected a familiar melody with a single repetitive verse that they could use to structure their ballad. The teacher illustrated music–literacy connections by playing a musical ballad, singing the lyrics, and comparing it to the ballad as a written story or poem. For example, she played *The Ballad of the Blue Bonnet,* a charming musical of a beautiful southwest flower (see "Additional Resources") and then read *The Legend of the Blue Bonnet* (de Paola, 1983). She also played music such as "The Legend of the Edmund Fitzgerald" (see Table 3-8) to show how storytelling interfaced with rhythm and rhyme.

Modern ballads are often protest songs ("Blowin' in the Wind" by Bob Dylan), outlaw songs (Jesse James), or songs about famous people, real or

TABLE 3-8　Putting Music to Poetry

Features to Consider	Sir Patrick Spens (Anonymous)
Theme/topic	Human drama; adventure
Voice and point of view	Narrator, first person; telling story to a listener who seems present; question and answer exchanges
Mood/lyrical beat	Melancholy; robust
Style	Legendary, colorful

Songs with Similar Features

"The Legend of the Edmund Fitzgerald" by Gordon Lightfoot; "Cat's in the Cradle" by Harry Chapin; "Bridge over Troubled Water" by Simon and Garfunkel

imagined (John Henry, Tom Dooley, Robin Hood). A classic children's ballad is *Casey at the Bat: A Ballad of the Republic, Sung in the Year 1888* (Thayer, 1991). The famous first verse is printed here.

> The outlook wasn't brilliant for the Mudville nine that day;
> The score stood four to two with but one inning more to play.
> And then when Cooney died at first, and Barrows did the same,
> A sickly silence fell upon the patrons of the game.

Traditional

Ballads represent many cultures. For example, *Ducks and Dragons: Poems for Children* (Kemp, 1983) contains English, Scottish, and American ballads. The book *The Little Mohee: An Appalachian Ballad* (Troughton, 1970) narrates episodes from rural southern Appalachia in song, poem, and pictures. Irish ballads such as "Danny Boy" or Australia's "Waltzing Matilda" are well known and loved. Probably the most famous ballads are those about the sea, such as Samuel Taylor Coleridge's *The Rime of the Ancient Mariner* and *Sir Patrick Spens* (Coleridge, 1997). Children will enjoy reading and writing ballads as they discover different ways of presenting narrative about adventure and diverse peoples from around the world.

Chants

A chant is a type of verbal performance, half speech, half song, and in monotones. This short musical ritual, phrase, or verbal text makes use of phonetic, lexical, or phrasal repetition, organized internally by language and externally by music (Merriam-Webster, 1995). Spanning cultures and traditions, some of the best known chants go back to the early periods of history, such as the temple chanting of Buddhist monks, or the dance songs of Eskimo villagers, or the aboriginal rituals of Australia. In Western churches, Anglican chant, Byzantine chant, and Gregorian chant (named after Pope Gregory I) were part of religious services. Sacred chants were also part of the Native American culture. These often took the form of legends or tales of their great ancestors. *My Drum* (Meyerowitz et al., 1988) is an unusual collection of poetry, song, native sound making, and chants in both native Zulu and English. Another multicultural collection is *Songs for Survival: Songs and Chants from Tribal Peoples Around the World* (Smith, 1996).

Children write, read, and sing chants in chorales or singing groups. Using chants in the classroom can expand children's traditional view of what constitutes a poem. They may want to use repetition, prose elements, or refrains to help structure their chant. They can begin with simple chants to accompany daily rituals in the classroom. These may be affirmations such as "I enjoy learning from others" or rules such as "Now I put my books away."

Spirituals

Spirituals are powerful religious folk songs that once centered on the daily lives and concerns of the slaves. Sung in the fields or in small country churches and one-room schoolhouses, people sang messages that expressed ideas of inner strength, belief in life after death, and the Old and New Testaments. Today, this communal form extends to jubilees and lullabies and is an important type of musical poetry performed and often choreographed as gospel music and hymns sung by choirs and religious congregations everywhere. Spirituals are part of our American heritage, celebrating diversity and instilling a deeper understanding of our historical legacy.

Spirituals often make use of repetition or call-and-response forms. The soloist might step out to "testify," making a personal show of faith by singing a phrase or verse and then blending back into the group as the phrase is repeated by others. This free and spontaneous expression is like a question-and-answer dialogue in which "all the speaker's statements (calls) are punctuated by expressions (responses) from the "listener" (Smitherman, 1986, p. 104). Most often the response is latched to the final word:

Call: There is a need for *freedom*

Response: *freedom* (overlapping the words of the call)

or it can be a completion of the speaker's pronouncement, such as:

Call: There is a need . . .

Response: *for freedom* (following the words of the call)

In the classroom, you might start with a collection of this verse, such as the beautifully illustrated children's book *This is My Song* (Higginsen, 1995). Familiar titles such as Louis Armstrong's "When the Saints Go Marchin' In," or chorales such as "Down by the Riverside" prompt children to move, dance, and sing to the melody, rhythm, and repetition of words. Since the songs are "elastic," children can improvise or repeat lyrics, insert a musical question or comment at the end of a musical line, or respond in movement to the improvisation along the way.

Leader: L   Group: G

L: Oh when the saints

G: Oh when the saints

L: Go marchin' in

G: Go marchin' in

L: Oh when the saints go marchin' in

L: Let's sing it louder!

G: I want to be in that number

L: Oh yea

G: When the saints go marchin' in

L: What do you want?

G: I want to be in that number

G: When the saints go marchin' in

As children sing, they use melodies and voice to inflect notes, twist notes, turn notes, bend notes, and blend notes to make spontaneous creations that the group can accompany with hand clapping or foot stomping (Preminger and Brogan, 1993).

Odes

The ode is a longer form of lyrical verse with one central theme. The ode usually commemorates public events or state ceremonies such as dedicating a building, celebrating an athletic victory, or lamenting tragedy. The tone, exalted, emotional, intense, or sentimental, reflects tribute to an object, person, or idea. Studying the ode enhances children's appreciation of the musicality of words and the functions they serve.

The children discuss the use of language for paying homage to an object of affection. The teacher helps them brainstorm ideas about the object's sentimental value. Ordinary, everyday items and events can be celebrated. Think of honoring your favorite ice cream.

DUM da DUM da DUM da DUM
Oh dear ice cream, perk me up
DUM da DUM da DUM
Flavors in a row

DUM da DUM da DUM da DUM da
Chocolate chip, mint creme and cherry
DUM da DUM da DUM
What a tasteful show!

See if children can clap to the common meter (alternating stresses of 3 and 4 beats) before experimenting with other musical odes.

The most famous odes ever written were those by Keats: "Ode to Psyche," "Ode on a Grecian Urn," "Ode to a Nightingale," and "To Autumn" (Keats, 1987). In music, Schiller's "Ode to Joy" in the final movement of Beethoven's Ninth Symphony is probably most notable.

Poems Set to Music and Music-Inspired Poems

The marriage of music and poetry has a long history. The poems of great writers were often recreated in musical terms (e.g., the lyrics of Ogden Nash recreated in music by Saint-Saens' *Carnival of the Animals*) and great music often became the inspiration for poetry (e.g., Debussy's *Prelude to the Afternoon of a Faun* as inspiration for the symbolic poetry of Mallarme). Children select music that produces the poetic image they are trying to convey. Creative music offers older children an ideal way to understand concepts of "mood" or "tone" in poetry. For example, the classical compositions by Debussy (e.g., *Arabesque*) evoke an airy, impressionistic, and delicate blend of melody and movement. Play the music through for the first time, and have the children write down initial impressions based on their five senses:

What I See	What I Feel	What I Hear	What I Taste	What I Smell
Shadows	Mist on my face	Footsteps	Sweetness	Fresh air

Then have children write a poem and draw a picture to accompany the music. Use some of the captivating musical selections in the first part of this chapter to help children match words, pictures, and sounds.

STORY STRAND: MUSICAL STORIES

Like poetry, stories have a strong relationship to music. The earliest stories were set to music and sung about heroic events (e.g., *Aida* by Verdi) narrative settings (e.g., *The Four Seasons* by Vivaldi), and cultural traditions (e.g., folk songs like "Arabian Nights" by Russian composer Rimsky-Korsakov).

The symphonic fairytale classic *Peter and the Wolf* by Sergio Prokofiev tells a story about a young boy named Peter who outsmarts a wolf (Prokofiev, 1987). It is told with musical instruments representing the characters: Peter is portrayed by a string orchestra, his grandfather, by a bassoon, the cat, by a clarinet, the duck, by an oboe, the bird, by a flute, the wolf, by a bass drum, and the hunters, by the horns. Each time the designated characters appear, the musical instruments of the characters are played while the actors role-play their parts. The popular musician Sting narrates the story. In this section the teacher introduces children to the ways in which musical stories are told and performed with and without words.

Folk Song Stories

Folk songs are traditional simple melodies and words that tell a story. Like folk literature they are steeped in oral tradition and learned from hearing rather than reading. Timeless and anonymous, folk music was rural in nature, frequently accompanied by dances venerating peasant life. This music belonged to the entire community and was passed down orally from person to person across generations.

Early American folk songs were about family life, religious faith, hard work, and survival. Many of these songs, rooted in English and Scottish ballads, were used not only for entertainment but also for expediting work. Imitating the motions, rhythm and tempo of the tasks to be done, songs such as "I've Been Working on the Railroad" (traditional), "Pick a Bale of Cotton" by the folksinger Leadbelly, and "Working in a Chain Gang" by Bob Marley used melodies tailored to the job (driving in railroad spikes, chopping wood) to increase efficiency and unify actions (Boni, 1947). Patriotic songs like the "Star-Spangled Banner" by Francis Scott Key, "Yellow Rose of Texas " by George Cohan, and "Stars and Stripes Forever" by John Philip Sousa provided valuable insights into America's past, its values and traditions. Two exemplary collections are *From Sea to Shining Sea: A Treasury of American Folklore and Folk Songs* (Cohn, 1993) and *Singing America: Poems that Define a Nation* (Philip, 1995).

In addition to American folk songs, multicultural stories such as "Abiyoyo" by Pete Seeger, which is based on a South African lullaby, and *The Magic Story Singer: From the Finnish Epic Tale Kalevala*, retold by McNeil (1993), use narrative to create a musical ambiance that becomes associated with the country, its customs and traditions, its landscape, and its social mores. Writing and performing folk music stories stimulate interest in cultural history and extend children's understandings of how music conveys the feelings of common, everyday people. For example, consider teaching an Irish story poem with Celtic music. You play this music softly in the background during the schoolday. Then when children become familiar with the lilting lyrics and melody, you turn the volume up and have them listen attentively to the words. Children discuss this Irish folk tune and then substitute words to create alternative versions. In order to write their lyrics, they study Irish customs and history so that the folk songs tell about social and cultural events. If children are not ready to write a story, they can limber up with the story limericks or rhymes embedded in the folk song. Writing folk songs helps children use music as a scaffold to structure their writing and shows them how to produce a thicker texture and rhythm to the words they are creating. The performance of their folk songs helps them learn about particular ethnic groups.

Children's Opera

An opera is a drama set to music and made up of vocal pieces with orchestral accompaniment, overtures and interludes. The first opera was performed in the seventeenth century at La Scala Opera House in Milan, Italy. This Opera House is still the home of today's famous tenor, Luciano Pavorotti, whose recent CD entitled "My Favorite Opera for Children" introduces children to the opera form. Although one of the most striking aspects of the opera's storytelling is the voices of the singers, with their exceptional expressive powers, many children's operas are more like musical plays. One of the best known operas for children of all ages is *Amahl and the Night Visitors,* by Gian-Carlo Menotti, a lovely Christmas classic (Menotti, 1986). There is also a book version illustrated by M. Lemieux. Like the opera, it tells about a poor widow and her crippled son. On Christmas day, a splendid miracle occurs when the boy meets the three kings and finds that he is able to walk again. There are many short opera plays for the elementary classroom, such as the mini musical *Three Piggy Opera* (a musical spoof of the three little pigs) or *Stone Soup* (a "rock" opera). The teacher will find many adult operas rewritten as stories for children such as *Aida* (Price, 1990), which tells about an Ethiopian princess captured during a war with the Egyptians, or *Lamb's Tales from Great Operas* (Elliott, 1984), a collection of popular operas of the twentieth century. *The Magic Flute,* a famous opera by Mozart, is available as a picture book with piano arrangement.

Reading the stories behind the great operas gives children another literacy choice for enriching their lives and acquainting them with Western culture. Children can also perform familiar stories opera style by "telling" or narrating parts, singing the dialogue, and using the sounds of musical instruments for actions in the story. Older children may actually be ready to write portions of an opera. They do not have to write original scores but might use a favorite storybook as a model. They ask themselves:

◆ "What settings or feelings in the book can be conveyed by music? Suspense? Gaiety?

◆ How do I want the music to make the audience feel? What types of music might portray the characters? Do I want them to be capricious and fairylike, dark and brooding?

◆ Does the book show more than one character? What do they do, alone and together? How can my story reveal the actions of these characters through music?

◆ What is the conflict or dramatic high point of the story? How can I imbue my words with this drama? What music will capture this feeling?

If children write original operas, they will need to generate ideas for a story line by moving back and forth between the words and music. As they assemble the narrative for a single act, they may find it necessary to read and act out the story first before adding the music or improvising the words. When the opera is finished, they write the words in small books called *librettos*. Librettos were once provided to members of the audience so that they could follow along. Since operas are known for their great pagentry and spectacle (Gannon, 1994), the children can discuss the high emotions they wish to portray in the delivery of the opera and identify a few props they might use, such as a wig, a fan, a beard, or a dagger. Teachers inclined to try out this form of literacy will find that plenty of support materials (e.g., filmstrips, cassettes, lesson plans, and handouts) are available from the Metropolitan Opera Guild.

Oratorios

An oratorio is a vocal dramatic work originally conceived for popular entertainment and based on biblical subjects. Handel's *Messiah* is the world's best known and best loved. Usually performed in a concert hall or church, the oratorio tells a story based on scenes from the Bible and is usually a chorus of praise. It is music and poetry set for solo voices, chorus, and orchestra. An oratorio includes recitatives and arias, which are songlike settings of a story, musically expressed. A book for children by Moser (1992) details the story and its music. Children can write celebrative stories that show triumphant accomplishments using words like "hallelujah" and "amen" in the closings. They can also take stories with spiritual themes such as the popular children's books *After the Flood* (Geisert, 1994) or *God's Gift* (the creation story; Richards, 1993) to inspire their own writing and explore the many different religions of the world.

Broadway Stories

Today's children are more in touch with music, video, and rap than they are with the show tunes of Rodgers and Hammerstein or Andrew Lloyd Webber. Yet because these stage plays are a piece of Americana, they provide children with a social history as well as a taste for theater music.

Children should be exposed to Broadway favorites such as *The Pirates of Penzance, Mary Poppins, Annie, Peter Pan, The Sound of Music, My Fair Lady,* or *Phantom of the Opera.* In most cases, teachers will be able to find book versions of these as well as videos. In fact, the children may want to compare the music videos with storybooks of the same title such as *The Surrey with the Fringe on Top* or *South Pacific* (Michener, 1992), both Rodgers and Hammerstein musical plays. Since most children enjoy musical stories of film and popular culture such as *Lion King, Willie Wonka and the Chocolate Factory,* and the classic *Wizard of Oz,* more will be said about them in Chapter 6.

Stories about Music and Musicians

Numerous children's books have music as a theme. Several books cleverly introduce names of musical instruments into the plots of their stories, such as *Meet the Orchestra* (Hayes, 1991), *The Musical Life of Gustav Mole* (Meyrick, 1993), or *Meet the Marching Smithereens* (Hayes, 1995). Others, such as *Grandma's Band* (Bowles, 1989) or *Ty's One-Man Band* (Walter, 1987) show children how sound-making instruments can originate from ordinary objects such as washing machines or pots and pans. In many of these books, the main character is accused of making noise and ends up making music, as in *Musical Max* (Krauss, 1990). Other common themes are the struggle to become a musician (*Come Sing Jimmy Jo,* Paterson, 1985) or recognition of a hidden talent (*Two Piano Tuners,* Goffstein, 1970). However, the most captivating theme of all in children's books is that of music having magical power to influence, mesmerize, trick, or rescue, as in *The Bremen Town Musicians* (Grimm, 1992) and *The Pied Piper of Hamelin* (Browning, 1997).

Biographies about musicians appeal to children's desire for heroes. Children are usually very interested in rock stars and recording artists. Have them write life stories about their favorite musicians. To start, identify the artists, list the songs they have recorded, and years, and then jot down some key words about their type of music (see Table 3-9). Next have students read biographies of the musician they have selected, such as *Young Mozart* (Isadora, 1997), *Jazz, My Music My People* (Monceaux, 1994), and *Lives of the Musicians* (Krull, 1993). After they write biographies, have them select audio recordings of the artist's music to play during (or following) the reading of the biography to the class.

To introduce contemporary groups and recording artists, students might read magazines such as *Rolling Stone* and *High Fidelity.* They can also organize a fan club and write letters to some of their favorite artists.

INFORMATION STRAND: LYRICS FOR LEARNING

Music is an important context for learning with important connections to memory and cognition (Miller and Coen, 1994; Serafine, 1988). Listening

TABLE 3-9   Recording Artists

Recording Artist/Group	Music	Year	Theme
Bob Dylan	*The Times They Are A-Changin; Bob Dylan's Greatest Hits; Nashville Skyline*	1960s	Folk songs; protest songs; prophetic songs
Dolly Parton	*Best of Dolly Parton; Coat of Many Colors*	1970s	Country; old fashioned virtues
Kiss	*Creatures of the Night; Unmasked; Dynasty*	1980s	Heavy metal; hard rock; theatrics; evil cartoon characters; mystery image
Puff Daddy and the Family	*No Way Out*	1990s	Rap

to rhymes, rhythms, and repetitions of song lyrics makes remembering information easier and helps anchor experiences for fine tuning memory (Maute, 1987). It is also an important tool for cultural transmission (Elliott, 1990) and influences our lives whether it is used as persuasion, as an emotional outlet, or as a source of entertainment. In this section you will become familiar with musical messages as a way to help children learn content material and critically assess and analyze ideas.

Singing Songs

Lowell Mason (1792–1872), an educator from Boston, Massachusetts, was responsible for the inclusion of music in the school curriculum. He believed that young children should use songbooks for learning to read because it allowed them to express rhythms of language in enjoyable ways. Older children, too, enjoy singing songs as a way of reading to learn and gaining insights into social, historical, and cultural events (Kolb, 1996). For example, they might begin hypothesizing about historical events reflected in song titles as shown in Table 3-10. In Table 3-11, children list all the songs that have a particular word or concept in the title (e.g., love). They compare two different eras to see how the meaning of the concept has changed.

Both of these activities would be followed up with background research to trace the sociohistorical origins of these song titles. Many music books contain interesting information about music compositions and their composers. There are also many collections of songs to help children learn about their own and other cultures. Some of these are collections of patriotic songs such as *America the Beautiful* (Bates, 1993) or *Yankee Doodle* (Chalk, 1993). Others are large collections of cross-cultural songs such as *Arroz con Leche: Popular Songs and Rhymes from Latin America*

TABLE 3-10   Song Titles and Sociohistorical Events

1920s: Roaring Twenties	1945: World War II	1960s: Hippies; Vietnam
"Ain't Misbehavin"	"I'll Be Back"	"He's a Rebel"
"Boogie Woogie"	"Homesick—That's All"	"Gimme Some Lovin"
"Here Comes My Ball and Chain"	"Don't Let Me Dream"	"Stairway to Heaven"
"Big City Blues"	"Love Letters"	"He's Not Heavy, He's My Brother"
Depression Era	**Woman's Movement**	**Hostage Crisis: 1970s**
"Brother, Can You Spare a Dime?"	"I Am Woman"	"Tie a Yellow Ribbon Round the Ole Oak Tree"

TABLE 3-11   Song Titles for Two Different Time Periods

1920s	1980s
"I'd Love to Fall Asleep and Wake Up in My Mammy's Arms"	"Love on the Rocks"
"I Love the Land of Old Black Joe"	"Love Me Over Again"
	"Love T.K.O."
	"Love Makes Such Fools of Us"

(Delacre, 1989), a variety of Hispanic-American songs and poems, and *Lift Every Voice and Sing* (Johnson, 1993), an inspirational set of African-American songs.

How to Teach a Song
To teach a song (and reading at the same time), the teacher selects one of several approaches.

Wholistic Approach.   In this approach, try out the song ahead of time and make sure it has a strong melody that is easy to learn. When introducing it to the class, give a brief story about it. Then play the entire song through. Provide for repeated listenings before expecting children to learn the entire song. During each repetition, call attention to the content or various musical elements such as rhythms or melodic patterns. The teacher might also want to turn down the volume of the recording slowly so that the children sing independent of it. Indicate by hand gestures the rise and fall of melodies. When the song is learned all the way through, give a starting pitch and tempo, record the children's voices, and then have them critique the tape. After rehearsing the song again and feeling satisfied with it, children can place it at a learning center.

Parts Approach. This approach involves singing a phrase or verse at a time and having children repeat it. Using a large chart or songbooks, teach a certain section; remember that you don't always have to begin at the beginning. Children can use lip-synch reading, moving lips to the words without hearing the voice, to develop fluency and rhythm with the support of a record or tape. Gradually they learn the entire song and are given the music to accompany the words. After a while, children observe how voices rise and fall as the notes move up and down the musical staff. They may even learn to read simple rhythmic and melodic notation (e.g., the musical alphabet, notes, staff, and clefs) as well as the expressive symbols (>, <, pp, f) necessary for knowing "how" to sing tempo, dynamics, and expression. Have the children select simple accompaniments to the songs they sing (clapping spoons, a triangle, or a drum). Forming "glee clubs" in which groups of children join together to practice songs they wish to perform for the class can help students build fluency in speech and reading.

Songwriting

The word *composition* literally means putting things together. Children's songwriting is a marrying of writing and music to enhance fundamental concepts about language, musical rhythm and sound (Cockburn, 1995). Children can substitute their own words to familiar melodies and songs. Before children are asked to write lyrics, they will need to do repeated listening and singing of the songs. During these repeated listenings, they jot down images, colors, and feelings that the music elicits rather than thinking about words to write. The music should create pictures in their minds and ideas that they can translate into words. Songs can be about anything. To get ideas, good songwriters read a lot; they draw on legends, ancient tales, newsworthy ideas, and biblical imagery. Sometimes what they read becomes the first line of the song or chorus. Keeping a musical notebook of collected phrases, idioms, slang, poetry, and ideas for songs and song titles comes in handy when getting ready to write.

If students start with words and wish to write their own music, they might learn a few basic chords and simple notes to match the words. Sometimes they might start with a rhythm they like and turn that into music. Learning to play music by ear, that is, humming a musical tune and then trying to match it (through trial and error) to an instrument is another way to experiment. Of course, students should listen to the radio or their own musical collections for lyrics, melody, poetry, and structures.

Suggested Steps for Writing Lyrics

1. After listening to songs, reading a lot, and coming up with a set of ideas related to a theme, the children write a poem or story with a conflict. They attempt to carry ideas over from one verse to the next to create one continuous tale. If they have music in mind for their words, they can try to match the words to the melody (by meter, length of lines, and other sound beats). Children can practice matching stressed syllables with stressed notes. Through experimentation they discover that using strings of stressed syllables slows rhythms down while the opposite accelerates them.

2. Children make decisions and experiment with some stylistic elements; for example, rhyming to connect phrases, or adding ideas to the content, or using imagery to make the words come alive and "show" rather than "tell." The first-person point of view is most common, but second and third person is also used. Writers should remember that if they decide to mix points of view, they will need to "neutralize" the chorus, that is remove verbs and point of view so that the verses will agree with the shifts in perspective (Pattison, 1995).

3. Children discuss what song structure they will use for their story and melody: The song structure may be one of two types: (1) verse/ chorus and (2) verse/bridge. The verse/chorus structure looks like this:

> Verse, verse, chorus, verse, verse, chorus (the structure repeats itself about three times)

An example is provided in Figure 3-3. The verse/bridge structure looks like this:

> Verse, verse, chorus, verse, verse, bridge (repeats itself) or verse, chorus, verse, chorus, verse, bridge, chorus

An example is provided in Figure 3-4.

The bridge is a section that steps out from the regular structure and content of the song to provide another angle on the song both musically and lyrically (Davis, 1988; Zollo, 1993). It is sometimes called a "hook" because it draws the listener in. For instance, sometimes the title of the song will not appear within the verse or chorus and then appear only at the very end. Usually, it connects verses, verses and choruses, or choruses with choruses. Most often it is placed between the last two repeats of the chorus (this way it breaks up the pattern and sounds more exciting).

You can develop the song as a whole story or as an episode. The song usually begins with at least one verse, sometimes two, then a chorus. The verses usually set the scene, give basic information, introduce the main character, and build up a chorus. The verses repeat

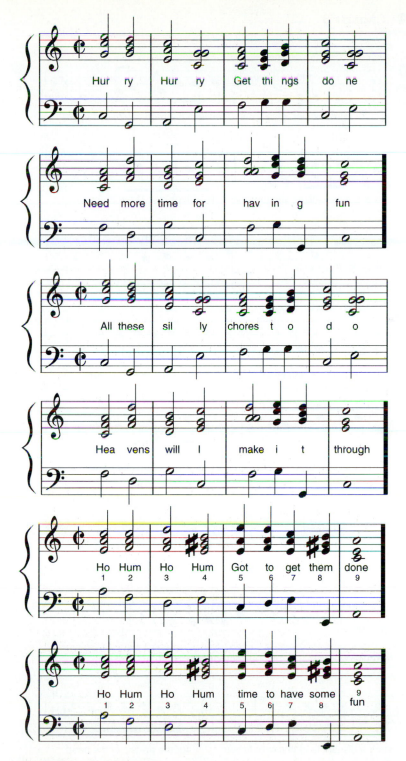

Figure 3-3 *"In a Hurry"*

Figure 3-4 *"Ragpicker Man" (Courtesy of Joseph Caruso, Sally Kendra, and Joseph Kendra)*

It's been said you on-ly made it through the third grade

But oh what a dif-fer-ence your life has made

Rag-pick-er man doing the best that you can

I love you rag-pick-er man I love you rag-pick-er man

mak-ing this land yours From the pri-zes of the heart

= rest equal to a quarter note

= 2 eighth notes

= 2 sixteenth notes

= 2 thirty-second notes

Figure 3-4 *(continued)*

Ragpicker man you with the hard calloused hands

Saving everything you touched saving prizes of the heart

Ragpicker man doing the best that you can

Wandering here and there for the prizes of the heart

I love you ragpicker man I love you ragpicker man

Always doing the best that you can my ragpicker man

Ragpicker man so misunderstood

Such a distant land that calls to you for the prizes of the heart

It's been said you only made it through the third grade

But oh what a difference your life has made

Ragpicker man doing the best that you can

Making this land yours from the prizes of the heart

Figure 3-4 *"Ragpicker Man" (continued)*

themselves musically and lyrically. This means they have a similar metrical pattern repeated throughout the song but with different words. There are usually two verses and a chorus and one or two repeats. Usually lyricists try to achieve brevity and simplicity and limit their verses so that playing time is about 3 minutes. The chorus usually repeats the title of the song or generalizes from the concrete details in the verses.

4. Finally, lyricists must learn the tools of the trade. They must revise for better rhyme, structure, and word choice, and avoid clichés and plagiarism. Above all, they make sure they are not using words that draw too much attention to themselves, distracting from the music. Table 3-12 offers three genres of music that are good starts for children because of the importance of the lyrics. But just about any type of music that is of interest to the children is suitable.

Media Melodies

Media melodies are TV and film music. They impress upon us many ideas, attitudes, and feelings and often mark the beginning of a motion picture, sit-com, or soap opera. These melodies are used to build suspense or touch

TABLE 3–12   Selected Songwriting Genres

♦ *Country-Western.* Country music began as the traditional music of the rural southern United States. It was first heard among pioneers during the nineteenth century. In its beginning, country and western music was influenced by English, Irish, and Scottish ballads brought to this country by immigrants and was combined with the blues music of southern African-Americans. It was simple and narrative. Today's country music blends rock and popular music with traditional tunes and themes and uses acoustical and steel guitar, fiddle, bass drums, piano, and keyboard.

♦ *Karaoke.* Karaoke is a recorded musical accompaniment for a sing-along. To create a karaoke tape, the children sing the lyrics with the music on side one and record the musical accompaniment only on side two. They follow along using lyrics on cue cards first with side one, then proceeding to side two.

♦ *Carols.* These are songs that celebrate festivals, particularly religious ones. Children can take popular carols from many countries and create new lyrics to familiar melodies.

emotions and are the lifeblood of commercial advertising. Consider the power of a commercial when accompanied by a catchy tune, the kind that has us humming it throughout the day. These messages use words and music that tap into our personal psyches and appeal to us as consumers. Children who view TV commercials can practice critical and creative thinking by responding to and generating questions such as these:

♦ What is the message? What is the product? Who or what represents the product?

♦ How does the combined use of music and words create meaning, sell an idea, sell an emotion?

♦ What particular appeal do the music and words have? How do they imprint an idea on your mind (through repetition, humor, suspense, familiarity, and common sense)?

♦ How does the commercial grab the audience's attention immediately?

♦ How is the volume of the music manipulated to punctuate speech, to fill conversational space, or to create background ambience?

♦ What is the mood of the music? How can mood music establish an association with the product? What effect does it have?

This thoughtful line of inquiry, applied to other real-life situations, increases the likelihood that children will be able to see through what is hidden or misleading. The children and teacher can videotape some commercials and bring them to class to discuss. How does sound serve as a signature tune for television favorites and commercials? When you hear a familiar melody or signature tune, can you identify it automatically with a person or product? Can music reflect the essence of a generation? Using a camcorder, children may want to make their own commercial. Along with a visual and written display (see Chapter 1) children can add music and lyrics to persuade others of an idea. Keep in mind some of the following tips:

◆ Use the music and lyrics to spotlight your most crucial ideas.

◆ Line up words and notes, match stressed syllables with stressed notes.

◆ Communicate your strongest messages in the first and last line of the jingle.

◆ Make your verses work together to accumulate power and build momentum.

◆ Use catchy phrases or a memorable melody to set your product apart from others.

◆ School–Community Links

Children should attend live music concerts. Beforehand, however, they learn to read program notes, the summary of the evening's performance, the names of key players (with photos or profiles), the names of the patrons, sponsors, or benefactors, and the names of the conductor, the scene director, and the artistic staff who helped create costumes, set, or scenes.

Inviting musicians into the classroom for special performances or having children apprentice with musicians-in-residence can show the school's appreciation for the unique qualities and talents of people from the community. Music is a way of life for many people. Children will come to value work done by recording artists, DJs, and local bands by observing them at work whenever possible. Exchange programs and partnerships with music educators and community musicians can result in children's participation with professionals in practice sessions, concerts, and contests. It may also lead to scholarships and sponsorships that result in paid tuitions for children to attend music camps or receive private instruction. Collaborative projects with musicians are likely to lead to an enriched literacy curricula and increased enthusiasm for music on the part of children and teachers.

Finally, children should have their own performances whether they are choral readings, musical concerts, or musical theater. The teacher might wish to start with small-scale performances, those given for classmates at school assemblies and events. The children can celebrate a "musician of the month" by honoring a classmate for special talents and hard work.

◆ Activities for Professional Development

1. Evaluate a children's popular musical audiotape such as that of *The Lion King* and prepare a written review. Prepare a list of questions so that your reactions can be written. For example:

◆ What voices are used? Are they in unison, or do they vary?

◆ How would you describe the sounds made by the instruments? Were they soft or loud, eerie or pleasant, joyful or sorrowful?

◆ Did you like the lyrics? Why or why not? How would you describe the lyrics? Are they a story, nonsense poetry, an imitation of something?

◆ How did you feel after listening to the music? If it created a picture in your mind, what was it? Did the music remind you of anything?

◆ How did you feel about the melody? the beat? Was the melody catchy? What made it so?

◆ For what age group would this activity be best suited?

2. Listen to a variety of different types of songs and create categories based on unique and shared features: for example, those that repeat a melodic idea or rhythm pattern; those with harmonizing parts; those that include traditional expressions passed on from song to song; those made from poems; those beginning with words; those beginning with music; performance style (e.g., choppy or smooth); types of songs (e.g., folk songs, work songs, popular songs). Then discuss such questions as: How did each song make me feel? Which did I like best? least? Why? What images came to mind when I heard these songs? How did the images differ among songs? How would I describe the lyrics of each song? In which songs were the lyrics crucial? In which was the music more important? How might I show the beat of these musical selections or songs?

3. Practice "ear training" activities to sharpen your abilities to evaluate and respond to musical ideas. Select one song, written in three different arrangements, or three songs each from a different genre (e.g., country and western, rock and roll, classical), or three songs each from a different country of origin (e.g., folksongs from Italy, Russia, and America). As you listen to each song, draw the approximate shape of what you hear and then compare and contrast your shapes with others (Figure 3-5).

Figure 3-5 *Sound Mappings*

◆ *Works Cited*

Professional References

Abrahams, R. D., and Gay, G. (1975). Talking black in the classroom. In P. Stoller (Ed.), *Black English: Its use in the classroom and in the literature* (pp. 158–167). New York: Dell Publishing.

Baldick, C. (1990). The concise Oxford dictionary of literary terms. New York: Oxford University Press.

Bamberger, J. (1982). Growing up prodigies: The mid life crisis. *New Directions for Child Development, 17,* 61–78.

Barclay, K. D., and Walwer, L. (1992). Linking lyrics and literacy through song picture books. *Young Children, 47,* 76–85.

Boni, M. B. (Ed.) (1947). *Fireside book of folk songs.* (illus. Alice and Martin Provensen; arrangements Norman Lloyd) New York: Simon & Schuster.

Burgie, I. (1992). *Caribbean Carnival: Songs of the West Indies.* New York, NY: Tambourine Books.

Burns, M. T. (1988). Music as a tool for enhancing creativity. *Journal of Creative Behavior, 22,* 62–69.

Cockburn, V. (1995). The uses of folk music and songwriting in the classroom. In M. R. Goldberg and A. Phillips (Eds.), *Art as education.* Cambridge, MA: Harvard Educational Review.

Coleridge, S. T. (1997). *Samuel Taylor Coleridge: The complete poems.* New York: Penguin.

Copland, A. (1988). *What to listen for in music.* New York: New American Library.

Dandy, E. B. (1991). *Black communications: Breaking down the barriers.* Chicago: African American Images.

Davis, S. (1988). *Successful lyric writing: A step by step course and workbook.* Cincinnati, OH: Writer's Digest Books.

Elliott, D. J. (1990). Music as culture: Toward a multicultural concept of arts education. *Journal of Aesthetic Education, 24,* 147–166.

Failoni, J. W. (1993). Music as means to enhance cultural awareness and literacy in the foreign language classroom. ERIC document reproduction services ED355796.

Gannon, M. J. (1994). *Understanding global cultures: Metaphoric journeys through 17 countries.* Thousand Oaks, CA: Sage Publications.

Gardner, H. (1993). *Frames of mind: The theory of multiple intelligences* (10th anniv. ed.) New York: Basic Books.

Glenn, K. (1992). The many benefits of music education—Now and in the future. *NASSP Bulletin, 76,* 1–4.

Heath, S. B. (1982). *Ways with words.* Cambridge, MA: Cambridge University Press.

Jackendoff, R. (1995). *Languages of the mind: Essays on mental representation.* Cambridge, MA: MIT Press.

Jeremiah, M. A. (1992). Rap lyrics: Instruments for language arts instruction. *Western Journal of Black Studies, 16,* 98–102.

Jolly, Y. (1975). The use of songs in teaching foreign language. *Modern Language Journal, 59,* 11–14.

Keats, J. (1987). *The complete poems,* 2nd ed. London: Penguin.

Kochman, T. (1981). *Black and white styles in conflict.* Chicago: University of Chicago Press.

Kolb, G. R. (1996). Read with a beat: Developing literacy through music and sound. *Reading Teacher, 50,* 76–77.

Lamme, L. L. (1990). Exploring the world of music through picture books. *Reading Teacher,* 44, 294–301.

Lerdah, F. (1996). *A generative theory of tonal music.* Cambridge, MA: MIT Press.

Macklis, K. (1989). Fifth graders "rap" English elements. *Reading Teacher, 42,* 340.

Maute, J. (1987). Tune in memory. *Middle School Journal, 18,* 3–5.

Merriam-Webster (1995). *Merriam-Webster encyclopedia of literature.* Springfield, MA: Merriam-Webster.

Miller, A., and Coen, D. (1994). The case for music in the schools. *Phi Delta Kappan, 75,* 459–461.

Pattison, P. (1995). *Writing better lyrics.* Cincinnati, OH: Writer's Digest Books.

Preminger, A., and Brogan, T. V. F. (Eds.) (1993). *The new Princeton encyclopedia of poetry and poetics.* Princeton, NJ: Princeton University Press.

Serafine, M. L. (1988). *Music as cognition: The development of thought in sound.* New York: Columbia University Press.

Smitherman, G. (1977). *Talkin and testifyin: The language of Black America.* Detroit, MI: Wayne State University Press.

Snow, C. (1977). The development of conversation between mothers and babies. *Journal of Child Language, 4,* 1–22.

Wiseman, A. (1979). *Making musical things: Improvised instruments.* New York: Charles Scribner's Sons.

Zollo, P. (1993). *Beginning songwriter's answer book.* Cincinnati, OH: Writer's Digest Books.

Children's References

Aardema, V. (1991). *Traveling to Tondo: A tale of the Nkundo of Zaire* (illus. W. Hillenbrand). New York: Alfred A. Knopf.

Axelrod, A. (1991). *Songs of the wild west* (arrang. D. Fox). Metropolitan Museum of Art with the Buffalo Bill Historical Center. New York: Simon & Schuster.

Bates, K. L. (1993). *America the beautiful* (illus. N. Waldman). New York: Macmillan.

Bowles, B. (1989). *Grandma's band* (illus. A. Chan). Owings Mills, MD: Stemmer House.

Browning, R. (1997). *The pied piper of Hamelin* (illus. T. Small). Mineola, NY: Dover Publications.

Carlstrom, N. (1992). *Baby-O* (illus. S. Stevenson), Boston: Little, Brown.

Chalk, G. (1993). *Yankee doodle.* New York: Dorling Kindersley.

Cohn, A. L. (compiler) (1993). *From sea to shining sea: A treasury of American folklore and folksongs* (illus. Caldecott Award Artists). New York: Scholastic.

Curtis, C. P. (1995). *The Watsons go to Birmingham—1963.* New York: Delacorte Press.

Delacre, L. (1989). *Arroz con leche: Popular songs and rhymes from Latin America.* New York: Scholastic.

de Paola, T. (1983). *The legend of the blue bonnet.* New York: Putnam.

Elliott, D. (1984). *Lambs' tales from great operas* (illus. C. Arrowood). Harvard, MA: Harvard Common Press.

Fleishman, P. (1992). *Joyful noise: Poems for two voices* (illus. E. Beddows). New York: Harper & Row.

Geisert, A. (1994). *After the flood.* Boston: Houghton Mifflin.

Goffstein, M. B. (1970). *Two piano tuners.* New York: Farrar, Straus & Giroux.

Greenberg, K. E. (1991). *Rap*. Minneapolis, MN: Lerner Publications.

Greenfield, E. (1988). *Nathaniel talking* (illus. J. S. Gilchrist). New York: Black Butterfly Children's Books.

Grimm, B. (1992). *The Bremen town musicians* (illus. J. Stevens). New York: Holiday House.

Hayes, A. (1991). *Meet the orchestra* (illus. K. Thompson). Orlando, FL: Harcourt Brace.

Hayes, A. (1995). *Meet the marching Smithereens* (illus. K. Thompson). Orlando, FL: Harcourt Brace.

Higginsen, V. (1995). *This is my song* (illus. B. Joysmith; music arrang. W. Naylor). New York: Crown Publishing.

Highwater, J. (1981). *Moonsong lullaby* (illus. M. Keegan). New York: Lothrop, Lee & Shepard.

Isadora, R. (1997). *Young Mozart*. New York: Viking Press.

Jekyll, W. (compiler) (1994). *I have a news: Rhymes from the Caribbean* (illus. J. Mair). New York: Lothrop, Lee & Shepard.

Johnson, J. W. (1993). *Lift every voice and sing* (illus. E. Catlett). New York: Orchard Books.

Joseph, L. (1992). *Coconut kind of day: Island poems* (illus. S. Speidel). New York: Puffin.

Kemp, G. (1983). *Ducks and dragons: Poems for children*. London: Puffin.

Kennedy, X. J., and Kennedy, D. M. (1982). *Knock at a star: A child's introduction to poetry*. Boston: Little, Brown.

Krauss, R. (1990). *Musical Max* (illus. J. Aruego and A. Dewey). New York: Simon & Schuster.

Krull, K. (1993). *Lives of the musicians* (illus. K. Hewitt). Orlando, FL: Harcourt Brace Jovanovich.

McNeil, M. E. A. (1993). *The magic storysinger: From the Finnish epic tale Kalevala* (retold and illus. M. E. A. McNeil). Owings Mills, MD: Stemmer House.

Menotti, G. C. (1986). *Amahl and the night visitors* (illus. M. Lemieux). New York: William Morrow.

Meyerowitz, B., Copans, J., and Welch, T. (1988). *My Drum: South African poetry for young People*. Parklands, South Africa: Hippogriff Press, Abecedarius Books.

Meyrick, K. (1993). *The musical life of Gustav Mole*. New York: Child's Play International.

Michener, J. (1992). *South Pacific* (illus. M. Hague). New York: Harcourt Brace Jovanovich.

Monceaux, M. (1994). *Jazz: my music, my people*. New York: Alfred A. Knopf.

Moser, B. (1992). *Messiah* (paintings and word book for the Oratorio of George Frederic Handel). A Willa Perlman Book. New York: HarperCollins.

Paterson, K. (1985). *Come sing Jimmy Jo*. New York: Dutton.

Philip, N. (1995). *Singing America: Poems that define a nation* (illus. M. McCurdy). New York: Viking Press.

Pomerantz, C. (1982). *If I had a paka: Poems in eleven languages* (illus. N. Tafuri). New York: Greenwillow Books.

Prelutsky, J. (1983). *The Random House book of poetry*. New York: Random House.

Price, C. (1973). *Talking drums of Africa*. New York: Scribner.

Price, L. (1990). *Aida* (illus. L. and D. Dillon). New York: Harcourt Brace Jovanovich.

Prokofiev, S. (1987). *Peter and the wolf* (retold J. Riordan, illus. V. Ambrus). New York: Oxford University Press.

Raschka, C. (1992). *Charlie Parker played be-bop.* New York: Orchard Books.

Richards, J. (1993). *God's gift* (retold); (illus. N. Gorbaty). New York: Doubleday.

Rodgers, R., and Hammerstein, O. (1993).*The surrey with the fringe on top* (illus. J. Warhola). New York: Simon & Schuster.

Smith, N. S. (1996). *Songs for survival: Songs and chants from tribal peoples around the world.* New York: Dutton.

Thayer, E. L. (1991). *Casey at the bat: A ballad of the republic, sung in the year 1988.* New York: Putnam & Grosset.

Troughton, J. (1970). *The little Mohee: An Appalachian ballad.* New York: Dutton.

Vozar, D.(1995). *Yo hungry wolf? A nursery rap.* (illus. B. Lewin). New York: Doubleday.

Vozar, D. (1997). *MC turtle and the hip hop hare: A happenin' rap.* New York: Doubleday.

Walter, M. P. (1987). *Ty's one-man band* (illus. M. Tomes). New York: Macmillan.

◆ *Additional Resources*

Note: Asterisks indicate resources that are cited in the chapter.

Videotapes and Catalogs

Amahl and the Night Visitors
Music in Motion
P.O. Box 833814
Richardson, TX 75083
800-445-0649
(Gian Carlo Menotti, 60 minutes, all ages)

The Ballad of the Blue Bonnet
Multi-S Music Company
3317 Knights Have Lane
Garland, TX 75044
800-530-7360

Beethoven Lives Upstairs
BMG Distribution
Children's Group
Ontario, Canada
800-668-0242
(Platinum Award, 51 minutes, all ages)

The House of Magical Sounds
Sony
(narrated by Raul Julia, 1994, 50 minutes, all ages)

Marsalis on Music
Marsalis on Music
P.O. Box 2284
South Burlington, VT 05407
WNET:
  A Series: Why Toes Tap (Rhythm)
  Listening to Clues (Forms in Music)
  Sousa to Stachmo (Jazz)
  Tackling the Monster (Practice)

*Mary Poppins
Walt Disney Home Videos
P.O. Box 126
Brea, CA 92622
(139 minutes, all ages)

The Music Box
Children's Video Collection
Films for the Humanities
P.O. Box 2053
Princeton, NJ 08543

Pete Seeger's Family Concert
Sony
550 Madison Ave.
New York, NY: 10022
800-270-6800
(Platinum Award, 45 minutes, all
ages) 1992

*Prokofiev Fantasy with Peter and the
Wolf
Deutsche Grammophon Video
825 Eighth Avenue
New York, NY 10019
(narrated by Sting, 53 minutes,
all ages)

The Red Balloon
Box C-137
Sandy Hook, CT 06482
(a Video Yesteryear recording, 34
minutes, all ages)

Stone Soup
Music in Motion
P.O. Box 833814
Richardson, TX 75083
800-445-0649

Three Piggy Opera
Music in Motion
P.O. Box 833814
Richardson, TX 75083
800-445-0649

Music Games and Resources

*Metropolitan Opera Guild
1865 Broadway
New York, NY 10133-0023

Music Maestro I
Aristoplay Games
P.O. Box 7529
Ann Arbor, MI 48107
(identification of instruments with
sound; board game and cassettes)

Music Maestro II
Aristoplay Games
P.O. Box 7529
Ann Arbor, MI 48107
(advanced identification of
instruments; board game and
cassettes)

Scores and Sheet Music

Arabesque
No. 1 Art Publication Society
7801 Bonhomme Avenue
St. Louis, MO 63105
(Debussy)

Beethoven's Pastoral Symphony
Deutsche Grammophon
825 Eighth Avenue
New York, NY 10019
(Karajan Berlin Philharmonic, 1984)

Kitten on the Keys
Mills Music
1619 Broadway
New York, NY 10019
(Zez Confrey)

Recordings, CDs, and Audiocassettes

*Abiyoyo and Other Story Songs for
Children*
Smithsonian/Folkways
955 L'enfant Plaza Suite 2600
Washington, DC 20560
(Pete Seeger, 1989)

Arabian Nights
Scheherazade
Rimsky-Korsakov
Sony
550 Madison Ave.
New York, NY 10022

Big Willie
Sony Columbia
550 Madison Ave.
New York, NY: 10022
(Willie Smith, rap, CD)

Brahms Lullaby
An Introduction to the Classics
Vox Music Group
560 Sylvan Avenue
Englewood Cliffs, NJ 07632
(Johann Brahms)

Carnival of the Animals
EMI Angel,
1750 N. Vine St.
Hollywood, CA 90028
(Camille Saint-Saens)

Cat's in the Cradle
Harry Chapin
Story Songs LTD
Huntington, NY 11743

A Child's Celebration of Broadway
Music for Little People
Department FGR
P.O. Box 1720
Lawndale, CA 90260
800-727-2233
(CD or cassette)

Classic Disney
Vols. I and II
Department FGR
P.O. Box 1720
Lawndale, CA 90260

Classics by Classical Kids, Vol. I
Music for Little People
Department FGR
P.O. Box 1720
Lawndale, CA 90260
  Mr. Bach Comes to Call
  *Mozart's Magic Fantasy: A Child's
  Journey through the Magic Flute*
  *Vivaldi's Ring of Mystery: A Tale of
  Venice and Violins*
  Beethoven Lives Upstairs
  Tchaikovsky Discovers America

The Four Seasons
Deutsche Grammophon
825 Eighth Avenue
New York, NY 10019
(Vivaldi; Orpheus Chamber
Orchestra; Gil Shaham, violin)

Magic Flute
(Die Zauberflote)
Wolfgang Amadeus Mozart
EMI Classics
21700 Oxnard St. #700
Woodland Hills, CA 91367

Maple Leaf Rag
(Scott Joplin; Max Morath,
piano; 1973)
Vanguard Records

Messiah: An Oratorio
(George Frideric Handel)
Kalmus Music
New York, NY

Welk Music Group
Omega Records, Inc.
27 West 72nd St.
New York, NY 10023

Music from Zambabwe
Tracey Recording
Pacific Palisades, CA

My Favorite Opera for Children
London Records
825 Eighth Avenue
New York, NY 10019
(Luciano Pavorotti, 1996)

Nash, Ogden
Peter and the Wolf/Prokofiev, The
Carnival of the Animals/Saint Saëns,
verses by Ogden Nash CD,
EMI/Angel
1750 N. Vine St.
Hollywood, CA 90028

No Way Out
Bad Boy Entertainment
Arista Records
12882 107th Ave
Surrey BC
Canada
V3t2E7
(Puff Daddy and the Family, rap, CD)

Phenomenon
Polygram Records
825 8th Ave
New York, NY 10019
(LL Cool J, Def Jam; rap; CD)

Prelude to the Afternoon of a Faun
Claude Debussy
CBS Sony Classical
51 West 52nd St.
New York, NY 10019

Soundtracks around the World
UNICEF
1 Children's Boulevard
P.O. Box 182233
Chattanooga, TN 37422

Symphony of Fanfares
Symphonies and Fanfares for the
King's Supper
John Joseph Moray
Nonesuch Records
51 West 51st St.
New York, NY 10019

The Bridge Over Troubled Water
Simon and Garfunkel
Sony Music
550 Madison Ave.
New York, NY 10022

The Legend of the Edmund Fitzgerald
Gordon Lightfoot "Gord's Gold Vol. 2"
Warner Brothers Records
400 Warner Blvd.
Burbank, CA 91522

Waltz of the Flowers
EMI Records Limited
1133 Avenue of the Americas
New York, NY 10036
(Tchaikovsky; The Seraphim Classical
50, Vol. 5; 1983)

Computer Software and Technology

Making Music, The Voyager Co.
Edutainment
800-338-3844

Musical Instruments
CD (IBM and MAC formats)
800-323-3577

*NetMusic: Your Guide to the Sound of
Music in Cyberspace*
Music in Motion
800-445-0649

Rock & Bach Studio
Binary Zoo (IBM format)
800-521-6263

Dance Literacy: Communicating Nonverbally

Vignette: The *Nutcracker*

In Miss Richards' sixth-grade class, the students are studying the Nutcracker *(music by Tchaikovsky), one of America's favorite holiday ballets, performed in most cities around the world at Christmas time. It is the tale of a young girl named Marie who receives a nutcracker doll for Christmas from her godfather, Herr Drosselmeier. In the land of fantasy, the nutcracker is really a prince who must battle a mouse king if he is to be magically transformed. The sixth-graders read and compare two unabridged versions of the book (Hoffman, 1984, 1985), one illustrated by Patricia Seminara, the other by Maurice Sendak, whose inspiration comes from the original stage designs and costumes he created for the Pacific Northwest Ballet. After reading and discussing the books, the children view excerpts from two different video versions of the dance. The first one, by Electra Entertainment, stars Macaulay Caulkin as the Nutcracker and Jessica Lynn Cohen as Marie; the other, by the Pacific Northwest Ballet, stars High Bigney and Vanessa Sharp. Over several days, the children view these video segments and compare each choreographed version. Now, in one of several discussions, they are ready to compare the dance with the book versions. The teacher leads the discussion:*

- *Which versions of the story (written/performed) did you most enjoy? Why?*
- *Which parts of the dance did you particularly like? Why?*
- *How was each organized? (Books are presented in chapters, ballet in "acts." Acts are in real time and allow the stage crew to change the set while the actors change costumes; a book can be read at any time and for as long as one likes.)*
- *How did the books and ballet present the settings, characters, and major events? (The book uses pictures and words; the ballet uses movements, costumes, props, and stage sets.)*
- *At what points did the dance elaborate the book version? (at celebrations or festivities; to show moods of enchantment, gaiety, solemnity). For example, when the Nutcracker prince and Marie go on their magical journey, the audience enters an enchanted world through the Dance of the Snowflakes. Soon the children become the guests at a banquet in their honor where dances are performed for them: the Hot*

Chocolates of Spain, the Chinese Tea, the Coffee of Arabia, the Candy Canes, the Marzipans (dance flowers), Mother Ginger (a kind of Mother Goose), and others.

♦ *At what points did the book elaborate the dance version? (In the book, a subplot details information about a beautiful child, born to the King and Queen, who is hideously deformed when the mice get near her cradle and place a curse on her. As she grows into womanhood, her only chance at restoring her beauty is to eat the seed kernel of the Crackatuck nut. But it is too hard. The Nutcracker is the only one able to crack the nut and perform the disenchantment. He cracks the nut, feeds it to the princess, and her beauty returns. When he does so, however, he becomes deformed and ugly. When the King sees the results, instead of rewarding the Nutcracker, he throws him out because of his deformity. The Nutcracker must now fight the Mouse King to regain his former self.)*

This discussion raises awareness of different interpretations of the same story: one expressed in movement, the other in narrative. Because each form of literacy has its own inventive techniques, means of expression, and interpretations (Birdwhistle, 1970; Kendon, 1985; Wood, 1981), they reveal the verbal and nonverbal choices available to children for symbolizing and representing meanings.

In this chapter we focus on movement and nonverbal expression as metaphors of dance. Past research suggests that encoding and decoding movement is an important part of language development (Bruner, 1966; Piaget and Inhelder, 1969; Vygotsky, 1978; Werner and Kaplan, 1964). As children acquire language, they rely on gestures and bodily expression to make statements at least 65 percent of the time (Birdwhistle, 1970). Moving and exploring space, they also develop rudimentary motor skills and a range of motion that helps them appreciate the use of space and social distance. Perceptual studies guide our understanding of how children process this movement information and knowledge of temporal and spatial dimensions (Kerr, 1982; Magill, 1989).

In addition to constructing knowledge through movement, children consciously control and select movement responses, depending on the functions they wish their movements to serve. Functional studies from descriptive analysis in dance (Laban, 1948) and nonverbal communication, (Ekman and Friesen, 1969; Wood, 1981) illustrate the possible ways in which children use movement and gesture as communicative and symbolic tools.

Before we explore further the interpretive and functional power of dance and movement, we consider ways that movement can lead to active problem solving (Montessori, 1949; Piaget and Inhelder, 1969; Vygotsky, 1978), flexibility and concentration, and memory and imaginative powers (Eisner, 1981; Gardner, 1991, 1993; Greene, 1988). By practicing the versatility of movement that gives birth to inventive strategies and ideas, children discover what the nonverbal channel has to offer.

INQUIRY STRAND: IDEAS IN MOTION

For most children, living is synonymous with moving (Fleming, 1990; Gilbert, 1992: Stinson, 1993; Wall and Murray, 1990; Wood, 1981). Often, they enjoy moving just for the sheer experience of it. Body travel through space helps children think in terms of directions and orientation. They move their bodies forward, backward, sideways, left, right, forward, and behind; they move in unison or successively; they move with form and structure, shape, and energy. The teacher can organize material so that students can experiment with body movements and nonverbal communication. While we explore movement literacy, we pay particular attention to motion as a form of inquiry that stimulates new ways to see, think, and wonder. As with the other inquiry strategies outlined in Chapters 2 and 3, our aim here is to consider movement as an aesthetic choice for generating ideas even though the strategies may be used as literacy tasks in their own right.

Dance Improvisation

Improvisation inspires children to become spontaneous creators and performers as they express themselves and explore ideas through movement without modification and revision. Although improvisation is unpredictable, operating in essence without a score or script, there is usually a creative framework provided by a set scenario or problem that the performer has in mind. For instance, children can represent a personal experience through plot development (e.g., conflict, climax, resolution). They assign emotions to each element of the plot and explore movements for them. When finished they go back to the plot line, translating the physical experience into words that capture actions, emotions, and feelings.

A problem solving improvisation that might also help children experiment with movement is to place a box in the center of the room and pretend it is a swamp inhabited by a hungry alligator. Children must figure out a way to avoid the creature and still get across the swamp. What is the process they go through to create their movement solutions?

Finally, an improvisation, that lends itself to introspection, is dancing an autobiography. Children introduce themselves in movement, showing their personality, ideas, and interests without the use of words (e.g., my dream vacation; my idea of hard work; my favorite pastime). In this activity they reflect on action while asking themselves to think about who they are at an emotional level. Reflecting on an inner life and molding it to movement is a wonderful exercise of intrapersonal intelligence (Gardner, 1991).

Movement Prompts

Side coaching and directive prompts are a scaffold for children who need support in performing extemporaneously. The teacher stands on the side-lines and cues children in the movements they are to execute: "Pretend you are holding a box. The box is shrinking. It's getting soft and squeezing through your fingers. It slips to the floor. It hardens. You pick it up. It's getting wider. It's getting longer. It's getting heavier." Children are translating words into action and making associations.

Students also write action scripts that they can try out with their peers. For example:

> *You are walking barefoot on the beach and the sand is very hot. You run as fast as you can to the water and jump in head first. The water is cold and you shiver all over. You swim back to the shoreline, and while standing there, you feel a sand bug crawl through your toes. You wiggle your toes and look down. While you are looking down at your feet, you notice a beautiful shell. You pick it up and run back to your friends to show them.*

Easy-to-follow "process" prompts that specify movement phrases are a good way to practice writing and following directions. Children can create prompts to cue a movement sequence such as "how to care for a cat," "how to spend Sunday afternoon," or "how to make lemonade." Directive questions can also help children think through movement ideas:

- ◆ *Create* a movement (What does it look like?)   Figure 4-1
- ◆ *Change* it (What does the movement become? How is it transformed?)   Figure 4-2
- ◆ *Associate* it (What connections between a movement and something else comes to mind?)   Figure 4-3
- ◆ *Combine* it (What parts can be blended together? What transitions connect them?)   Figure 4-4

Figure 4-1   *Stick Figure 1*

Tree

(arms straight up over head)

Figure 4-2 *Stick Figure 2*

Wind

(arms swaying overhead, left to right)

Figure 4-3 *Stick Figure 3*

Table

(bending over to touch toes)

Figure 4-4 *Stick Figure 4*

Runner's
startup

(bending over to
touch toes)

Winning the race

(arms straight up
over head)

Waving to the crowd

(arms swaying over head)

Figure 4-5 *Movement Puppet*

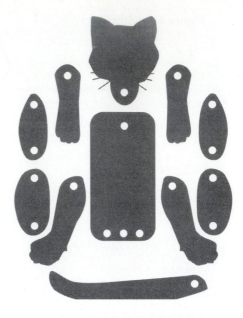

While one person performs the answers to the questions, the children at their seats work along with the performer arranging their own poses and changing actions using pipe cleaner figures or paper puppets assembled with movable arms and legs (like the one in Figure 4-5). As the children create visual displays of movement, they associate words and phrases with their actions. Translating movements to words builds vocabularies through free association and idea formation.

Movement Webs

While the directive prompts change movements to words, the movement web changes words to movement for the purpose of brainstorming ideas. Children start by creating a web of words that take into consideration the major elements of dance (see the elements in Table 4-1). Using these elements as anchors, the children think of a theme (such as bubbles), a movement (such as skipping), or a feeling (such as anger) to place in the center of the web. A delightful book for generating dance themes is *Dance with Me*, (Esbensen, 1995), a set of poems that conceptualize the dance as wind, bubbles, shadows, and other ordinary actions. Here we use our own bubbles poem (see Figure 4-6), to show how the elements of dance evoke a web of ideas for movement.

Prop Play

Play is a natural part of literacy development and a powerful context for helping students construct meanings through movement (Corsaro, 1985;

TABLE 4-1   Elements of Dance

Dance Element	Definition	Examples
Body	The instrument of dance	Includes movement of head, arms, feet, legs, hands, elbows, wrists, shoulders, hips, knees, ankles, or torso
Space	Where the body moves	In a maze, lines, patterns, pathways
Actions	What the body does	Gestures, jumps, kicks, falls, turns, twists, collapses
Relationships	Stance toward others	Meeting, parting, passing, surrounding, leading, far or near
Dynamics	How the body moves	In rhythm, fast or slow, a long or short period of time, energy level

Figure 4-6 *Movement Web*

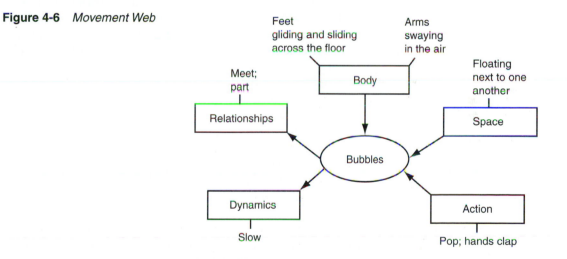

Bubbles

Delicate bubbles
lifting themselves skyward
in a dance of
fancy footwork,
gliding, sliding and turning
touching, popping, and disappearing
ever so softly
without a sound.

TABLE 4-2   Fabric Feelings

Fabric Swatch	Movements, Sensations, and Associations
Silk	Grace, languid, gentle, flowing, free-spirited
Canvas	Hefty, rugged, rustic, stiff, taut
Flannel	Heavy, warm, outdoors, folksy, comfortable, wilderness
Batik	Fluid, graceful, cool, elegant, exotic
Voile	Transparent, languid, sensual, flowing, romantic
Cotton	Cool, fresh, informal, soft
Linen	Cool, casual
Rayon	Ritzy, flowing, lyrical, rhythmic

Garvey, 1977). Researchers repeatedly point out the importance of senso-rimotor play with materials and objects, spontaneous activity, and socio-dramatics in helping children represent objects and construct symbolic meanings (Bruner, 1966; Garvey, 1977; Smilansky, 1968). Keep a box filled with hats, scarves, fans, canes, baskets, jump ropes, pillows, and other paraphernalia to stimulate imagination and action. Simple props such as a white mantilla and fan inspire a Spanish dance, a red cape sig-nifies a matador's mantra, and a flowing scarf of many colors becomes a rainbow.

Older children can discuss clothing and costumes, not just for move-ment but for communicative effects. Clothes convey what is appropriate at-tire for certain occasions and often communicate a character's status, per-sonality, or gender (Schnurnberger, 1991). Provide children with samples of fabrics pasted onto cards and have them list movement words that char-acterize these fabrics, as shown in Table 4-2. This will not only help them understand movement but will give them a set of sensory vocabulary words with which to describe motion and character.

Next, have them cut out pictures of people wearing various kinds of clothes to illustrate a character's personality traits (sloppy, carefree, fas-tidious), a setting (a picnic, a wedding), an historical era (the silk embroi-dered cloaks of kings in the Middle Ages), or social roles (e.g., the habits of monks or nuns) (Table 4-3).

Show how the clothes make some sort of statement about a person and see if the children can interpret customs, status, ego or gender from the words generated. They may want to draw a picture of the person whose clothing has conjured up an image in their minds.

Dance Mime

Mime is a kind of body speech that requires a keen physical awareness on the part of the actor and a recognition by the audience that they must lis-

TABLE 4-3   Clothes Talk

Item of Clothing	Movements, Sensations, and Associations
Bandana	Folksy, lively, joyful
Khaki pants	Slow, deliberate, walk, casual
Tutu	Toes, airy, bouncy
Blue jeans	Casual, grungy, western, rough and tumble
Wool blazer	Classic, preppy, country club, chic
Crinolines	Fashionable, ostentatious, victorian, hooped
Bell-bottoms	Hippie, reactionary, funky
Spandex	Athletic, biking, exercising, aerobicized

ten to what silence has to tell. Mime within dance is a way of expressing ideas, feelings, and plots with gestures rather than words. Some mime is conventional in all ballets (e.g., the fright gesture in Act II of *Swan Lake*). Mime is a wonderful movement activity for dance and drama because it integrates thought with action. An easy mime to act out is *The Pied Piper of Hamelin* (Browning, 1998). As the legend goes, a Pied Piper rids the German town of Hamelin from an infestation of rats and rescues the townsfolk. Unfortunately, the mayor reneges on his word and refuses to reward the Piper financially. In retaliation, the Piper plays a tune that leads the town's children to follow him. The children, including the mayor's daughter, disappear forever.

Select children to play the parts of the main characters. The rest of the class can participate in group scenes in the role of the "townsfolk," "rats," or "children of the town." Children try to communicate meanings, feelings, and thoughts through their movements. Acting out movement ideas in motifs and mimetic action sharpens student's ability to relate to the subject of the work in a way that reading alone cannot. Some other expressive exercises that you might try out are provided in Table 4-4. For further reading, see the *Handbook of Creative Dance and Drama: Ideas for Teachers* (Lee, 1992).

LANGUAGING STRAND: ACTIONS TALK

We have all heard the familiar saying that "actions speak louder than words." As children grow linguistically, they continue to develop their body grammar as an important communicative channel. This means that they are able to produce meanings through actions (a touch, pinch, poke, or tug), facial expression (a smile, frown, or wrinkled nose), body language (arms folded, knees bent, hands on hips), or through movement (running, galloping, walking). The section "Actions Talk" showcases a set of symbols

TABLE 4-4 Expressive Movement Exercises

- One student stands in the middle of the room or in a corner of the room while the others orient to her and show distance, closeness, overlap, piling, touching.
- Children use their elbows to scribble in the air, see with their hands; see with their feet; see movement; reach out into space; move like they are entangled in a spider web; push a rock up a mountain.
- Children pretend they are a mirror, copying exactly what they see a partner do.
- Children have a movement conversation with a partner. They copy action phrases adding intensity or speed. One makes a gesture and the other answers it with another gesture. A motion is started (e.g., nod head, rub hands together, tap feet) and the others respond in kind.
- Children perform the movements of animals, objects, or activities such as the procession of ants or watercolors dripping down the page.
- Children make alphabet letters out of their bodies: twisted lines, angular, zigzag lines, curved circular lines, and straight linear lines (e.g., L with arms)
- Children write directions on cards to be acted out spontaneously. They can be simple statements such as "show fear or joy," "make gestures to say hello" (take a bow, wave, tip your hat), "run down the street; throw a ball; crawl like a snake; fly like a bird." Have the children act these out and see if others can guess what they are. Students can interpret others' actions and decode body language and gesture.

for conveying ideas and feelings as movement messages. Used alone or in combination with other strands, actions and nonverbal gestures are valuable components of a language arts curriculum.

Sign Language

The language of the hearing impaired highlights a natural way to expand all children's communicative and interpretive powers. Students who are deaf or hard of hearing use sign language to convey messages but rely on interpreters to be heard. When "hearing" children learn to sign, they can engage in communicative exchanges with students who are physically challenged. Hearing children might also use signing as a strategy for spelling or encoding words and concepts. Signing words to a song or poem can add an expressive dimension to literacy.

"Talking hands" communicate messages beyond words. Have children compose a story using their hands and gestures as the accompaniment. They will discover the many ways of creating action phrases with their hands: turning the lid of a jar, beating a drum, molding a clay pot, or playing the piano. Actions that express emotions and feelings are also discovered (e.g., How would you use your fingers to show rain? grace? tiptoeing? swaying? nervousness?)

An introduction to sign language is found in *Handsigns: A Sign Language Alphabet* (Fain, 1993), 26 beautiful illustrations that show letters of the alphabet accompanied by the signs. Another beginning book is

Handtalk: An ABC of Finger Spelling and Sign Language (Charlip et al., 1974) or, for children who enjoy working at the computer, there is *Interactive Sign Language: 101 Basic Signs* from Palatine Incorporated.

Another valuable sign language to explore is that of the Native American. The book *Indian Signals and Sign Language* (Fronval and Dubois, 1994) introduces the communication of the Plains Indians using signs that exchange messages about travel and trade. Children will enjoy writing messages using Indian signs as shown in Figure 4-7.

Nonverbal Expression

Practicing nonverbal communication and explaining its functions develops children's awareness of voluntary movement patterns. If children watch TV with the volume off, they will discover interesting gestures and movement patterns of actors and actresses, evangelists, or news reporters. Taping TV shows and turning the volume on and off can serve as a stimulus for critical discussions: How do actions communicate attitudes, emotions, messages? How do actions signal questions? How does a nonverbal message complement or contradict a verbal message? Does the nonverbal message help the viewer process a message, or does it purposely distract?

In addition to describing nonverbal communication, have children produce or show moods, interpretations, and messages in concrete ways. Help them "see" how words are mapped onto movements to express action in prose, poetry, or speech events. For example: How would you place your hands on your face to show boredom, fear, stress, pensiveness? Write about a character showing these expressions in words. What body shape best describes worry? self-confidence? anxiety? Write about a character who experiences all of these feelings.

Nonlinguistic behaviors, gestures, facial expressions, and body language differ from culture to culture. Some gestures are easily understood because they are universal; others, although not imbued with shared meanings, pave the way for a study of cross-cultural communication. For instance, there are many ways to show respect, honor, willingness to negotiate, leave taking, and other communicative signals. Some possible interpretations of these as they exist in our culture are shown in Table 4-5. Viewing subtitled foreign films is one way of developing an awareness of the different communicative gestures across cultures (e.g., do the actors wave with palm outward or with the back of the hand outward?).

Game Dances

Children's game dances are an ideal way of learning to read, move, and write. They help children to coordinate with others (especially partners) and to pursue communal relationships in lines, circles, or other well-ordered patterns (Steiner, 1984). As part of children's oral heritage, game dances celebrate customs, the seasons, and other symbols that have traditionally made their way into childhood lore. Many of the game dances are

Figure 4-7 *Indian Signs*

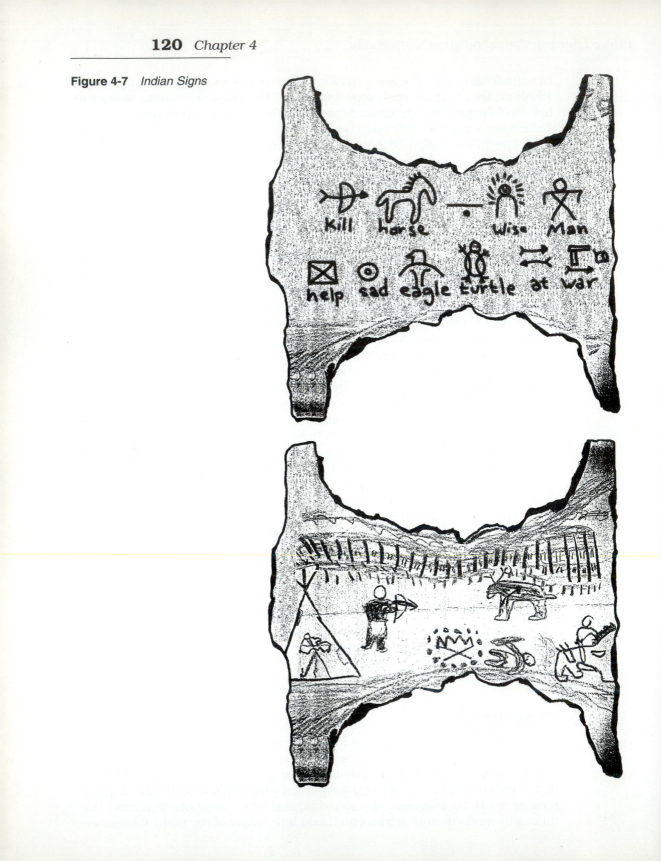

TABLE 4-5   Nonverbal Expression and Possible Interpretations

Nonverbal Expression	Possible Meanings or Effects
Facial expressions: smile, eye gaze, wink, frown, blink, nod, tug on ear, pursed lip, raised eyebrows	Self-confidence, reinforces what we are saying; distractions; anger, disappointment, happiness
Gestures: rubbing hands, a thumbs-up sign, shake head, point finger, head held high	Animates conversations; amplifies information; clarifies information; replaces voice commands; shows moods and self-confidence
Posture and movement: repetition of gesture, curved spine	Shows a sense of purpose; shows energy, speed; shows interest or boredom; clarifies time elements and sequence; shows confidence or lack of it
Position and spatial grouping: closeness, overlap, distance, formations	Shows control; shows attention; shows safety; social relationships

closely aligned with poetry and music. For instance, there are any number of familiar children's singing games and dances, such as "Ring around the Roses" and "The Hokey-Pokey" (Knapp and Knapp, 1976), as well as such cultural favorites as "Arroz con Leche" (Rice with Milk) from Argentina and "Naranja Dulce" (Sweet Orange) from Mexico (Yurchenco, 1967).

Another source of game dances are the play party games. During the nineteenth century, play party games were a popular multigenerational event in the rural areas and frontier regions of the United States. Held once a week, play party games involved children and their neighborhood peers in singing, handclapping and foot stomping. Because play party games involve the customs and activities of past generations, children learn history through song lyrics and the cultural movements that accompany them (e.g. draw a bucket of water). For a compilation of these historical game dances see *Folk Music in America: A Reference Guide* (Miller, 1986).

Children can make up dance routines to go with play party games, poems, or game dances using the different types of movements (locomotion—run, leap, skip; stationary actions—bend, stretch, shake, swing, or sway; directional—sideways, forward, backward, pathways; or effort and energy movements—squeeze, relax, tense up). Have children write lists of action verbs for later use in writing their own game songs and poems.

POETRY STRAND: THE DANCE OF POETRY

The dance of poetry is the movement of words on the page. Like dance, it expresses images, feelings, and emotions through movement and space. In this section we consider the fluidity and rhythm of words and discuss how the poem can serve as a metaphor for motion.

Movement on the Page

Dance can take a visual form in print. Translated into poetry, characteristics of a particular dance can look like the very movement it represents. For example, breakdancing, popular in the 1980s, typically involved headspins, backspins, acrobatics, floorwork, windmills, and complex leg movements. Notice how Lillian Morrison shows break dancing on the page by its format and the clipping and twisting of words in a distinct break-dancing rhythm.

The Break Dance Kids
or
No More Gang Wars

No more gangs
      now they are crews
    who dance the news
        of the street
            the Rock Steady Crew
     the Dynamic Breakers
  compete
      on the pavement
         in impossible feats
     of gyration
       to rhythm of rap
         to beat of hip hop
   like corkscrews
       they spin,
     on heads, backs, shoulders
     legs racing,
  then stop   in a freeze.

Maniac whirls
   into a hand glide
Crazy Legs does his
    automaton's slide.

Float like a zephyr
   slither   in waves
   like a snake
rocket like a robot
    tick like a clock
   their fights
are mock now   their fights
   are rock now
    Rock Steady.

Morrison (1985)

After reading the poem, the children might look at pictures of break dancing or watch films and TV programs that include the dance. Then they discuss the poem.

- How did the writer include a variety of movements in the piece?
- How did the movements manifest themselves (format, repetitions, exaggerations, alliteration)?
- How did the poetry flow?
- How would you translate Morrison's poem into a dance?
- What would you call this dance or written piece?

Dance provides a framework for writing poetry since they share visible and rhythmic elements. Taking a dance and transforming it into words creates poetry in motion. Students may want to practice with familiar dances. For example, have them watch the "Mexican Hat Dance" and then try to recreate it in print (see Figure 4-8).

Poems as Metaphors of Dance

Although the features of dance can create visual moving poetry, so can the content of the poem represent the dance metaphorically. Listen to the dance quality of this poem as Morrison writes again about break dancing:

B Boy

As onlookers clap
and rap and shout
I curl up and turn myself
inside out.

I can jig horizontal
as I lean on one hand;
I'm a spin-top, a pinwheel,
a one-man dance band,

inventing new moves
when I get a notion.
I can take out the best.
I'm graffiti in motion,

a sidewalk tornado
to the rhythm of rock.
meet the baddest break dancer
(that's me) on the block.

Morrison (1985)

WE DANCE	*AND SING*	*A SONG*
WITH EACH STEP	*WE GO*	*ALONG*
TWIST ROUND	*AND ROUND*	*AND ROUND*
SOMBREROS	*TOSSED TO*	*THE GROUND*

 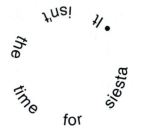 

Grab your partner and join the fiesta

It isn't the time for siesta

Feel the rythm and shake the maracas

JOIN	THE	CHORUS
AND	SHOUT OUT	

¡OLÉ!

Figure 4-8 *"The Mexican Hat Dance"*

The poem recreates the rhythm and beat of the dance and captures the lingo and movement. The music of poetry can be felt in our bodies even if only snapping fingers or nodding and swaying heads. It's as though the poem is shouting to be performed. The teacher asks:

- ◆ Did you like this poem? Why or why not?
- ◆ How would you move to this poem? Show me.

◆ What interior visions and meanings did the poem suggest?

◆ What is the time movement or time element in the piece?

◆ How does the poem display an openness of possibilities to meaning?

◆ In what ways does the poem offer dance directions through content?

STORY STRAND: DANCE STORIES

Many dances are based on the plots of great plays, romantic legends, classical myths, and other contemporary literature. Like literature, dances build in intensity and interest to reach a climax followed by a resolution. The beginning, middle, and end, however, are told by juxtaposing and combining dance elements such as body, dynamics, space, actions, and relationships. Repetition is often an effective way to structure the dance and unify its various sections. The sequence of the movements is purposefully connected through transitions such as an entrance or exit, stillness, a solo embedded in an event, a musical interlude, or the mechanical drop of a new stage set. Children should have opportunities to transform stories into dance, and vice versa. Stories based on dance must also have a clearly defined story line, lots of activity, contrasting moods, imagery, words or phrases with strong rhythmic content, and memorable characters.

Fairytale Ballets

Ballets are stories in movement, e.g., the magic of the fairy godmother changing a peasant girl into a beautiful princess (*Cinderella*), the mythical creature, a sylph, who enchants someone's lover and lures him away (*La Sylphide*), a foolish puppet whose jealousy leads to disaster (*Petrushka*), or a handsome prince looking for a magical tree (*Firebird*). These fairytales of dance include supernatural characters, magic, royalty, romance, and witches. The plot usually involves conflict and action, with some resolution or moral to be learned at the end (like a fable).

Dancers must create the plot line, conflicts, and actions using gestures and movements to music. For example, in *Petrushka* the dancer pretends to make his body like a lifeless straw puppet; in *Swan Lake*, the dancer's body trembles, extends, and grows limp as her arms move in romantic elegance like that of a swan. Children should read and become familiar with the plots of the fairytale ballets because they illuminate themes of Western dance and literary culture. With older students, teachers can use ballets as the basis for critical discussions. For example, they can ask:

◆ What did you think about the modern notion of princes and princesses?

◆ What do you think this story is trying to teach? Do you agree?

◆ Is the ballet beautiful? What is beauty?

◆ How do you feel about boys dancing?

◆ Is there gender bias in dance? what kinds of dance? Are the dancers represented by various races and ethnic groups? How might you argue that the ballet is or is not a stereotype?

◆ What was the role of ballet in history?

◆ Why is the ballet considered "high culture"? Why is it considered "elitist" by some? Do you think it is?

Children might also view segments of videotaped ballets as a way of generating ideas for another tale. The class may wish to act out dance segments or respond in other ways. Selected ballets that also have book adaptations are listed here.

Cinderella

Cinderella lives with her three stepsisters and cruel stepmother who are preparing for an upcoming ball. Cinderella will not be attending and instead is confined to the house to clean and sweep. Meanwhile, a beggar woman appears at the house asking for alms. Everyone turns her away except Cinderella, who gives her some bread. Later, after everyone departs, the beggar woman reappears as a beautiful fairy godmother. She changes Cinderella into a princess and arranges for a magical carriage to take her to the ball. The fairy godmother cautions her to return home before the clock strikes midnight or she will turn back into a rag girl. At the ball, Cinderella meets and dances with a handsome prince. They fall magically in love, forgetting all about the time. When the clock strikes midnight, Cinderella begins to turn back into rags. As she runs away, one of her glass slippers is left behind. The prince finds it and travels far and wide to find the owner of the slipper, his true princess. (choreography by Rotislav Zakharov; music by Sergei Prokofiev)

Children view the ballet and read the classic versions of *Cinderella* by the Brothers Grimm and Charles Perrault. They also read and interpret several different variations of the same tale from around the world, such as *Yeh-Shen: A Cinderella Story from China* (Louie, 1988); *Mufaro's Beautiful Daughters,* an African tale (Steptoe, 1987); or *The Brocaded Slipper and Other Vietnamese Tales,* a collection of Asian fairy tales including Cinderella (Vuong, 1982). To present these stories through movement, children start with a "movement" prop or key object central to the story and present it from the object's point of view. For instance, in the Western version of Cinderella, this might be the clock, the glass slipper, the broom, or the magic wand. The children select an object and write out a set of questions that personify an object (e.g., the clock) and dance the actions accordingly.

The Clock

1. Warn Cinderella with your eyes and body that it is almost midnight.
2. Struggle to keep your hands from moving toward the 12.
3. Ring loudly.

The Magic Wand

1. Move like the wand.
2. Show how you might move if held by a wicked stepmother, a fairy princess, a mouse.
3. Pretend that you have eyes. Look for something to transform, and touch it.

The children may want to replay scenes and use different prop improvisations for the other cultural versions of *Cinderella*. After the children move like objects, they can generate personification poems or riddles that mirror the movements. For example:

I sway both to and fro
Change a pumpkin to a carriage, you know
If Cinderella is smart
At twelve she'll depart
For my magic is merely on loan.
Who am I?
(The wand)

Sleeping Beauty

A child named Princess Aurora is born and it is the day of her christening. As she lies in her cradle, the fairy godmothers, the ladies in waiting, the royal fairies, and the maids of honor pay homage. However, Fairy Carabosse, the hunchbacked godmother, has accidentally been left off the invitation list, so she places a curse on the child. While at her spinning wheel, Aurora pricks her finger and dies! The King and Queen are distraught. But the Lilac Fairy consoles them, saying that the princess only appears dead—she is really asleep. One day a prince will wake her from her sleep and they will live happily ever after. (choreography by Marius Petipa; music by Tchaikovsky)

Again the children view the ballet and read several versions of *Sleeping Beauty:* for example, *The Sleeping Beauty: The Story of Tchaikovsky's Ballet* (Richardson, 1991) or *The Sleeping Beauty* (Walker, 1986). To compare dance and book versions, they might select a particular scene or idea, such as the dream sequence of the main character. They can write diary entries for the dreams of Sleeping Beauty and enact these dreams in dance, thereby adding another dimension to the dance story.

Swan Lake

This is a popular ballet of a beautiful princess named Odette, who is turned into a swan by an evil sorcerer named Von Rotbart. Odette is Queen of the Swans except for the time between midnight and dawn, when she becomes a beautiful woman. A prince named Siegfried is hunting at the lakeside and sees the beautiful creature that is half woman and half swan. Odette explains her plight and that of her swan maidens, who are under an evil spell. Siegfried promises to love and marry her. When he must select a princess bride at the palace ball, Rotbart tricks Siegfried into thinking that his daughter Odile is the beautiful Odette. When Odette hears of this, she is overwrought. She knows that if she dies, she will be released from the power of the evil sorcerer. Love finally triumphs when she throws herself into the water and Siegfried follows. (book by V. P. Begitchev and Vasily Geltzer; music by Tchaikovsky)

Lovely book versions of *Swan Lake,* such as the one by Helprin (1989), are available for children to compare to the dance versions. They ask themselves the following questions:

◆ How is a dance story written?

◆ What is included that is not in a text version?

◆ What words tell you that this is about dance?

◆ How can you write a book version of another ballet (e.g., *Petrushka* or *Giselle*)?

Children can also read reviews by dancers and choreographers and discuss how they compare to music, movie, or sports reviews. For example, note how Balanchine and Mason (1975) describe the character of Odile, the antagonist of *Swan Lake:*

Odile follows with a quick final dance designed to whip Siegfried's passion still further, and she succeeds in this brilliantly. Her variation contains a dazzling circling of the stage with small, swift turns, a series of quick, close movements performed in a straight line from the front of the stage to the back and finally a series of 32-fouettés. These relentless, whipping turns sum up her power over the prince and, with disdainful joy, seem to laugh at his passion. (p. 446)

As this example shows, a dance review often highlights movements with a special vocabulary that accentuates emotions and dance elements (timing, space, relationships). We see less emphasis on story line and more on technical descriptions of actions and emotions that carry the story line. Children can learn to write dance reviews in the role of a dance critic or choreographer. Now is the opportune time to refer back to the inquiry strand and use the vocabulary of movement that children have been studying and developing.

The Firebird

This is a story about a prince named Ivan who searches for a magical tree of unsurpassed beauty. When he arrives at the magical tree, he sees the Firebird, a creature that is half woman and half bird with feathers as bright as flames. The prince captures the Firebird, but feels compassion for it and releases her to freedom. In appreciation, the Firebird gives the prince one of her brilliant red feathers as a magic charm. When an evil sorcerer meets up with Ivan, he uses the red feather for his survival. The feather becomes a golden sword and saves him from evil. (choreography by Mikhail Folkine; performed by Ballet Russes led by Serge Diaghlev; music by Stravinsky)

The *Firebird* (San Souci, 1992) is a wonderful children's book that can be interpreted in different dance motifs and tempos such as jazz, hip-hop, or rock and roll. Children can work out dance routines interspersed with tiny vignettes of acting.

Writing Moving Narratives

Like dance, written stories involve movement but do so through the pace of the sentences and passages, quickening action through dialogue or summaries and slowing it down with elaborate detail. Specific words (especially action verbs) and other language devices create movement, as shown in Table 4-6. Let's look at a sample from the table. Start with a football photograph from the sports page of the newspaper and create a web of words to describe the action that takes place (e.g., thrashing, leaping, dashing, squirming). Next, have children write a caption to show the action.

. . . Smith leaped into the air and caught the football in midflight.

Have children enact the movements that they write about, noticing how the strong action verbs cue the movements. Children can write an entire sports article on football using several different action pictures and captions.

Writing a narrative of motion requires children to translate actions and movement into words. As writers, they ask themselves the following questions:

◆ How can I create action or mood in a written work (e.g., can I create energy by using strong action verbs, placing emphatic words at the end, using short rather than long sentences?)
◆ How can I portray a sequence of actions? (logical order, hierarchical order, compare and contrast, transitions)

TABLE 4-6 Translating Language to Movement

Language Device	Translating Language to Movement
Show, don't tell. This strategy is used to create pictures of action in someone's mind, showing concrete actions or giving concrete directions.	Have children think of 10 ways to use a hula hoop and show these to the class
Figures of speech. Similes are comparisons using the word "like" or "as."	Have children move like a rag doll, wiggle like a cooked noodle, melt like snow, rise like a balloon
Action grammar. This includes verbs, adverbs, adjectives, and prepositions that create visual meanings, suggest direction, or show spatial relations.	Teach the recognition of lively action verbs by displaying words used in dance reviews or newspaper headlines for the sports page. Have children show these actions.
Verbs of action: squirm, thrash, twist, fidget, saunter, promenade, bounce	
Verbs of relationships: mingle, meet, merge, mirror, shadow, depart, pounce, disperse, congregate	
Verbs of expression: meander, creep, writhe, linger, stretch, bend, shake, swing, twist, dawdle, dart	
Verbs of motion: walk, crawl, leap, gallop, hop, slide, skip, step-hop, roll, flee, rush, dash, kneel, sit, spring	
Adjectives of effort: firm, strong, fine, delicate, slow, fast, relaxed, flexible, uncontrolled, strained	
Adverbs: wave boldly, jump daintily, slide smoothly	
Prepositions: toward, away from, sideways, around, near, far, over, under	

♦ How might I describe the movement of my written piece? (advancing, receding, circling, flowing, repeating)

♦ How can I show versatility and flexibility in prose? (in word choice, sentence variety, movement and innovative language patterns, fluency)?

Children can also write moving poetic narratives. The example of the rag doll in Table 4-6 is a good case in point. Have children move like a rag doll and then find words for it. Use the "adjectives of effort" to describe the doll's actions (delicate, relaxed, uncontrolled) or the "verbs of expression" to show how it moves (writhes, lingers, bends). Write a poem about the doll and then express it in movement.

Dancing a Story

To introduce children to "dancing their understanding of a book," share with them the story *Song and Dance Man* by Karen Ackerman. Begin by identifying personal and general space on an imaginary "attic" stage (the setting of the book). Then have a narrator read the story while the others enact movements modeled by the teacher. The teacher uses the words and pictures to improvise the movements. The children discover another visual means for portraying a story without pictures. Here's how it might go.

1. The narrator reads excerpts as the children enact the movements. The first episode considers *spatial concepts.*

[Children stand in a horseshoe circle as the narrator recites these words]

"Grandpa was a song and dance man who once danced on the vaudeville stage. When we visit, he tells us about a time before people watched TV, back in the good old days, the song and dance days . . . ."

[Children lift legs in high marching form as if going up the steps]

"We follow him up the steep wooden steps. . . ."

[Children pretend to move objects around by swaying their arms and hands from left to right]

"He moves some cardboard boxes and a rack of Grandma's winter dresses out of the way, and we see a dusty brown, leather-trimmed trunk in the corner. . . ."

[Children pretend to place a hat on their heads and they nod from left to right]

"Inside are his shoes with the silver, half-moon taps on the toes and heels, bowler hats and tophats, and vests with stripes and matching bow ties. We try on the hats and pretend we're dancing on a vaudeville stage, where the bright lights twinkle and the piano player nods his head along with the music."

2. In the next episode, the children learn about *body movement and energy concepts.* Grandpa will do the soft shoe for them. The teacher asks for someone to play Grandpa.

"Grandpa turns on the lamps and aims each one down like a spotlight."

[One child comes forward to do a solo tap dance]

"All we can hear is the silvery tap of two feet, and all we can see is a song-and-dance man gliding across a vaudeville stage."

[All the children start tapping in place faster and faster]

"Slowly he starts to tap. His shoes move faster and faster and the sounds coming from them are too many to make with only two feet. He spins and jumps into the air. Touching the stage again, he kneels with his arms spread out, and the silk tophat and gold-tipped cane lie side by side at his feet. His shoes are still and the show is over."

[All the children stop tapping and clap and laugh as the soloist continues the tap dance]

Now the soloist moves and dances with a cane (as shown in the book's illustration). The child is directed by the story narrative to produce body movements while the group sits and watches, clapping and laughing. The dance starts out slowly, escalates to a feverish pitch, and then comes to a sudden halt.

3. In the final episode, children show *temporal concepts* by virtue of the story ending and actions.

[The children clap their hands and shout "hurrah" and "more." They slow down their tapping, bow their heads, and begin to sway their arms]

"We stand up together and clap our hands shouting "Hurrah!" and "More!," but Grandpa only smiles and shakes his head, all out of breath. He takes off his tap shoes, wraps them gently in the shamming cloth, and puts them back in the leather-trimmed trunk. He carefully folds his vest and lays the tophat and cane on it, and we follow him to the stairway."

[The soloist takes a bow and moves back into the half circle. All the children bow and in marching fashion, descend the "pretend" stairs in single file]

The soloist acts out the ending actions and the children exit at the steps, this time going down. They have closure by virtue of the staircase's symbolic opening and closing.

[the end]

This book also has other vaudeville acts that children can enact: singing "Yankee Doodle Boy" with a banjo, doing magic tricks, juggling, and telling jokes.

Stories about Dance and Dancers

Books about dance and biographies of dancers add richness to the language arts curriculum. For instance, in addition to the books that accompany such fairytale ballets as *Cinderella, Swan Lake, Sleeping Beauty,* and *Firebird,* there are many books with dance as a theme, such as *My Pretty Ballerina* (Backstein, 1991), *Boy, Can He Dance* (Spinelli, 1993), and *Chin Chiang and the Dragon's Dance* (Wallace, 1984). These books typically focus on animal shenanigans and dance fantasy, multicultural celebrations featuring dance, or heroic attempts to ensure that "the show will go on." There are also series books that celebrate dancing, such as that of Gauch's books about Tanya, Katharine Holabird's books about Angelina ballerina, Giff's Rosie stories, and Isadora's books of ballet (see the titles in the "Additional Resources" section at the end of the chapter). Although these authors feature girls in their stories, some authors are beginning to break stereotypes, with books such as *Boy, Can He Dance* (Spinelli, 1993) and *Baseball Ballerina* (Cristaldi, 1992).

There are interesting life stories of dancers and dance companies [e.g., the story of *Katherine Dunham: Black Dancer* (Greene, 1992), *Alvin Ailey, Jr.: A Life in Dance* (Lewis-Ferguson, 1994), and *Agnes De Mille: Dancing off the Earth* (Gherman, 1990)].

If children are interested in other nonfiction books about dance, a good place to start is *My Ballet Class* (Isadora, 1990), which describes a young girl going to ballet class, or *Dancing on the Dusty Earth* (Price, 1979), an excellent introduction to African, Indian, Polynesian, Thai, and other dances around the world.

INFORMATION STRAND: LEARNING THROUGH DANCE

Over the years there have been many forms of dance; those that tell stories, those that reject storytelling and focus solely on expressive and free form, and those that follow classics and tradition. As a result, children have a rich heritage for exploring and understanding dance. Moreover, as one of the oldest and most primal of arts (Fonteyn, 1978), dance helps students explore civilizations and peoples across cultures, a kind of window into values and beliefs, traditions, customs, and religion (National Dance Association, 1996). In the next sections we think about dance for learning.

Choreography for Children

Choreography is the detailed planning of a dance and pantomime sequence. The word *choreography* comes from the Greek *khoros*, meaning "dancing," and *graphia*, meaning "writing." Dance notation, the art of how to "write down" a dance, was used initially in 1701 by Raoul Feuillet. These stories helped dancers preserve specific movements for posterity. Children can learn to write visually and spatially by trying their hand at choreography. First, however, they need to come up with ideas for a movement sequence. Let's use an example from a fifth-grade classroom called *Street Talk*. Taping butcher paper to the floor, children use chalk to create a large figure eight.

Next, they brainstorm movements and actions to use along the figure eight path (e.g., jumping, walking, pausing). These movements are translated into a symbolic code and the codes are drawn along the figure eight floor plan to help them remember the routine (see Figure 4-9). In this dance number, *Street Talk,* they use props such as paper traffic signs, mounted on cardboard and glued to sticks (e.g., stop signs, yield signs, do not pass signs, slow down signs, move forward) to direct movements. They use embroidery hoops as steering wheels to role-play drivers. The children move along the figure eight floor plan in single file. Along the way they perform the actions represented by the codes drawn on the figure eight. When they

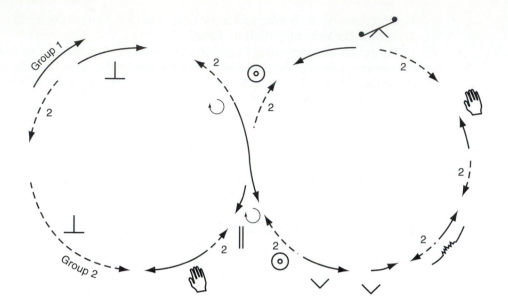

Travel	Fall	Turn	Twist
→	⊥	↻	ℰ
Pause	**Contract**	**Expand**	**Transfer Weight**
⊙	‖	〜	⚊
Jump	**Gesture**		
⌄	🖐		

Figure 4-9 *Choreography Map and Dance Code*

reach the intersection, they hold up their signs to show the others who has the right of way and how they should pass the intersection. When children know the routine, they can remove the paper and dance the routine from memory.

Folktales and Folk Dance

In the medieval unit in Chapter 1, children performed peasant folk dances as part of medieval wedding and celebratory feasts. These dances provided a way for children to express their understanding of historical events through movement enactments. They used books and story lines to help them convey the social dances of the masses, which originated outside the courts or elitist circles of power. Folk dances are a part of every country, and through them we learn about the history and life of people around the world (Table 4-7). The children can practice movement and dance to study cultural and historical events. An example dance card is shown in Figure 4-10. The children are asked to research specific questions and share their findings with others. A research guide helps to scaffold the task for them.

Research Guide: Native American Dances

◆ *History.* Study the many forms of dance and the lifestyles and beliefs of the Native American. Read about the dance and then show how movements help symbolically and rhythmically to identify the natural environment in which particular groups lived. For example, why might a leaping dance flourish on the hillsides, while running and chain dances flourish in large spaces such as the plains? How did the climate affect the dance? Did it restrict or free it, based on the clothes that were worn (in arctic versus tropic)? Did the dance

Native American Tribal Dance

• What is the history of the dance?

• What can you learn about the Native American people's beliefs through dance?

• What costumes and props are appropriate?

• What books can we read?

• What music can you select to represent this dance?

• Demonstrate the dance.

Figure 4-10 *Dance Card*

TABLE 4-7 Ideas for Multicultural Dance Cards

Folk Dance	Country of Origin
Tarantella	Italy
Flamenco	Spain
Cossack dance	Russia
Sailor's hornpipe	England
Scotch reel	Scotland
Waltz	Germany
The jig	Ireland
Hula hula dance	United States (Hawaiian Islands)
Snake dance	United States (Hopi Indians)
Turkish sword dance	Turkey

symbolically represent animals and nature? day and night? the sacredness of the earth, sun, stars, fire, land, and water? the gifts of the gods? Consider the functions of these dances to gain insights into the thinking and beliefs of the people. Why were peacetime dances created: to bring the rainfall, to temper the natural disasters, to make the earth fertile, to revere ancestors, to ward off danger, or to celebrate rites of passage? Ask yourself a series of questions about what you would like to know.

◆ *Costumes and props.* The Native American dance is characterized by costumes, body painting, and masks, which also are symbolic of the dance. Find samples of these and try to create them.

◆ *Recommended books.* Read books about your topic, such as *The Sacred Path: Spells, Prayer and Power Songs of the American Indian* (Bierhorst, 1983) and *Pueblo Storyteller* (Hoyt-Goldsmith, 1994), both of which discuss dance.

◆ *Music selection.* Find music or create a rhythmic beat to accompany your dance (see Chapter 3). How might you use rhythmically repeated steps, leaps, or gestures to perform a Native American dance?

◆ *Demonstration.* Perform your dance for the class. Mime-dance a hunt or sacred ritual. Perform magical dances.

◆ ## *School–Community Links*

Teachers will want to take advantage of special experiences for sharing the importance of dance. After all, one of the goals of the dance literacy program is to help all children enjoy leisure time and a rich quality of life. Based on the dance card activity, the teacher might arrange a folk festival for a school assembly so that the children can explain and perform their various dances for the entire school.

The specific cultural interests of the local community should also be reflected in the school program and include participation by dance companies, universities, and dance studios. Mentor-apprentice programs can team children with dancers to explore the creative and artistic skills necessary for enjoying dance. If feasible, schools can be kept open as community learning centers during nontraditional school hours, and children and parents can be invited to movement and fitness classes. These classes can help parents release stress and, more important, help them spend quality time with their children. The teacher can also send students into the community as ethnographers to interview individuals in the dance business or to talk with high school students or young adults about popular dance. They can question their parents or grandparents about the popular dances of their youth, asking them what dances were their favorites, who taught them, who their dance partners were, and where they went to dance. The children ask these people to show them the dance and tell them a little about its history. For example, one of the students returned with the notes shown in Figure 4-11.

Teachers should encourage students to attend community events such as dance recitals and musical theater. Many of these events are free to the public, and the dance community is always eager to have schoolchildren attend.

◆ *Activities for Professional Development*

1. Attend a dance performance. When you arrive at the theater, read the program—the story of dance and the biographical information about the dancers, choreographers, musicians, and other performers. Note the physical aspects of the performance, such as the theatrical space, lighting, and acoustics. While the dance is being performed, savor important impressions so that when you return home, you can write about them in your journal. Write about your first reactions:

Dance	How It Is Performed	What I Learned about the Dance
Disco	(demonstration)	I learned that disco was popular in the 1970s. One important movie, *Disco Fever* with John Travolta, and a rock group, the Bee Gees, influenced this form of dance. This was the era following the hippies and the 1960s.

Figure 4-11 *Dance Research Notes.*

moments you most enjoyed, how the music made you feel, or the quality of the dancers' performance. Describe what you remember about the story, the set, the props, the costumes, the dance movements, the relationships of dancers (solo, duets, groups), and the way that space was used. Also think about any historical or cultural insights that the dance or music may have elicited in you. Share your experience with colleagues and your students.

2. Collect and study dance art prints and the poses and movements they illustrate. Many artists have portrayed dancers in their artwork. Brueghel's work shows peasants dancing and Toulouse-Lautrec shows dancing at the Moulin Rouge in Paris. Mitchell (1993) has a beautiful book of black-and-white photographs of the Alvin Ailey Dancers that reproduce the movements and poses of the dancers. Dance artwork can also be found in children's literature. For example, one of the most famous of the dance painters, Degas, has a collection of ballerinas and ballet statuettes that are well known. Anholt's (1996) book *Degas and the Little Dancer* shows how the artist immortalizes dance in sculpture. Collect and study dance art prints as well as ordinary poses found in magazine pictures. See if you can imitate the still poses and nonverbal gestures (facial, body, or kinesthetic). Then ask yourself: What movement might have preceded this one? followed it? Try putting the movements together in an action phrase. Then share the picture you are trying to convey.

3. Do an investigative report on childrens' contemporary dance. Identify the popular dances enjoyed by today's children and ask them about the music, the movements and/or steps, the relationship with partners, the clothing worn, and the settings or contexts where the dances take place. Meanwhile, find examples of these dances on television or videos or in real life. Have the children teach you the dance and videotape your practice sessions. Share the dances with others.

◆ *Works Cited*

Professional References

Balanchine, G., and Mason, F. (1975). *101 stories of the great ballets.* New York: Doubleday/Anchor Books.

Birdwhistle, R. (1970). *Kinesics and context: Essays in body motion communication.* Philadelphia: University of Pennsylvania Press.

Bruner, J. (1966). *A theory of instruction.* Cambridge, MA: Harvard University Press.

Corsaro, W. (1985). *Friendship and peer culture in the early years.* Norwood, NJ: Ablex Publishing.

Eisner, E. W. (1981). The role of the arts in cognition and curriculum. *Phi Delta Kappan, 63,* 48–52.

Ekman, P., and Friesen, W. W. (1969). The repertoire of nonverbal behavior: Categories, origins, usage, and coding. *Semiotica, 1,* 49–98.

Fleming, G. A. (Ed.) (1990). *Children's dance.* Reston, VA: American Alliance for Health, Physical Education, Recreation, and Dance.

Fonteyn, M. (1976). *Margot Fonteyn: Autobiography.* New York: Alfred A. Knopf.

Gardner, H. (1991). *The unschooled mind: How children think and how schools should teach.* New York: Basic Books.

Gardner, H. (1993). *Creating minds: An anatomy of creativity seen through the lives of Freud, Einstein, Picasso, Stravinsky, Eliot, Graham, and Gandhi.* New York: Basic Books.

Garvey, C. (1977). *Play.* Cambridge, MA: Harvard University Press.

Gilbert, A. G. (1992). *Creative dance for all ages.* Reston: VA: National Dance Association/American Alliance for Health, Physical Education, Recreation, and Dance.

Greene, M. (1988). *The dialectic of freedom.* New York: Teachers College Press.

Kendon, A. (1985). Some uses of gesture. In D. Tannen and M. Saville-Troike (Eds.), *Perspectives on silence* (pp. 215–234). Norwood, NJ: Ablex Publishing.

Kerr, R. (1982). *Psychomotor learning.* Philadelphia: Saunders College Publishing.

Knapp, M., and Knapp, H. (1976). *One potato, two potato: The folklore of American children.* New York: W.W. Norton.

Laban, R. (1948). *Modern educational dance.* London: Macdonald & Evans.

Lee, A. (1992). *A handbook of creative dance and drama: Ideas for teachers.* Portsmouth, NH: Heinemann.

Magill, R. (1989). *Motor learning: Concepts and applications.* Dubuque, IA: Wm. C. Brown.

Montessori, M. (1949). *The absorbent mind.* Madras, India: Kalakshetra Publications.

Miller, T. E. (1986). *Folkmusic in America: A reference guide.* New York: Garland Publishing.

Mitchell, J. (1993). *Alvin Ailey American dance theater.* A Donna Martin Book. Kansas City, MO: Andrews and McMeel.

National Dance Association (1996). Reston, VA: American Alliance for Health, Physical Education, Recreation, and Dance.

Piaget, J., and Inhelder, B. (1969). *The psychology of the child.* New York: Basic Books.

Schnurnberger, L. (1991). *Let there be clothes.* New York: Workman Publishing.

Smilansky, S. (1968). *The effects of socio-dramatic play in disadvantaged pre-school children.* New York: Wiley.

Steiner, R. (1984). *Eurythmy as visible speech.* London: Rudolf Steiner Press.

Stinson, S. W. (1993). *Dance for young children: Finding the magic in movement.* Reston, VA: American Alliance for Health, Physical Education, Recreation, and Dance.

Vygotsky, L. (1978). *Mind in society.* Cambridge, MA: Harvard University Press.

Wall, J. A., and Murray, N. R. (1990). *Children and movement.* Madison, WI: Brown & Benchmark.

Werner, H., and Kaplan B. (1964). *Symbolic formation.* New York: Wiley.

Wood, B. (1981). *Children and communication: Verbal and nonverbal language development.* Upper Saddle River, NJ: Prentice Hall.

Children's References

Ackerman, K. (1988). *Song and dance man* (illus. S. Gammell). New York: Alfred A. Knopf.

Anholt, L. (1996). *Degas and the little dancer: A story about Edgar Degas.* London: Frances Lincoln.

Backstein, K. (1991). *My pretty ballerina* (illus. C. Beylon). New York: Tyco Inc.

Bierhorst, J. (1983). *The sacred path: Spells, prayer and power songs of the American Indian.* New York: Morrow.

Browning, R. (1998). *The pied piper of Hamelin* (illus. T. Small). Orlando, FL: Harcourt Brace.

Charlip, R., Charlip, M. B., and Ancona, G. (1974). *Handtalk: An ABC of finger spelling and sign language.* New York: Four Winds Press.

Cristaldi, K. (1992). *Baseball ballerina* (illus. A. Carter). New York: Random House.

Esbensen, A. J. (1995). *Dance with me* (illus. M. Lloyd). New York: HarperCollins.

Fain, K. (1993). *Handsigns: A sign language alphabet.* San Francisco: Chronicle Books.

Fronval, G., and Dubois, D. (1994). *Indian signals and sign language* (illus. J. Marcellin, transl. E. W. Egan, photos G. C. Hight, period paintings G. Catlin). New York: Wing Books.

Gherman, B. (1990). *Agnes De Mille: Dancing off the earth.* New York: Atheneum Books.

Greene, C. (1992). *Katherine Dunham: Black dancer.* Chicago: Children's Press.

Grimm Brothers (1954). *Cinderella* (illus. M. Brown). New York: Harper & Row.

Helprin, M. (1989). *Swan lake* (illus. C. Van Allsburg). Boston: Houghton Mifflin.

Hoffman, E. T. A. (1984). *The nutcracker* (illus. M. Sendak, trans. R. Manheim). New York: Crown Publishing.

Hoffman, E. T. A. (1985). *The nutcracker* (illus. P. Seminara, trans. A. R. Hope). New York: Crown Publishing.

Hoyt-Goldsmith, D. (1994). *Pueblo storyteller* (illus. L. Migdale). New York: Macmillan/McGraw-Hill.

Isadora, R. (1990). *My ballet class.* New York: Greenwillow Books.

Lewis-Ferguson, J. (1994). *Alvin Ailey, Jr.: A life in dance.* New York: Scholastic.

Louie, A. L. (1988). *Yeh-Shen: A Cinderella story from China.* New York: Putnam.

Morrison, L. (1985). *The break dance kids: Poems of sport, motion, and locomotion.* New York: Lothrop, Lee & Shepard.

Perrault, C. (1985). *Cinderella* (illus. S. Jefers). New York: Dial Press.

Price, C. (1979). *Dance on the dusty earth.* New York: Charles Scribner's Sons.

Richardson, J. (1991). *The sleeping beauty: The story of Tchaikovsky's ballet* (illus. F. Crespi). Boston: Little, Brown.

San Souci, R. D. (1992). *Firebird* (illus. K. Waldherr). New York: Doubleday.

Spinelli, E. (1993). *Boy, can he dance* (illus. P. Yalowitz). New York: Four Winds Press.

Steptoe, J. (1987). *Mufaro's beautiful daughters: An African tale.* New York: Lothrop, Lee & Shepard.

Vuong, L. D. (1982). *The brocaded slipper and other Vietnamese Tales* (illus. V. Mai). New York: Harper & Row.

Walker, D. (trans. and illus.) (1986). *The Sleeping Beauty.* New York: Thomas Y. Crowell.

Wallace, I. (1984). *Chin Chiang and the dragon's dance.* New York: Atheneum Books.

Yurchenco, H. (Ed.) (1967). *A fiesta of folk songs from Spain and Latin America* (illus. J. Maidoff). New York: Putnam.

◆ Additional Resources

Note: Asterisks indicate resources that are cited in the chapter.

Videotapes and Catalogs

Alice in Wonderland: A Dance Fantasy
Stage Step
P.O. Box 328
Philadelphia, PA 19105
800-523-0960

Ballet Is Fun
NCM
Walnut Hill Lane
Irving, TX 75038
(CD-ROM video dictionary)

Chime Time
1 Sportime Way
Atlanta, GA 30340
800-477-5075

*Cinderella
75 Rockefeller Plaza
New York, NY 10019
(Paris Opera Ballet; Electra Nonesuch
Dance Collection; Rudolf Nureyev,
choreographer)

Music for Little People
Dept. FGR
P.O. Box 1720
Lawndale, CA 90260
    Folk Dance Fun
    Square Dance Fun

Dancing
HomeVision
4411 N. Ravenswood Ave., 3rd FL.
Chicago, IL 60640
(eight-part series includes: 1. The
power of dance, 2. Lord of the dance,
3. Sex and social dance, 4. Dance at
court, 5. New worlds, new forms, 6.
Dance centerstage, 7. The individual
and tradition, 8. Dancing in one
world; 58 minutes each; overview for
teachers)

*Firebird
Stravinsky's Firebird, Petrushka and
Fireworks

*La Sylphide
Pas De Deux
Stage Step
P.O. Box 328
Philadelphia, PA 19105

English Country Dances for Children,
2nd ed.
Riverside Productions
Music in Motion
P.O. Box 833814
Richardson, TX 75083
(Martha Chrisman Riley, 1994)

Miss Christy's Dancin': Jazz
Music for Little People
Department FGR
P.O. Box 1720
Lawndale, CA 90260
800-727-2233
(35 minutes, all ages)

*Petrushka
Stravinsky's Firebird, Petrushka and
Fireworks
Music in Motion
P.O. Box 833814
Richardson, TX 75083-3814

Romeo and Juliet and Giselle
Music in Motion
P.O. Box 833814
Richardson, TX 75083-3814
(60 minutes; "Footnotes: The classics
of ballet" with Frank Augustyn)

Sleeping Beauty
Kultur Videos
195 Highway 36
West Long Branch, NJ 07764
(prince: Rudolf Nureyev, 90 minutes,
all ages, 1972)

Stage Step
P.O. Box 328
Philadelphia, PA 19105
800-523-0960
(videos on dance and dancers)

Swan Lake
Kultur Videos
195 Highway 36
West Long Branch, NJ 07764
(60 minutes, all ages)

Swan Lake Story: A Dance Fantasy.
Stage Step
P.O. Box 328
Philadelphia, PA 19105
800-523-0960

The Nutcracker
Electra Entertainment
Division of Warner Communications
4000 Warner Blvd.
Burbank, CA 91522

The Nutcracker
The Maurice Sendak Production
Music in Motion
P.O. Box 833814
Richardson, TX 75083
(84 minutes, all ages)

The Nutcracker and Sleeping Beauty
Stage Step
P.O.Box 328
Philadelphia, PA 19105
800-523-0960
(60 minutes, all ages, footnotes: The
Classics of Ballet with Frank
Augustyn)

Children's Book Series (Selected Titles)

Gauch, P. L. (1989). *Dance Tanya* New York: Philomel Books.
Gauch, P. L. (1992). *Bravo, Tanya* (illus. Satomi Ichikawa). New York: Putnam.
Gauch, P. L. (1994). *Tanya and Emily in a dance for two* (illus. Satomi Ichikawa).
    New York: Philomel Books.
Giff, P. R. (1996). *Rosie's nutcracker dreams* (illus. Julie Durrell). New York:
    Viking Press.
Giff, P. R. (1997). *Not-so perfect Rosie* (illus. Julie Durrell). New York: Viking Press.
Giff, P. R. (1997). *Starring Rosie.* New York: Viking Press.
Giff, P. R. (1998). *Rosie's big city ballet.* New York: Viking Press.
Holabird, K. (1988). *Angelina ballerina* (illus. Helen Craig). New York: Crown
    Publishing.
Holabird, K. (1992). *Angelina dances.* New York: Random House.
Isadora, R. (1976). *Max.* NY: Macmillan.
Isadora, R. (1984). *Opening night.* New York: Morrow.
Isadora, R. (1991). *Swan lake.* New York: Putnam.
Isadora, R. (1993). *Lili at ballet.* New York: Putnam.

Recordings and Audiocassettes

The Hokey Pokey
Educational Record Center
3233 Burnt Mill Drive, Suite 100,
Wilmington, NC 28403

World Dance Series
(set of six)
Music in Motion
P.O. Box 833814
Richardson, TX 75083

Computer Software and Technology

*Interactive Sign Language: 101 Basic
Signs
Palatine Inc. through Edutainment
P.O. Box 21210
Boulder, CO 80308
800-338-3844
(CD for MAC or Windows)

Internet Addresses

Dance Archives and Discussion
Anonymous FTP
Address: ftp.cs.dal.ca
Path:/comp.archives/rec.arts.dance/
(all materials and discussions of
interest to dance fans of all kinds of
dance)

Theater Literacy: Performing Language

5

Vignette: The Storyteller

Nine-year-old Michael stands in front of the class holding a toy ax and a stuffed blue cow. Today he is Paul Bunyan and he is telling his story.

When I was a baby, I was s-o-o-o big that when I sneezed I blew the birds right out of the air. If I rolled over in my sleep, I'd knock down a mile of trees. I was a danger to the whole state of Maine. Things were rough at first, but when I grew older, I found I could really swing an ax.

["swing an ax": takes the toy ax and swings it in front of his chest in a half circle]

I was s o-o-o- good at this that the lumberjacks wanted me to help them cut down trees. I would swing my ax *and bundle the trees under my arm.*

["swing my ax": repeat gesture]

But you see, I was lonely. No one could understand what it was like to be so big. Till one day, in the winter of the blue snow, I stumbled over something with hair as big as a mountain. It was this ox *and his ears were blue from the snow.*

["this ox": shows the blue stuffed cow]

I decided to call him Babe the Blue Ox. The Babe was so o o big *you needed*

["so big": holds arms apart, palms of hands facing inward to show size]

field glasses to see from one end of him to the other. He was big like me.

["he was big like me": makes fist with left hand, pointing thumb to chest]

One time, the cooks at the logging site couldn't find a grill big enough to cook all the pancakes for the lumberjacks. I built one so big that they had to strap bacon on the lumberjacks' feet and have them skate over the griddle to keep it greased. I hitched Babe to the handle and he went round and round, *diggin a big hole for the fire. We made tons of pancakes.*

["round and round": Make a fist with right hand and circle round and round, counterclockwise like stirring cake batter]

No one knows this, but when Babe and I moved on to the west, I had this sharp spike draggin behind me and it made a rut that is now the Grand Canyon!

    Babe and I finally ended up in Alaska. That's what most folks say. Today, you can still hear the whirling of my ax and my shouting T-I-M-B-E-R-R-R through the trees. The end.

Based on *American Tall Tales* (Stoutenburg, 1976)

A moment of silence fills the air. Then the children huddle around Michael asking: "Are those stories you told really true?" "Whatever happened to Babe?" "Where did you get that blue cow?" "Can I see your ax?"

Michael is proud of his performance and delighted with the audience's reactions. Mr. Beasley is pleased too. When he first decided to try out this storytelling activity, he immediately thought of Michael, who was a natural-born storyteller with an interest in tall tales. At Mr. Beasley's suggestion, Michael watched a video of Paul Bunyan (see "Additional Resources") and read the story from American Tall Tales *to select favorite episodes. Then Mr. Beasley showed him how to improvise the lines of his episodes and add gestures and expressions so that the fictional character might come alive. They talked about a few simple props to set the mood, and Michael went off to rehearse his story. The tale was easy to learn. Exaggeration and humor made it possible for Michael to improvise and embellish the story if he forgot actual lines. The episodes were short enough to remember and followed no strict order. By simply recalling the subject of the episode (i.e., finding the blue ox, making pancakes, creating the Grand Canyon), Michael could mix the order if necessary. The entire storytelling event was short with minimal preparation.*

Now that the story had been told, Mr. Beasley was eager to try out a peer-teaching technique. Like the original storytellers of long ago, Michael would pass down the story, orally, to other classmates.

Mr. Beasley asks Michael to work with others just as he had done with him. Because Paul Bunyan, like other tall tales, has many extraordinary events (cornstalks growing to the sky) and superhuman feats (pulling the kinks and curves out of a road), the novice can retell the same story, with slightly different renditions. Mr. Beasley promises that everyone will get a chance to perform a tall tale. As the number of experienced storytellers multiplies and grows, Mr. Beasley eventually transfers complete ownership and expertise to the children.

As this class experience shows, storytelling provides a way for children to extract important dialogue and details for performance (Moffett and Wagner, 1992), comprehend and recall stories (Hamilton and Weiss, 1990) and practice oral language strategies such as exaggeration and vocal expression (Flynn and Carr, 1994; Fox, 1986; Straczynski, 1987; Wagner, 1988). It also gives children actual experience handing down literary tradition from one classmate to another.

Storytelling is just one of the many drama tasks that teachers have at their disposal. Drama performances range from reader's theater, to storybook enactments, to poetic drama, to professional plays. All of these performing arts help children experience literature in a new way and provide a workable bridge to storywriting (Jett-Simpson, 1989; Kardash and Wright, 1987). Performers must take abstract story elements such as character, setting, conflict, or plot and translate them into the concrete, easily understood world of the senses. In so doing, they learn the meaning of "show don't tell" and begin building texts based on performed dialogue. They develop a character or point of view not simply by recognition or definition but by actively constructing concepts through words, nonverbal gestures, movements, settings, and costumes. The production of drama engages children as creators whose raw materials are words, visuals, sounds, and actions. Integrating all the story elements with words and extralinguistic cues builds on the interdependent nature of multiple literacies. Teachers who regularly make time for drama tasks support basic reading, writing, and oral language skills by opening up several communicative channels for exploring the concept of story. Before we examine this further, we begin with visual, auditory, and kinesthetic aspects of theater that enhance imagination and new ways of thinking.

INQUIRY STRAND: ACTING ON IDEAS

To invent realities, children manipulate actions and dialogue for a participating audience. Before doing so, however, they must dig deep into sensory memories of sights, sounds, smells, and feelings to enact ideas and interpretations. Acting on ideas provides another aesthetic choice for formulating and responding to the invented realities of drama. Throughout the inquiry strand, children use action (movement and words) to interpret events and develop characters. Some of the dramatic strategies woven throughout this strand and others are summarized in Table 5-1. Remember that you can use these literacy tasks independently or for purposes of inquiry as characterized here.

Reader's Theater

Reader's theater is a group language activity in which "two or more readers present a piece of literature by reading aloud from a hand-held script" (Robertson, 1990, p. 2). Engaging in reader's theater casts an interpretive posture on the act of reading and deepens comprehension of known stories (McCaslin, 1980; Stewig, 1983). Because children use a book or script, they don't have to worry about forgetting lines and can concentrate on the overlapping use of voice and gestures to develop characters.

To introduce reader's theater, prepare a sample script for children with print notations (punctuation, italics, bold print) to help them read and jointly interpret how to emphasize words, when to slow down, or how to convey a line. Group read-alouds can help them practice fluency, expression, and shifting perspectives through different voices. Next, have children image the characters thoroughly so that they can project sounds and expression into their words. Reader's theater offers a rich experience for showing how a character comes to life through voice. Proposing an initial set of exploratory questions can be a springboard for interpreting and inventing a character.

TABLE 5–1   Drama Strategies

◆ *Questioning.* Probing questions allow script writers and actors to test characters for a performance. To try out a character, one might ask: How does this character talk? walk? react to others? What are her habits? How does she spend her free time? What does she wear? Who are her friends? How do her parents treat her? What does she look like?

◆ *Speculating.* Speculating is the ability to extrapolate and make predictions from past experiences to produce and manipulate what will happen next. Actors often speculate about hypothetical situations and act them out. For example: A crowded beach. A shark is sighted. Parents notice their child is missing. Frightened, they run to the water. The lifeguard jumps into the ocean. What can reasonably happen next? How might the people on the beach react? Will the lifeguard become a hero? Will the child be all right? A series of books, published by Scholastic and written by Ann McGovern, help children speculate about the past: *If You Lived in Colonial Times; If You Lived with the Sioux; If You Sailed on the Mayflower in 1620; If You Grew up with Abraham Lincoln.*

◆ *Experimenting.* Experimenting, a process of trial and error, allows actors to explore different interpretations of a play. In classrooms where children are not penalized for making mistakes they take chances and tolerate the necessary ambiguity that always occurs in the initial stages of the drama process.

◆ *Interpreting.* Interpreting comprises the point of view and choices the actor makes to understand a character and story. All actors bring their own special interpretations to a script and enact them accordingly. Children will bring a personal imprint to their work if they participate frequently in a number of different performances.

◆ *Reflecting.* All performers reflect on their work through introspection and self-study. Introspection through reflection is the practice of inspecting our experiences and examining them privately. It is an opportunity for the actor to be both the observer and the observed, both judge and jury. Since audience reactions are also powerful stimuli for actor reflection, children are advised to pay attention to the audience on a continual basis.

◆ What is this character like?

◆ What does this character value?

◆ Who does this character remind you of? Why?

◆ How is this character like you? different from you?

◆ What does this character say that you would say differently?

◆ How is this character different from other people you know? other fictional characters?

Finally, children volunteer as narrators and characters to perform the reading in small groups. The teacher will want to set up several concurrent groups so that many children have the opportunity to participate. Children can experiment writing their own scripts for reader's theater. The teacher assists them in the selection of extended stretches of dialogue and main ideas from children's books and prepares a set of guidelines for them to follow. The generic script directions are based on two excellent books:

Reader's Theater for Children: Scripts and Script Development (Laughin and Howard, 1992) and *Reader's Theater for Beginning Readers* (Barchers, 1993). Use the guidelines in these books as a model and adapt them according to the literature you have selected.

- Write the title of the book and author.
- Tell what part of the book you are adapting for the script (either a chapter or a scene).
- In words or symbols, tell or show us where the narrator stands and where the readers are situated.
- Write a stock opening paragraph for the narrator to introduce the story. Follow this format: Our scene today is from _____. The characters are _____, read by _____, _____ read by _____, and so on. The scene we are about to perform shows _____ .
- Write the script:
  1. Go to the place in your book where _____ asks (shouts, teases).
  2. Omit the next part (description).
  3. Copy the dialogue and provide instructions so that the readers can communicate _____.
  4. Insert the following lines for the narrator: _____.
  5. Skip the rest of this page.
  6. Go to the place in your book where _____ asks (demands, begins).
  7. Continue this part.
  8. Write a closing paragraph for the narrator.
  9. End the scene after _____.

For each book, the teacher can create a new set of script directions and narrator inserts. Before long, children will create dynamic dramas independently and may even write their own reader's theater guides for others to follow.

Puppetry

Most children know Kermit the frog and Miss Piggy, the famous Jim Henson puppets. Every generation has its time-honored favorites, such as Punch and Judy, Pinocchio, or Lambchop. Today's puppets are animated like those in *James and the Giant Peach* or *Toy Story*. As part of childhood folklore and entertainment, puppets are wonderful props for narrating stories, trying out ideas, or exploring content material. For example:

- *To narrate stories:* Multicultural folk stories and fables using puppets of the culture (e.g., the stick puppets the make silhouettes for shadow plays in China).

◆ *To try out ideas:* Marionette puppets manipulated through strings inspire ideas through movement messages.

◆ *To explore content areas:* Traditional hand and stick puppets, made from any variety of materials, introduce a social studies or science unit (e.g., famous personalities).

The puppets themselves evoke oral language. The commingling of verbal and nonverbal messages endows puppets with distinct and complex personalities. Figure 5-1 shows simple puppets that children can make. They range from socks, Popsicle sticks, and paper plates to bags, papier-mâché and Styrofoam and take very little time to assemble.

Traditional use of the puppet as a prop allows children to project creativity publicly while concealed behind a stage. The stage can be as simple as a cardboard box with the back cut out, or the top of a desk with a make-shift curtain around the sides. As in reader's theater, children assume a voice other than their own to match the physical and emotional attributes of the puppet. They also concentrate on manipulating puppet movements to show affect and nonverbal messages (e.g., claps, bows, throwing kisses, and rubbing foreheads or eyes). In an experiential way, children discover how dialogue and movement shapes interesting characters and how oral language can carry meaning in its intonations, volume, speed, and inflections.

Mime

The silent art of mime uses body gestures, action, and expressions to convey thoughts and emotions. Famed entertainer Marcel Marceau dedicated his life to pantomime and was a genius in communicating and articulating movement. (Teachers should refer to Chapter 4 for additional mime activities). The fact that mime is one of the few arts that rely heavily on the symbiotic transaction between sender and receiver bears repeating. A simple exercise will illustrate. Have children use their five senses to create word lists of body and facial movements. Table 5-2 shows some examples.

After compiling a list, they can mime these behaviors and have others guess the word they are performing. Call their attention to the role played by both the performer and audience. Children will see how they play off one another using feedback for revision. In other words, they are reading the audience and modifying actions accordingly to deliver their message. Mime is certainly a valuable tool for impressing upon children the concept of audience.

From a dramatic standpoint, mime teaches the power of tapping into emotions, feelings, and inner action. Asking children to "show" what they look like when they are worried, angry, happy, or tired prepares them for lively writing. It is more exciting to see someone "shiver" than it is to say "she was cold."

1.

Paper plate puppet: Staple plate to stick, add features (or use ice cream cup lid or foam meat platter). Cut out eyes for a face mask.

2.

Finger-through puppet: Cut egg shape for Humpty. Cut holes for two fingers. A happy face on one side, sad on the other tells the story.

3.

Tennis ball puppet: Put a mid-way slit in a tennis ball. Draw mouth around slit. Decorate. Squeeze sides to open and close mouth.

4.

Matchbox puppet: Slip a toothpick through a matchbox drawer to open and close mouth.

5.

Index card puppet: When thumb is opposing, squeeze the card; the mouth moves. Add yarn for arms and hands.

6.

Dishmop puppet: Flatten one side of mop and glue on features, pom-pom ball nose.

7.

Whisk broom puppet: Glue on features and necktie.

8.

Tube sock puppet: Glue features on a green sock. Add black and orange yarn hair, hat, and bow. Sock slips over hand.

9.

Tongue depressor puppet: Simply draw or glue on features, hair, earrings, beads, feathers. Can also use ice cream spoon.

Figure 5-1 *Puppets*

Improvisation

Improvisation is impromptu invention that allows you to make up communication as you go along. Plans are often made in advance, but detailed action and dialogue is left to the moment (Ward, 1957). In Chapter 4 we discussed the importance of improvisational structures for dance and

TABLE 5-2   Five Senses Drama Vocabulary

Seeing	Hearing	Tasting	Smelling	Touching
Blink, scan, gaze glance, peep, squint, stare, gawk, gape	Eavesdrop, overhear, listen, harken, heed, detect	Sip, savor, lick, smack, drink, guzzle, gulp, nibble, suck, gnaw, chomp	Sniff, whiff, sneeze, snort, inhale, breathe in and out	Grasp, hit, pinch, rub, strike, scratch, squeeze, tickle

TABLE 5-3   Spot Improv

◆ An audience member can be brought to the front of the stage and included in the act. Children will joke with this person, ask questions, or call for information.

◆ The audience member can participate with one actor (in a two-person improv) by saying the same one or two statements over and over when the actor calls for an answer or remark. For example, the audience member says "sounds good to me" or "I like that."

◆ The audience member(s) offers a personal object to the actors and they must work up a scene around it.

◆ The audience member provides character traits or types for the improvisers to use in the scene (e.g., play "creepy").

◆ The audience member reveals three facts about himself and the actor makes up a story.

movement. The ideas presented are useful for theater improvisation as well. But in theater, actors also create dialogue to focus thought and inspire imagination. Children can begin with a familiar story to enact as they ad-lib along the way, extending or expanding the original material. A key feature of dramatic improvisation is building and reacting to scenarios by interacting with the audience. Using audience suggestions to shape the action that unfolds on the stage represents collaboration of the most fundamental kind. In fact, one popular form of improvisation, *spot improv,* has performers field questions and obtain suggestions from the audience to create short scenes. Examples of these scenes are listed in Table 5-3. Spot improv impresses on children a true understanding of audience. Audience awareness is essential to good writing and is often an abstract concept in print. Improvisation is a concrete way to impress on children the idea of audience.

For young children, improvisation might simply take the form of dramatic play, "the nonliteral (or symbolic) behavior that children use to transform the identities of objects, actions, and people" (Pellegrini, 1997, p. 486). Lost in its immediacy and make-believe, children encounter dramatic play as an important context for using the imaginative function of language and complex linguistic structures (Corsaro, 1985; Dyson, 1989; Halliday and Hasan, 1976).

Role-playing

Role-playing is an activity where children assume certain roles from real-life situations to resolve everyday conflicts, try out new solutions, experience another's point of view, or gain insight into the adult world. One of the important reasons for role-play in the classroom is that it allows students to get inside characters' intentions, motivations, and reasoning to better understand how emotions drive actions and thoughts. Children play off each other (acting and reacting) in a kind of theatrical duet. Situation storylines or subtexts become a scaffold for supporting the role-play. A few of these subtexts (some literary, some everyday events) are suggested in Table 5-4. Role-playing is essential to reading and writing because it gives

TABLE 5-4 Role-Playing

Conflict

◆ You are on the playground and the class bully, who has been needling you for some time now, purposely steps on your foot. Show us what you do or say to him.

◆ You have wandered into the house of the three little bears and one of them was home.

Trying out a new solution

◆ You are at summer camp and you are expected to know how to swim. The counselor sees you splashing and thrashing around in the water and refuses to allow you in the lake. Convince the counselor that you can remain safe in the water.

◆ You have traveled to <u>Where the Wild Things Are</u> (Sendak, 1991) and the forest is filled with little people. How do you recreate the story?

Point of view

◆ You are a new student at school. It is the first day and everyone has arrived. You hang back. A young boy sees that you are uncomfortable and tries to make you feel welcome. Show us this scene.

◆ You are the story character Miss Trunchbull, headmistress of the school in *Matilda* (Dahl, 1998). Many believe that you are a tyrant. You want to tell your side of the story. Portray this scene.

Tolerance: Walking in another's shoes

◆ Your best friend's parents have decided to divorce. Your friend is feeling very sad and abandoned. Show us how you would cheer her up.

◆ Your baby brother awakens in the middle of the night, screaming from a bad dream. Show us how you might comfort him.

Interview

◆ You are looking for a job at a local grocery store. Show us the job interview.

◆ You are a journalist interviewing Beverly Cleary's character <u>Ramona</u> (Cleary, 1984). Enact the interview.

Social practices and courtesies

◆ You spot someone new at school. Introduce yourself and a friend.

◆ You are the master of ceremonies at a variety show. Role-play how you will open and close the show. How will you introduce the comedy routines, songs, and dance?

children another opportunity to take a concept such as point of view and demonstrate it through words, actions, and situations. Also, the ability to "step into another's shoes" is an invaluable life skill.

LANGUAGING STRAND: THEATER TALK

Theater brings together a combination of many symbols (dialogue, narrative, props, costumes, makeup) to communicate ideas to an audience. In this section we focus on "talk," the spoken art, reserving the other meaning-making symbols for a later section. Again the literacy tasks in this section can be embedded into the next three strands or done independently.

Voice and written dialogue are meaningful drama elements that cue action and organize experience. Our voices provide insights into personality traits, geographic region, attitudes, and historical milieu: for example, the words we use, the way we say them, and the way in which they are delivered. According to literary theorist Bakhtin (in Emerson and Holquist, 1986), each person is imbued with multiple voices that reflect a mix of personal and social factors. These various points of view allow the audience/listeners to co-create the story and its meaning with the actor. In this strand we discuss the multiplicity of voices that theater uses to carry and inspire meanings. We begin with the three basic forms of talk used in drama: dialogue, soliloquy, and monologue.

Dialogue

The most distinguishing feature of plays is the emphasis on dialogue, conversations between two or more people. Many teachers like to introduce dialogue using cartoon strips with speech bubbles for children to fill in. Another favorite is to analyze photos and match the people pictured in the photograph to the words that describe their actions and moods. But beyond mapping words to pictures, teachers can emphasize the functions that dialogue serves in drama and writing. Dialogue that really works doesn't just fill in conversational space but assumes an important job in the story.

Take excerpts from children's literature and have children inductively figure out the function that dialogue takes on in a particular instance. Use an answer box of choices and examples to help scaffold the activity:

- ◆ *To identify character:* "He's right! Fudgie's teeth are gone!" [from *Tales of a Fourth Grade Nothing* (Blume, 1972)].

- ◆ *To keep narrative moving:* "I've been meaning to say to you how much I appreciate the way you've been making friends with William Ernest" [from *The Great Gilly Hopkins* (Paterson, 1996)].

- ◆ *To provide information:* "He's my uncle, my mother's brother. And he's a fisherman. They leave very early all the fishermen, each morning—their boats go out" [from *Number the Stars* (Lowry, 1998)].

- *To foreshadow a story:* " . . . old Gary and I go way back. . . . Until he lost his temper over a missing Tootsie Roll he thought I had taken . . . he pounded me into a pulp and threw me over the teeter totter" [from *Libby on Wednesday* (Snyder, 1991)].

- *To reveal conflict, plot, or setting:* "Look what you've made me do, you Bandit" [from *In the Year of the Boar and Jackie Robinson* (Lord, 1984)].

- *To create a sense of time or place:* "Come aboard! Come aboard! The gale's up, and changing direction. Let's fly! Let's fly!" [from *Augusta and Trab* (de Vinck, 1993)].

Dialogue allows the audience to hear personalities, emotions, storyline, history, and social norms through the spoken word. Children can listen to features of voice from books on audiotape and ask the following questions:

- How can you learn about the characters from the way they talk?
- What can talking too much and too fast say about a character?
- What if the character stutters over words in a disjointed fashion? pauses? uses fillers? (ah huh, you know)?
- What does the tempo or volume of the words suggest (excitement, anger, fear, or embarrassment)?
- How would you describe the speech (e.g, fluent, expressive, well phrased, loud enough, rhythmic, appropriately paced)?
- How can the gender of the characters be identified?

Finally, performed dialogue is invented speech that "sounds" natural. To illustrate the differences between raw speech and dialogue, ask the teacher children to capture snippets of language around them (e.g., eavesdrop on a conversation or listen to a TV news report). Remind them that real language has false starts, interruptions, inexact words, repetitions, and elliptical phrases. Now take some of the raw language that children have collected and craft it into dialogue, a more coherent, informative language that serves the purposes and functions discussed earlier. Have children practice performing dialogue. Table 5-5 shows a few oral and written activities for practicing dialogue.

Soliloquy

A *soliloquy* is a speech by a single character, a self-verbalization that gives the audience a way to hear the character's innermost thoughts and feelings. Special actions called *asides* are markers that signal a soliloquy. In an aside, a speaker steps out from the play and talks directly to the audience while the other characters keep on acting, whisper in crowds, or just silently "freeze." Soliloquies often augment the play's message and elicit a response from the audience.

TABLE 5-5 Dialogue Activities

◆ Clip a picture of someone from the newspaper. Interview as that character.

◆ Imagine a conversation between two people whose pictures have been clipped out of magazines.

◆ Use cue cards to act out characters' dialogue.

◆ Invent a character to interact with a historical or literary figure.

◆ Have a phone conversation.

◆ Make a guest list of four people in the news you would invite to a dinner party. Act out the conversation at the dinner table.

◆ Give a eulogy for an inanimate object (e.g., Dominoes pizza box).

◆ Enact a dialogue between two characters pictured in a magazine.

◆ Pretend to be a reporter interviewing a suspect or informer. Have the informer speak "on" and "off" the record. How are these different?

◆ Brainstorm a list of "ways of talking" (e.g., speaking in a combative way; speaking to create rapport or mollify a situation; being verbose or filibustering; using short, catchy, and clever words; speaking objectively with neutral verbs; using vivid, colorful, or very precise language)

◆ Speak the lines of characters from some of your favorite books. Then change the sound of your voice to create different personas. How might a giant utter those same words? a mouse? a little girl?

Soliloquies are another way to teach viewpoint and characterization by sharing thoughts with an audience. The children read a story together, stopping at key points for an aside. During the aside, a student gives a short soliloquy of the character's thoughts. For example, let's say that the story is about a character who is having a bad day at school. He is struggling over his math assignment when the reader/character stops and steps out of the book to give an aside. The soliloquy goes something like this:

> I remember when I had a problem reading. But nobody is good at everything. Even Albert Einstein didn't always do so well in school, and look at how he turned out. I don't have to be good at everything.

A soliloquy like this one allows the reader to extend, compare, or relate the story to himself. This practice builds on what teachers frequently do to help children negotiate and read stories. Learning to think aloud while reading is just one way of introducing the soliloquy for actual dramatic performances. From the teacher's standpoint, it also opens a window for observing the child's reaction and inner response to a story.

Monologue

A *monologue* is like a soliloquy but is often loosely defined as a long speech delivered by one character. Most teachers are familiar with the popular show-and-tell presentation in the primary grades, where a child brings in a special object to share or has something important to tell the class. In drama, the most popular monologue form is the speech or public address.

Monologues are sustained talk, a speech form that can serve children well when they must begin independent writing, with its continuing flow of words on the page. Although children may be familiar with the to-and-fro of conversations, monologue invites them to build words without the help of a conversational partner. Children can practice monologues by delivering famous presidential addresses, creating public service announcements, or delivering a political campaign speech for class election. A one-minute presentation is a good start. During this time the children try out an interesting quote, anecdote, testimonial, or tribute.

Another kind of monologue is an *interior monologue,* speaking aloud the character's emotions, thoughts, and attitudes in an uncensored, unedited way. Because interior monologues are associative and disconnected, children might record stream-of-consciousness in a journal and then read it aloud. Interior monologue allows the audience to hear thoughts running through the character's mind: "I'm furious. How could this be happening to me? What can I do? Think! Think!"

When children incorporate monologue into stories and drama, they practice sustained talk and at the same time hear and see mental action. Learning to translate unseen thoughts into concrete action is an essential technique for storywriting.

Writing Dramatic Talk

Playwrights skillfully compose and balance dialogue, monologue, and soliloquy as required by the play. They also enlist certain strategies for choosing and regulating different forms of oral delivery. In this section we consider the diverse linguistic choices available to playwrights for producing dialogue in written scripts. Children come to understand that the script is merely a blueprint from which the words will grow and take shape through voice.

Character Dialects

Dialects are regional or social modifications of language noted in pronunciation, vocabulary, syntax, or discourse routines. Children who assume the role of characters with dialects learn how to use voice to signal membership in a special geographic or social group. Children should read aloud dialogue from books written in dialects such as *Little Man Little Man: A Story of Childhood* (Baldwin, 1976) or *The Friendship and The Golden Cadillac* (two stories; Taylor, 1987). Then they can perform character sketches from the book using dialect or other prepared materials. So that children focus on the purpose and functions of dialect rather than on evaluating or stereotyping, they should listen to books on tape to identify language styles associated with various speech communities.

Register

Children should also have access to different *registers* or levels of language so that they can alter their words for different purposes and roles. For example, what do the following formal and informal statements convey?

◆ *Sample 1:* I, Catherine, of the royal family of Don in the Province of Toboso, wish to have your presence at the royal banquet.

◆ *Sample 2:* Wouldjou come to dinner at my house tonight?

Notice how the level of diction in sample 2 is toned down in register from sample 1 by eliminating "big" words, shortening the sentence, and substituting colloquial form for formulaic or ritualized language. In drama, register is a versatile and purposeful technique that actors use to invent their character's public persona. Have children draw or cut out pictures of different characters and use words to give them vocal personalities. Give them a sample list of phrases that extend along a continuum from slang and colloquial forms ("hafto," "I'm gonna," "didjou," and "wouldjou") to formal and ritualistic registers such as "by the power invested in me, I pronounce you husband and wife." Have children match pictures to statements written in different registers of talk to create appropriate or humorous matches. Identify which characters go with the words written in a particular register.

Diction and Pronunciations

As has already been mentioned, the sounds of the words and the way they are spoken say a great deal about characters (e.g., are they clumsy, exuberant, or shy?). Sometimes the actor wishes to use pronunciation and diction to emphasize how someone's voice is "coming across." For example, they accent a word (inSURance/ INsurance) or pronounce a word (tomayto/tomahto) to show a regional or cultural identity. The children can make lists of words with variable pronunciations to use for special character effects: (laBORatory/LABoratory; adVERtisement/adverTISEment; GArage/garAGE).

Voice

Voice is the unique stance that actors take to breathe life into a written script. The actor's voice print, gleaned from written words and conventions, helps the audience identify a character's physical and psychological identity, gender, age, personality, and geographic, ethnic, and national origin. Diction and pronunciation are part of one's unique voice. So is sentence structure, phrase, and word choice. For example, a young child might use simple declarative sentences, repetitions, uncomplicated syntactic structures, or pet phrases ("fraidy cat"). Children can try out familiar voices by reading material as though they were different characters (e.g., Bugs Bunny, Frankenstein, Dorothy of Oz, or any other book favorite).

Lexicon

Lexicon is the vocabulary or word choice that the actor uses to convey a certain persona. If, for instance, you were playing the part of a news reporter, you might expect to hear such words as *scoop, deadline, divulge,* and *cover the beat.* On the other hand, if you were playing a storekeeper or grocer, you might hear such words as *checkout, receipts, purchase,* and *grocery bags.* Children must learn how to shift their vocabulary in order to take on different roles, ages, and personalities. The lexicon chosen for characterization in drama is just as important as the one chosen for creating believable characters in written stories.

Paralanguage

Paralanguage deals with attributes of speech that signal linguistic qualities such as pitch, stress, volume, and other language modulations. These features wrap and enfold language and give it character and emotion. Have children identify markers called *tag lines:* the words or phrases that tell you not only "who is speaking" but "how someone is speaking" (e.g., he said, she replied quickly, shrieked Mildred). Then have them read these statements aloud to create certain vocal effects. For example, say "And then what happened?" as if you were angry, nervous, nagging, or judgmental. Say "This is my neighborhood" as though it were boring, exciting, or horrible.

Silence

What is not said may be just as important as what is said. Have an actor break off conversation in midsentence and you might be telling the audience that your character is tongue-tied, nervous, embarrassed, or surprised. Have a main character say very little, speak in broken utterances, or remain speechless, and you might intensify the plot as well as characters' feelings and actions. Silence has meaning and has a tendency to draw the audience into the story.

POETRY STRAND: PLAYWRIGHT'S POETRY

The drama forms in this section make use of poetic verse and lyrical qualities (e.g., onomatopoeia, alliteration, rhyme) for purposes of theatrical performance. A playwright's poetry joins the beauty of language with an impressive delivery of storyline. Because poetic drama uses rhythm and rhyme as well as dramatic action and nonverbal gestures, the actors' lines are easy to remember and perform. Children become familiar not only with Western classic plays but also contemporary ones.

Shakespeare and the Like

The classical Shakespeare plays are the best known poetic dramas in the world, and many of them have been modified and adapted for children.

Years ago, *Shake Hands with Shakespeare* (Cullum, 1968) introduced children to the works of the world's greatest playwright in a way that was accessible and genuinely enjoyable. In Cullum's newest book, *Shakespeare in the Classroom: Plays for Intermediate Grades* (Cullum, 1995), he has again translated Shakespeare for modern times. *Tales from Shakespeare* (Lamb and Lamb, 1988) is also a high-quality adaptation and happens to be retold by young readers. Shakespeare's works have endured the test of time and have been translated into film, rock music, and murder mysteries. Shakespeare has even been made into animated tales (Knowledge Unlimited, 1992). Because of timeless themes and new adaptations, Shakespeare is relevant to today's children and is an appropriate topic for the elementary grades. To underscore this point, preview the newly acclaimed film called *Shakespeare's Children* which shows how inner-city elementary students perform Shakespeare's plays and discover insights into their own lives (gangs, lover's quarrels, and custody battles).

Another notable byproduct of studying Shakespeare is readily available examples of the changing nature of language. With the upsurge of dialect study in school, performing Shakespeare can help children understand language diversity. Shakespeare's Middle English offers a way to show children how language and society interact and change over time. As Table 5-6 points out, Middle English dialect, although an oddity today, was the acceptable vernacular in the Middles Ages and has meanings that we can still

TABLE 5-6 Middle English

Verb Form	Middle English
To be	I am
	Thou art
	He/she/it is
	We/you/they are
To have	I have
	Thou hast
	He/she/it hath
	We/you/they have

Middle English	Modern English
Good morrow	Good day
Fare-thee-well	Goodbye
Aye	Yes
Mayhap, perchance	Maybe
Prithee/pray	Please
Fie	Curse

identify. Children can sprinkle these words into medieval ballads and plays to create the flavor and ambience of the times.

In Chapter 1, children involved in the medieval unit practiced poetic dramas through the Robin Hood adventures. Verses like "Allan-a-Dale" and "Robin Hood and Maid Marian" embellished stories with musical poetry and adventure, mystery, or morality. Embedded in the plays were opportunities for "reveling" and merrymaking (dance), thus portraying the poetic drama as fun to perform.

Exposure to classic poetic drama such as Chaucer's *Canterbury Tales* puts children in touch with their literary heritage and offers insights into the history and culture of unusual characters and ways of life. Francis Storr's classic *Canterbury Chimes: Chaucer Tales Retold for Children* (1895; 1914) is still a useful children's drama resource, as is the more contemporary *Canterbury Tales: A Participation Play for Children 9 and Up* (Branson, 1971).

Modern Verse Drama

Modern and contemporary verse also acquaints children with poetic drama and rhyme. The rhyme helps them to remember their lines and the alliteration and dialogues encourage language play. An excellent verse drama for children to perform is the modern fairytale *East of the Sun and West of The Moon* (Willard, 1989). A combination of dialogue and verse is delivered by memorable main characters such as the north, south, east, and west winds; a white bear/prince; a princess named Karen; and some nasty trolls. In three acts (with six or more scenes per act), the play offers opportunities for participation in more than one role. In addition to a cast of characters, there are also parts for "voices" such as the harp, the water folk, and the stars. Using "puppets" to tell the story brings added variety and enjoyment to the drama production.

Another verse drama from Ireland, "The Long Leather Bag" (Gerke, 1996), illustrates how verse and dialogue are intertwined to create delightful repetition and rhyme. The Irish-Gaelic words are accompanied by a pronunciation guide and include recommendations for settings, costumes, and props. These and other poetic dramas, whether classics like Robin Hood or contemporary stories like the Owl and the Pussycat, bring a new vitality to literacy lessons by providing rich contexts for practicing oral language competencies.

STORY STRAND: STORY DRAMA

Drama offers children many possibilities to present, organize, and perform stories. Children are always relaying stories to teachers on the playground, in class, and at incidental times of the day. But all too often, the potential of these stories goes unnoticed. To show children that their stories are a valued part of the curriculum, teachers can help them shape and craft their experiences for others. Some stories might be encoded in oral language such as storytelling, while others might rely heavily on text. But writing story scripts as the basis for performances is a worthy practice for discovering the human condition through dialogue and action. We begin with the oral act of storytelling and then move on to stories based on texts. Finally, we consider the published play and ways of writing a script of one's own.

Storytelling

Storytellers such as Livo and Rietz tell us that storytelling is a "distinctive art form" and an important way to revive a "lost dimension of human experience" (1986, p. xiv) that draws on cross-cultural performances and practices.

Although necessary for preserving our rich cultural heritage, stories written down do not substitute for practicing and performing a story. Unless learned orally, it is difficult to know just how the original storyteller presented an experience for listeners and how the audience may have contributed to constructing the story (Livo and Rietz, 1986).

As a starting point, the collective literature lets children revive the oral tradition and train in the unique applications of oral language. The vignette at the beginning of the chapter told why tall tales were excellent literary choices for storytelling. Certain other stories are also particularly suited for storytelling because they were originally told orally, have lots of action, and are predictable and familiar to children (Mallan, 1992; Sawyer, 1942). Table 5-7 offers some of these typical tales. A book that is excellent for beginning storytellers and includes audience participation is *Twenty Tellable Tales* (MacDonald, 1986). Also useful for performances is *Favorite Folktales from Around the World* (Yolen, 1993).

TABLE 5-7 **Tales for Storytelling**

Folk Tales

◆ A West African folk tale: *The Cow-Tail Switch,* retold by Courlander (1993)

◆ A Chinese folk tale: *The Emperor and the Kite,* retold by Yolen (1993)

◆ A Japanese folk tale: *The Crane Maiden,* retold by Matsutani (1968)

◆ An Icelandic folk tale: *Half a Kingdom,* retold by McGovern (1977)

Fables

◆ An Aesop fable: *The Lion and the Mouse,* retold by Jones (1997)

◆ A Jataka fable: *The Monkey and the Crocodile,* retold by Galdone (1969)

Legends and myths

◆ A Comanche legend: *The Legend of the Bluebonnet,* retold by de Paola (1996)

◆ Greek mythology: *The Furies,* retold by Evslin (1989)

◆ Vietnam legends: *Six Legends of Vietnam,* retold by Vuong (1993)

In addition to this literature, you will also want to involve children in their own family stories. They can get ideas for spinning out stories from a family scrapbook or picture album, as suggested in Chapter 2, or from writing an account handed down by an older family member. They may even create a lifeline of personal experiences by writing to future generations about their family.

After story ideas are gathered, the teacher needs to discuss the procedures storytellers follow to prepare for their stories. A few suggestions follow:

- Read and reread the story to get the incidents firmly and clearly in mind.
- Mentally list the sequence or episodes; then reread the stories to make sure that none have been forgotten.
- Rely on aspects of language repetition (and he huffed and he puffed and he blew the house down).
- Select cumulative story sequences.
- Use language ritual or patterns pertaining to the origin of the story [e.g., the number symbols found in European folklore (three: three sons, three wishes, three brothers) and in African and Native American folklore (e.g., magical significance of two and four)]. Young children can tell stories that have lots of repetition and songlike features.
- Learn verbatim lines that are essential for holding story plot or meanings together.
- Remember the overall story structure and then slot in information along the way.
- Practice the rules and conventions for oral language delivery, particularly ways to map paralinguistic elements to the narrative.

When storytellers have the story under control, they are free to decide how they wish to "work the story" with the audience. With the appropriate oral language techniques, the storyteller can transport the audience to another reality and focus their attention on the meanings behind the words. Here are a few of the ways that storytellers Livio and Rietz (1986) involve and interact with the listeners, making them co-creators of the story:

- Ask questions or make rhetorical comments (and what do you think of that!).
- Prolong eye contact with the audience (serves as an invitational cue to the audience to respond while you are pausing).
- Use repetitive lines that involve people in chanting, noisemaking, or movement and singing.
- Make editorial comments to encourage banter (i.e., a statement that is latched on to the story and told parenthetically, such as "and if

that wasn't politically correct" or "they were starting a regular old revolution." A typical response might be: "You have that right!"

◆ Use noises and sound effects to affect audience emotions (e.g., screeeeech, or clickety clack, clickety clack).

◆ Leave the audience with a question to answer or a curiosity to think about.

The story format can also engage audiences. Table 5-8 shows some typical formats for entertaining an audience during storytelling.

Along with a collection of written stories to practice and perform, children should have occasions where they learn how to pass down the storytelling tradition. Children can ask community members to share oral histories, stories, proverbs, and songs. As children learn this folklore and share it with others, they preserve the original intent of the storyteller as one who carries on history and tradition.

TABLE 5-8   Storytelling Formats

◆ *Chalk talks.* Children use the chalkboard and draw the story as they talk. Colored chalk can add to a story's appeal.

◆ *Story aprons.* The storyteller wears an apron and keeps props in each of the pockets. He or she numbers the props for easy identification and holds up the pieces as the story is told. Cereal boxes can be used in a similar fashion. Cover a cereal box and decorate it with the story title and picture. Place props inside the box and pull them out as you tell the story.

◆ *Flannel board talks.* Children use a flannel board decorated with story settings and background. As they tell the story, they add characters and emblems that will attract the audience's attention and engage their interest. Children should find flat material like an art canvas, desk blotter, or plywood and cover it with flannel. Use paper cutouts, pictures, letters, or drawings with backing on them that will stick to the flannel board. Certain natural stickers to flannel are velvet, corduroy, yarn, and sandpaper. Have children number the pieces the way the story is told.

◆ *Magnetic boards.* Magnetic boards are also useful for storytelling and there are countless types of magnets to purchase or make on your own. Again the storyteller uses the board as a prop for telling the story.

◆ *Diorama.* A scenic representation using ordinary objects becomes a stage. Children can line a shoebox with construction paper and color a background onto it. Then they use objects such as cotton, pebbles, or string to build a three-dimensional scene relating to the play pictured inside the box. Another possibility is to create a movie roll out of a cereal box and paper towel tubes. Children illustrate their stories on wide strips of paper and tape the ends around the tube. The tube is inserted into slits cut at each end of a cereal box positioned horizontally. Children roll out the various scenes as they tell the story.

◆ *Overhead transparencies.* Children can make picture transparencies of their story and place them on an overhead projector, showing each one as they tell their story.

Storybook Theater

Storybook theater involves using children's literature or published stories as the basis of an enactment or performance. It's a way to focus on the drama process, using a familiar story as a form of *narrative prop* (Heath and Branscombe, 1986). Familiar stories also inspire spin-offs, as in the example of *The True Story of the Little Pigs* (Scieszka, 1996).

Performing stories is an excellent experience for helping children learn to read, interpret, and negotiate text (Booth, 1985, 1996). To create dramas based on stories, children select parts to enact. The process requires tightening the plots, eliminating unrelated descriptive material and unnecessary details and retaining the most essential dramatic incidents from the story. It also involves looking closely at the punctuation and word choice for cues to voice projection, phrasing, timing, and emotional displays. Most stories contain important story elements of characterization, conflict, plot, and point of view. Let's consider some of the traditional story elements from the perspective of drama.

Characterization

Drama gives children the chance to try out characters who move, feel, and talk differently from themselves. Children should practice questioning techniques that concentrate on the insider's view of character. Notice how the questions go beyond describing the character and instead, center on the detailed behaviors and habits that allow the performers to truly know the characters they are portraying.

- What types of things does your character dislike?
- What does your character like to do?
- Would your character rather spend time indoors or outdoors?
- What problems does your character face?
- What events are memorable to your character?
- Does your character regularly read the horoscopes?
- What would an obituary say about your character?

In addition to reflecting on these questions, children can begin making lists of characters that they enjoy in theatrical performances, such as Dorothy of *The Wizard of Oz* (Baum, 1982). They can conduct auditions with these characters and, at the same time, familiarize themselves with the plot line. The casting director or teacher asks a question and the child actors answer "in character." For example:

Q: What is your name?

A: My name is Dorothy.

Q: Where are you from?

A: I am from Kansas.

Q: What happened to you?

A: A tornado came through our town and tossed objects into the air. I was hit in the head and knocked unconscious.

Q: What do you remember next?

A: I was swept away with my little dog Toto to a very special place called Oz. There I had many adventures.

Q: Do you recall your first adventure?

A: Well, I followed this yellow brick road like the good fairy godmother told me and came upon a tin man.

Q: What do you remember saying to the tin man?

Use of directive prompts, in addition to the audition, prepares students for acting out internal motivations or emotional states of a character. Refer to Table 5-9 for more examples of these prompts.

Story Conflicts

Story conflicts are the "hook" of most stories. They are the problem issues that hold the attention of an audience and move a story along. The use of words to develop story conflict reflects what writers must do. In other words, drama serves as a rehearsal for writing by translating action into words. The examples below are four types of conflict that speaker 1 (S1) and speaker 2 (S2) act out.

Conflict between the Character and Nature

S1: Wow, the sky is looking dark. We may be in for some bad weather. We best get this boat to shore.

TABLE 5-9   Directive Prompts

- Walk into the grocery store as though you forgot what to buy.
- Walk into a surprise party.
- Walk into the house as if you just received an F on your report card.

- Say your lines as though you were just presented the Nobel Prize.
- Say your lines as though you were being held captive by robbers.

- Show your character responding to bad news.
- Show your character startled.
- Show your character receiving a compliment.

S2: I know but I think it might be too late. Look over there. I see something like a tornado coming toward us.

S1: What's that sound?

S2: It sounds like a freight train.

S1: Oh, no! It IS a tornado and it's heading right for us!

Conflict between the Character and Society

S1: I can't. I just can't. I will never concede to this madhat decision to turn my pet into a robot.

S2: But why not? Don't you see how well behaved the other pets are. They are virtual reality. They sleep on demand, play on demand, eat on demand, and go outdoors on demand.

S1: But how can you do this? How will pets show their special personalities, their special love, or their special intelligence?

S2: It doesn't matter. What really matters is that they are easy to handle and obey orders.

Conflict between the Character and Self

S1: I must tell Mary how ashamed I am that I didn't stick up for her in the cafeteria. But if I had, the other kids would certainly have ganged up against me. I don't know what to do. Should I tell the teacher? What if the others find out? So what? Isn't it more important that I support my friend? What if I were to figure out a way to have the other children like Mary? But how would I change their minds? I don't even know why they are picking on her in the first place. Is it because they are jealous of her? Oh, I'm avoiding the issue? What is it I must do?

Conflict between the Character and Another Character

S1: I hate you. You are always setting curfews and restrictions that other mothers don't.

S2: I am not other mothers. I am *your* mother and I won't have you running around the neighborhood after 9:00 P.M.

S1: But I won't be running around the neighborhood. I'm going with John and Jeff to the pizza shop. We are going to hang out.

S2: No. You will not hang out. You may go to eat there, but I want you back by 7:00 P.M.. Do you understand?

S1: Yeah.

Story Plot

The plot is the artistic focus of a story in which characters resolve or fail to resolve a conflict. To enact a plot, children can begin by altering action sequences of familiar stories. For example, consider questions to initiate performance alterations of two stories:

King Midas and the Golden Touch

- What if King Midas had touched his head and turned himself to gold?
- What would have happened if the man told Midas that he would no longer have the golden touch and couldn't reverse those things that were already gold?

The Little Prince

- What could have happened if the little prince had decided to stay on his own planet?
- How might the prince have gotten to the planet if he had driven a spaceship?

Plot is essentially characters performing activities that include a struggle. Skits often selectively identify those essential aspects of plot for children to practice. In *The Skit Book: 101 Skits from Kids* (MacDonald, 1986) are examples of great warm-ups and resource material for enacting and expanding scenes, action, and endings.

Point of View

What would happen if children rearranged a story from a different character's point of view, much as the wolf telling his side of the story in the *True Story of the Three Little Pigs* (Scieszka, 1996). Point of view is the perspective from which the story is being told. Have children read several stories and see if they can identify point of view. Then have them perform texts such as the following to experience point of view from a dramatic standpoint.

First-Person Point of View. Enact a monologue in which the narrator and actor are one or adopt personas to tell the story. Remember that in first person you can comment on the actions and dialogue of others only when you are present to observe them.

> "I won Dribble at Jimmy Fargo's birthday party. All the other guys got to take home goldfish in little plastic bags."
>
> *Tales of a Fourth Grade Nothing (Blume, 1972, p. 1)*

Third-Person Objective Point of View. The narrator is the storyteller who presents the ongoing drama for us to observe and interpret as eyewitnesses. Have the narrator stand offstage and tell what the actors are doing and saying as they mime the actions and lip synch the dialogue.

> *"Her eyes were moist and some hair had loosened from the gray bun at the back of her neck. She stood over the stove but there was nothing to cook and she was just waiting."*
>
> "I'm sorry, Aggie," Clay said, still carving.

Tracker (Paulsen, 1984, p. 32)

Omniscient Point of View.   The narrator is not in the story but instead, floats above the stage and watches from afar to tell the audience what all the characters are saying, doing, or thinking. Have several different actors mime the actions <u>and</u> dialogue of their particular character while the narrator tells all.

> *"Winnie had her own strong sense of rightness. She knew she could always say, afterward, 'Well you never told me not to!' "*

Tuck Everlasting (Babbitt, 1975, p. 118)

Third-Person Limited Omniscient Point of View.   The narrator is telling the story from outside the action but can tell you about only some of the characters. Each of the characters leads the narrator through the story seeing and hearing what other characters experience. Have the narrator tell about one of the actors and have all the others perform on their own.

> *"Zeely asked that tomorrow you meet her at the entrance to the catalpa forest. She wants to talk to you."*

Zeely (Hamilton, 1967, p. 87)

Prior to these minilessons on the elements of story, children may want to use picture books in which the elements are already organized into a unified whole. A good example is *Where the Wild Things Are* (Sendak, 1991). Children enlarge the pictures on a transparency as a framework for enacting what they see. An enjoyable video series for learning story elements is the *Story Lane Theater* from Macmillan/McGraw-Hill. These stories are told by Hollywood stars and include a backstage documentary about the settings and drawings.

Published Plays

Along with the other forms mentioned previously, published plays have their place in the curriculum. Although the presence of a script in a theatrical production may, at first glance, seem to limit children to memorizing lines and following directions, if used sparingly, they may be valuable models in their own right. Memorizing language in its diverse and unique styles can help children experiment with its many functions and uses. A well-developed script exposes children to already crafted stories and introduces new topics. There are many available books of plays for children to perform. Helen Louise Miller has 15 plays on topics of interest to kids: circus, mystery, and outer space. Scholastic puts out *Plays Around the Year,* based on more than 20 themes (Scholastic, 1994).

Writing Your Own Script

A good script offers a distinct pathway to drama. Because of its significance in the theatrical design, we review a few basic steps for writing one. In many ways, theatrical scripts are similar to screenplays, discussed in Chapter 6. In theater, however, dialogue has a much more significant role to play, and thus the reasons for emphasizing the importance of language in this chapter. Teachers should consult professional handbooks for more detailed information on teaching script writing such as *How to Write a Play* (Hull, 1983) and *Successful Scriptwriting* (Wolff and Cox, 1991), two notable books published by Writer's Digest. As children think about writing their own original scripts, they should consider some of the following steps.

Step 1: Take Stock of Ideas
Playwrights remember ideas, feelings, or concepts from everyday experiences and then build stories. Sometimes they begin with a setting, sometimes a character, sometimes an emotion, or sometimes a snippet of interesting conversation between two people. An essential part of searching for ideas requires knowing the target audience and the purpose for the play.

Directors and stage managers often use a *prompt book* to think through the larger plan for the play. It often includes sample scripts, diagrams of the set, questions about the characters, and various other information. Children create their own prompt books, including necessary props, meeting deadlines, and other group responsibilities.

Step 2: Brainstorm a Literary Cast
Children brainstorm lists of literary characters associated with story genres (e.g., trolls, wizards, toads, princes, princesses, fairy godmothers, kings, and queens in folktales, fairytales, and fantasy) and give their characters names (e.g., LuLu or Rumpelstilkskin; Sleepy or Humpty Dumpty). Then they describe the character in terms of the following dimensions:

- *Physical characteristics:* height, weight, age, eye color, hair color, special visible marks of identification (scar, glasses, mustache, limps, uses a cane)
- *Backgrounds:* family life, job, education, ethnicity
- *Attitudes and beliefs:* interests, values, religion, morals, politics, philosophy

- ◆ *Dominant traits:* a noticeable characteristic of the person based on a pattern of behavior—stingy, clever, manipulative, happy-go-lucky
- ◆ *Character's attire and props:* red hood, basket with cloth over it, grandmother's bedcap—Red Riding Hood; cape, tuxedo—Dracula; soldier suit—Nutcracker.

Step 3: Write a Thumbnail Sketch of the Characters

Once students brainstorm ideas for the character, they write a character sketch. In the sketch they mention character personality traits and reactions to other players. For instance, what happens to your main character when someone insults her or when she is asked to do something she doesn't know how to do? How do these encounters advance the plot? Such questions aid in rounding out the character.

Step 4: Sketch a Synopsis

The next step is to draft a synopsis of the play. This involves writing a summary of characters (physical descriptions, occupation, or other information appropriate to the storyline) and action (the main messages of each scene and the information that moves the story forward). The general setting envisioned might also be placed in the synopsis. Writing summaries gives children practice with expository writing style, meaning that they can *tell* the reader in short statements who the characters are and the gist or substance of the play. Let's use a layout from the book *Paddington on Stage* (Bradley and Bond, 1977). The play is entitled "Paddington Paints a Picture" and the synopsis is reproduced in Table 5-10.

Step 5: Write Dialogue

Next, students write dialogue, conflict, and action to carry the plot and hold a viewer's attention. The protagonist and antagonist must be presented through dialogue, which allows the audience to eavesdrop on conversations and, in turn, helps them to understand the characters more fully. Dialogue moves the plot forward. It can increase immediacy and give the impression that events are really happening. Have children review the functions of dialogue and the strategies for creating it.

Step 6: Write Stage Directions

What characters do, where they stand, what nonverbal gestures and facial expressions they exhibit, and so on, are signified in the stage directions that accompany the dialogue. These elements, many of which have already been discussed in this chapter, provide actors with the cues they need to deliver their lines. Talk itself offers many examples:

Babble	Blab	Chatter	Drawl	Gossip
Grumble	Lisp	Mumble	Murmur	Mutter
Prattle	Preach	Rant and rave	Jabber	Stammer

TABLE 5-10   Story Synopsis

Cast of characters

◆ *Mr. Brown:* kind man who takes a bear, Paddington, home to live with him and his wife. Works in an office and has a mustache and glasses.

◆ *Mrs. Brown:* the warmhearted woman married to Mr. Brown.

◆ *Paddington:* a bear who has a strong sense of right and wrong. He wears a duffel coat.

◆ *Mr. Gruber:* Paddington's friend, who keeps an antique shop on Portobello road. He is an immigrant from Central Europe and speaks with a slight accent. He uses surnames with Paddington, and vice cersa. He wears glasses perched on the end of his nose.

◆ *Mrs. Bird:* The housekeeper at the Brown home. She is stern on the surface but is kind and soft-hearted. She wears her gray hair in a bun.

◆ *Jonathan:* One of the Brown children.

◆ *Judy:* One of the Brown children.

◆ *Miss Black:* the curator at the art exhibit.

Scene

◆ The Browns' sitting room and Mr. Gruber's antique shop.

Props

◆ A few chairs, table, easel, messy painting, paintbrush, red and green paint, marmalade jar, spoon, palette, three empty bottles painted to look like paint remover, handkerchief, sign saying "antiques," books, toys, china, Thermos flask, and two mugs.

Action

◆ *Scene 1.* Mr. Brown has just completed his masterpiece and he thinks it is his best yet. He plans to enter it in a contest. For now, he says goodbye to Paddington and goes off to work.

◆ *Scene 2.* Paddington sets out to visit Mr. Gruber's shop, where he is cleaning an oil painting. As he removes the paint it reveals another picture beneath. It shows two different pictures: half boat, half woman. Mr. Gruber suggests that he is removing the top layer to discover the work of an Old Master.

◆ *Scene 3.* When Paddington leaves Mr. Gruber's shop and arrives home, he takes Mr. Brown's painting and tries to clean it to see if there is an Old Master underneath it. Mrs. Bird, the housekeeper, walks in and finds him. She asks Paddington what he is doing. Mr. Brown's boats on a lake are turning into a storm at sea. Paddington is dramatically altering Mr. Brown's work, which he has planned to enter into the exhibition. Mrs. Bird says that the only thing Paddington can do is to try and touch it up before the painting is due at the exhibit. When Paddington arrives at the exhibit, he runs into Miss Black, who accepts the painting and says the judging will be that afternoon. The Brown family is having dinner when a man and Miss Black come to the door to announce that Mr. Brown's painting has won first prize because it is so unusual and imaginative. The man explains that it was the marmalade chunks that caught their attention. Mr. Brown is bewildered and Mrs. Brown comments that she didn't realize that Mr. Brown liked to do abstract art. Nor did I, says Mr. Brown. He calls out "Where's Paddington?" This question, by the way, ends up being the title of Mr. Brown's newly touched-up painting.

In the written stage directions, the writer draws on specific words to demonstrate how speech is to be expressed and delivered. The stage directions include important information about where to stand and how to move around. For the purpose of planning movements, the stage is divided into five main areas: up stage (the back of the stage), down stage (closest to the audience), stage right (the actor's right as she faces the audience), stage left (the actor's left as he faces the audience), and center stage (right in the middle of the stage). Children can learn how to make notations on the script to remind actors where to make entrances, exits, and how to move across the stage.

Step 7: Read, Rehearse, Revise

Reading rehearsals give children practice decoding print, understanding storylines, and hearing words spoken aloud. Groups of children sit around a table reading from a script to familiarize themselves with the play's characters and lines. On alternate days, children practice scenes together and hold drama workshops. In workshops they rewrite the scenes that are not working. They may want to make them funnier, clearer, more dramatic, or just better. The teacher communicates changes and choices to the class, and they, in turn, offer their opinions. The advice of the audience is always sought during these drama workshops.

Stories about Theater and Performers

To get a feel for how plays are written, students spend considerable time reading plays. There are many interesting stories told in dramatic form. For example, *The Sign of The Seahorse* (Base, 1992) is a morality play that includes a prelude, two acts, four scenes each, and an epilogue. It is about a grouper and a gang of swordfish who represent greed, violence, and deception. They attempt to gain power through force rather than cooperation. Seven plays about Paddington, complete with costume notes and staging, can be found in *Paddington on Stage* (Bradley and Bond, 1977). Three plays based on Patricia Reilly Giff's popular books are found in *Show Time at the Polk Street School: Plays You Can Do Yourself in the Classroom* (Giff, 1995). These and other collections are fun to read in play format. Theater is also a way to learn about the lives of famous people [see, e.g., *Langston: A Play* (Davis, 1982) or *An Actor's Life for Me!* (Lincoln, 1987)].

To show the multimodal nature of theater, have children read books such as *Acting and Theater* (Evans and Smith, 1992), *Theater Magic: Behind the Scenes at Children's Theater* (Bellville, 1986), and one of my favorites, *Putting on a Play* (Pryor, 1994). Teachers can review materials available through Heinemann Books (see "Additional Resources").

INFORMATION STRAND: ALL THINGS THEATRICAL

The drama performance gets its full meaning not only from human dialogue and action but also from the sights, sounds, spaces, and props that are part of the overall theatrical design. The literacy tasks in this strand might just as easily have been placed in the languaging strand, since "all things theatrical" are nothing more than communicative symbols for meaning making. However, since this section deals with inanimate objects and space–time dimensions, the information presented will center on how design elements communicate meaning and messages. Since much of what will be discussed in "all things theatrical" pertains to film as well as drama, these topics will not be repeated in Chapter 6. Instead, you are encouraged to refer back to this section when studying film design.

Creating a Space

Discussing performance space can begin with the current working area. A ministage or space partitioned by a curtain or screen is a simple, yet effective solution for classroom plays. When students wish to transform it into a formal stage, they can add furniture and arrange audience seating. Small spaces require simple sets and simple arrangements. Figure 5-2 offers two stage designs that a classroom can accommodate: the theater-in-the round and the thrust stage.

The *theater-in-the-round* has four entrances, with the audience wrapped around the stage. Although there is no wall for scenery, the space requires only a few modest props. The children can place their desks around the room, leaving the center open for the stage.

Theater-in-the-round   Thrust stage

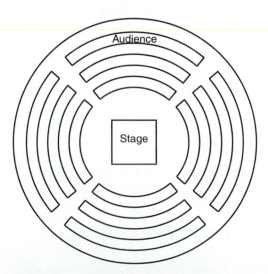
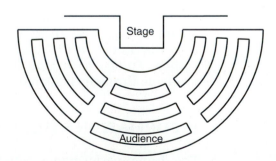

Figure 5-2   *Classroom Stage Designs*

To create a *thrust stage*, children use the back wall for scenery, and the audience surrounds the stage on three sides. Children place desks in a half-circle around the stage.

Scenery and Set Designs

In the classroom, children set up workstations to make the props and scenery designs. Home decorator magazines and descriptions of story settings from favorite books help children visualize ideas for furnishings, colors, textures, moods, and object arrangements. Scenery should be kept at a minimum, with no more than three scenes per play. The scenery should describe the setting and communicate important ideas about the play (when and where it took place, something about the characters and where these characters frequent). Easy-to-construct props for stage scenery are presented in Table 5-11.

The set design offers hints about the play's theme. It communicates the genre of the play, the location and time period, and the economic status of people (e.g., the slum, a royal palace). Children should spend time researching the location of their story. Some questions for the stage designer, culled from a set of exercises for theater (Green, 1981, p. 87), will remind you to keep the set *simple.*

- ◆ How can you identify just a few objects to give an idea of the context? What is the least you need to see in order to know the precise location?
- ◆ What symbols can be used to show time, place, or weather?
- ◆ How can you use your imagination to make substitutes for objects? (For example, can you make believe that a chair is a throne?; Can you hang written labels such as "chair" or "table" and use your imagination instead of the real object?)

TABLE 5-11   Simple Scenery Ideas

- ◆ Cover a door or wall area with a fabric and hang props such as trees, a sun, a few snowflakes, or other cutouts.
- ◆ Add an awning over the bulletin board and turn it into a shop window.
- ◆ Add paper shutters to the side of the bulletin board and make it a window for peering into a living room.
- ◆ Draw a scene on the chalkboard as background.
- ◆ Paint backgrounds on sheets of butcher paper and hang them across pegboard strips mounted along a wall or chalkboard area.
- ◆ Cover a bulletin board and draw scenery on it. For example, show night and day by covering half of the bulletin board with white paper and half with dark paper. If the setting is an underwater scene, use a wide strip of blue paper across the wall and attach drawings or glued objects such as sand, seashells, fish, plants, or rocks.

Costumes

In theater, costumes and attire are more than mere "window dressings" but make statements about age, occupation, personality (extrovert or introvert; keeping up appearances), and moods (happy, melancholy), historical era, geographic location (mountains, ocean, and social customs (including religious beliefs or sacred superstitions). They are also an artistic expression and mark of one's culture. When children are responding to literature or writing their own stories, they should consider how writers provide insights into the character and setting through costumes and descriptive techniques. To understand a character's personal identity and characteristics, the children talk about the language of clothes:

- What do the clothes say about someone?
- Which clothes most often "mark" a person (e.g., T-shirts, jeans, or polo shirts)?
- Does the way your character dress show that he is rich or poor? careless or careful? a person of good taste?
- Can you guess the setting of the story based on the way your character is dressed?

They can also come to understand sociocultural messages of dress by researching the costumes best suited to the type of play they are to perform. If, for example, they choose a period piece such as colonial days, it will be necessary to look in vintage catalogs or magazines, history books, old newspapers, or the Internet.

After students explore the world of clothing and its meanings, they gather costumes for their play. With a little imagination, children can locate costumes in their dress closets or Halloween storage chests. Borrowing costumes from a local theater company or university theater department is another possibility. If children wish to make their own costumes they might use sheets, tablecloths, pillowcases, and other large pieces of fabric. As a quick solution they can take large poster boards, draw human figures or animals, cut out circles for inserting their faces and arms, and paint their costumes onto the posters. Many craft books have patterns for making accessories such as paper hats, aprons, swords, and other drama paraphernalia.

Have children brainstorm costume possibilities in the four major categories illustrated in Table 5-12: clothing, headgear, accessories, and shoes. The clothing should help express the personal or social aspects of the character.

Makeup and Face Painting

Makeup accentuates an actor's normal features and helps create unusual and memorable appearances. A fine book, *Makeup Art* (Freeman, 1991), shows children how to create various effects: scary animals, cheerful

TABLE 5-12   Actors' Attire

Clothing	Headgear	Accessories	Shoes
Tunic	Crown	Scarves, sashes	High heels
Robes, togas	Nightcap	Jewelry	Boots
Dresses of various lengths	Beret	Bows, ribbons	Sandals
Cloaks	Top hats	Eyeglasses, sunglasses	Slippers
Armor	Baseball cap	Apron	Swim paddles
Gown	Turban	Parasol	Athletic shoes

clowns, ceremonial dancers, a black eye, a scar, wrinkles, a beard, or whiskers. They may also want to add a tattoo, a mask, or a wig to alter appearances. Children should use paints that will clean up easily using cold creams or soap and water. A little makeup can go a long way and need not take up a lot of school time.

Props

Props are inanimate objects that symbolize meaning or support the necessary messages and dialogue of the storyline (e.g., telephones, furniture, or set dressings). Often, they are ordinary items strategically placed to carry meaning, for example, the president's picture hanging on a wall, a football trophy on the television set, or a vase of plastic flowers on a broken kitchen table. These can say volumes about the characters. A clear understanding of character and storyline makes it easy to select the most appropriate props. Props organized and cataloged in kits allow easy access. They can be cataloged generically as period objects, symbols for settings, character items, and event or idea objects, or if you have a particular genre or title in mind, you might use thematic categories such as the scary play, the colonial play, or the broadway musical (Grease), as shown in Figures 5-3 through 5-5.

Since the props are assembled for a particular purpose, the development of the kits in and of themselves becomes a worthy classifying activity, one that shows comprehension of a particular genre and time period. Now is an ideal time to study artifacts for dramatizing history (e.g., washtubs, lanterns, slates and slate pencils, tin cans, quilts). Forming special committees to put these kits together is a valuable contribution to the play and teaches lessons about the past. Where possible, find books for children to consult, such as *Daily Life in a Victorian House* (Wilson, 1993). Children can also investigate cross-cultural symbols, and objects that characterize a particular sociohistorical era (i.e., cornhusk or corncob dolls, feathers, hoops, and sticks).

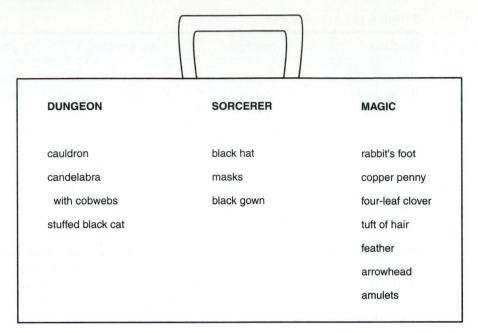

Figure 5-3   *Prop Kit for the Scary Play*

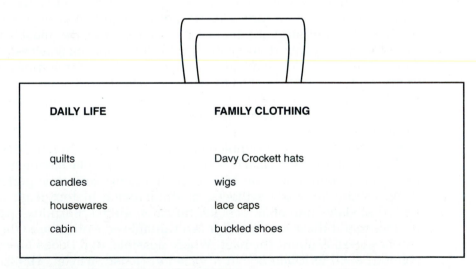

Figure 5-4   *Prop Kit for the Colonial Play*

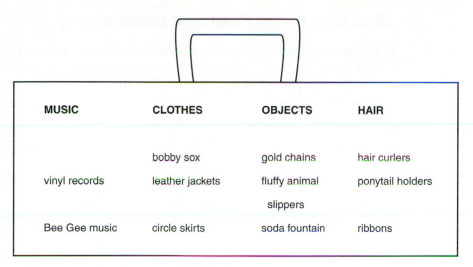

MUSIC	CLOTHES	OBJECTS	HAIR
	bobby sox	gold chains	hair curlers
vinyl records	leather jackets	fluffy animal slippers	ponytail holders
Bee Gee music	circle skirts	soda fountain	ribbons

Figure 5-5 *Prop Kit for the Broadway Musical*

◆ *School–Community Links*

Having the opportunity to attend live performances in the community theater or outdoor "theater on the square" is a welcome experience for all children. Before doing so, have them talk about the various aspects of theater and their general expectations of the play.

In addition to attending professional plays, the children can create their own performing troupes and companies and perform plays in homes for the elderly, civic organizations such as the local Kiwanis and Jaycees, community centers, church halls, public library, or hospitals. Notwithstanding community efforts, children can also perform theater in the school. School productions cultivate a sense of community in the classroom and capitalize on the team efforts and joint talents of all children as they plan and organize work to complete a project successfully. To involve as many children as possible, you might present two or more miniplays concurrently on different days or times. Parent volunteers can coach children as they practice scripts and make props and costumes. If the school is raising money for the event, the parents can handle ticket sales.

Involvement by theater companies in the school is also worthwhile. Children can apprentice with actors and storytellers to learn their crafts. Perhaps the teacher can initiate a joint community–school theater workshop during the summer or on weekends where children and professionals come together for practice and experimentation through theater games, body work, and dance.

◆ *Activities for Professional Development*

1. Prepare a drama simulation for children to enact for an entire school day. Come up with a theme and make certain that all activities and props are geared to it. Try to stay in the role for the entire day. For example, try a day in the life of a pioneer. Have children play games at recess such as sack races and leapfrog; cover the bulletin board with a covered wagon; do square dances and sing Early American pioneer songs; follow a recipe for making butter and have a spelling bee.

2. Interview family or community members and find out what stories they have to share. Have them teach their stories to you. You might videotape them and do repeated viewings. Practice the stories several times in front of a mirror. When you have learned the story thoroughly, tell it to your students.

3. Participate in a theater workshop. Invite community performers to work with you. Have the group sit around the table with a script. Practice reading the script aloud, then discuss the characters and their personalities. Now split into small groups with a leader. In each group discuss and do some of the exercises in this book to practice movements and mannerisms such as what to do with your hands? your face? your body?; vocal exercises such as enunciation and volume, sense of timing, or affectations; or use of different props. Return to the large group. Re-read the script, and this time add in some of the nonverbal and extralinguistic signs you used. As a group, decide and discuss what gestures made the character come alive, what props were the most practical and meaningful, and what vocal qualities were most effective.

◆ *Works Cited*

Professional References

Barchers, S. I. (1993). *Reader's theater for beginning readers.* Englewood, CO: Teacher Ideas Press.

Booth, D. (1985). Imaginary gardens with real toads: Reading and drama in education. *Theory into Practice, 24,* 193–198.

Booth, D. (1996). *Story drama.* Bothell, WA: Wright Group.

Corsaro, W. (1985). *Friendship and peer culture in the early years.* Norwood, NJ: Ablex Publishing.

Dyson, A. H. (1989). *Multiple worlds of child writers.* New York: Teachers College Press.

Emerson, C., and Holquist, M. (Eds.) (1986). *M. M. Bakhtin: Speech genres and other late essays.* Austin, TX: University of Texas Press.

Flynn, R. M. and Carr, G. A. (1994). Exploring classroom literature through drama: A specialist and a teacher collaborate. *Language Arts, 71*, 38–43.

Fox, M. (1986). *Teaching drama to young children.* Portsmouth, NH: Heinemann.

Green, J. (1981). *The small theatre handbook.* Boston: Harvard Common Press.

Halliday, M. A. K., and Hasan, R. (1976). *Cohesion in English.* London: Longman.

Hamilton, M., and Weiss, M. (Beauty and the Beast Storytellers) (1990). *Children tell stories: A teaching guide.* Katonah, NY: Richard C. Owen.

Heath, S. B., and Branscombe, A. (1986). The book as narrative prop. In B. B. Schieffelin and P. Gilmore (Eds.), *The acquisition of literacy: Ethnographic perspective* (pp. 16–34). Norwood, NJ: Ablex Publishing.

Hull, R. (1983). *How to write a play.* Cincinnati, OH: Writer's Digest Books.

Jett-Simpson, M. (1989). Creative drama and story comprehension. In J. W. Stewig and S. L. Sebasta (Eds.), *Using literature in the elementary classroom.* Urbana, IL: National Council of Teachers of English.

Kardash, C. A. M. and Wright, L. (1987). Does creative drama benefit elementary school students: A meta-analysis. *Youth Theatre Journal, 1*, 11–18.

Laughlin, M. K., and Howard, K. (1990). *Reader's theater for children: Scripts and script development.* Englewood, CO: Teacher Ideas Press.

Livo, N. J. and Rietz, S. A. (1986). *Storytelling: Process and practice.* Littleton, CO: Libraries Unlimited.

Mallan, K. (1992). *Children as storytellers.* Portsmouth, NH: Heinemann.

McCaslin, N. (1980). *Creative drama in the classroom.* New York: Longman.

Moffett, J., and Wagner, B. J. (1992). *Student-centered language arts, K–12.* Portsmouth, NH: Boynton/Cook.

Pellegrini, A. D. (1997). Dramatic play, context, and children's communicative behavior. In J. Flood, S. B. Heath, and D. Lapp (Eds.), *Handbook of research on teaching literacy through the communicative and visual arts* (pp. 486–491). New York: Macmillan.

Robertson, M. E. (1990). *True wizardry: Reader's theatre in the classroom.* Rozelle, Australia: Primary English Teachers Association.

Sawyer, R. (1942). *The way of the storyteller.* New York: Penguin.

Stewig, J. (1983). *Informal drama in the elementary language arts program.* New York: Teachers College Press.

Straczynski, J. M. (1987). *The complete book of scriptwriting.* Cincinnati, OH: Writer's Digest Books.

Wagner, B. J. (1988). Research currents: Does classroom drama affect the arts of language? *Language Arts, 65*, 46–55.

Ward, W. (1957). *Playmaking with children.* New York: Appleton-Century-Crofts.

Wolff, J., and Cox, K. (1991). *Successful scriptwriting* (1991). Cincinnati, OH: Writer's Digest Books.

Yolen, J. (1986). *Favorite folktales from around the world.* New York: Pantheon Books.

Children's References

Babbitt, N. (1975). *Tuck everlasting.* New York: Farrar, Straus, and Giroux.

Baldwin, J. (1976). *Little man, little man: A story of childhood.* New York: Dial Press.

Base, G. (1992). *The sign of the seahorse.* New York: Harry N. Abrams.

Baum, F. (1982). *The wizard of Oz* (illus. M. Hague). New York: Henry Holt.

Bellville, C. W. (1986). *Theater magic: Behind the scenes at children's theater.* Minneapolis, MN: Carolrhoda.

Blume, J. (1972). *Tales of a fourth grade nothing.* New York: Dutton.

Bradley, A., and Bond, M. (1977). *Paddington on stage* (illus. P. Fortnum). Boston: Houghton Mifflin.

Branson, B. (1971). *Canterbury tales: A participation play for children 9 and up: Adapted from Geoffrey Chaucer.* New York: New York Plays.

Cleary, B. (1984). *Ramona forever.* New York: William Morrow.

Courlander, H. (1993). *The cow-tail switch and other West African tales.* Boston: Houghton Mifflin.

Cullum, A. (1968). *Shake hands with Shakespeare.* New York: Scholastic.

Cullum, A. (1995). *Shakespeare in the classroom: Plays for intermediate grades.* Carthage, IL: Fearon Teacher Aids.

Dahl, R. (1998). *Matilda.* New York: Puffin Books.

Davis, O. (1982). *Langston: A play.* New York: Delacorte Press.

de Paola, T. (1996). *The legend of the bluebonnet: An old tale of Texas.* New York: Putnam & Grosset.

DeVinck, C. (1993). *Augusta and Trab.* Toronto, NY: Four Winds Press.

Evans, C., and Smith, L. (1992). *Acting and theatre.* Philadelphia: Stage Step.

Evslin, B. (1989). *The furies.* New York: Chelsea House Publishers.

Freeman, R. (1991). *Makeup art* (illus. C. Fairclough). Fresh Start Series. Danbury, CT: Franklin Watts.

Galdone, P. (1969). *The monkey and the crocodile: A Jataka tale from India.* New York: Clarion Books.

Gerke, P. (1996). The long leather bag. In P. Gerke (Ed.), *Multicultural plays for children* (pp. 87–108). Lyme, NH: Smith & Kraus.

Giff, P. (1995). *Show time at the Polk Street school: Plays you can do yourself in the classroom* (illus. B. Sims). New York: Yearling Books.

Hamilton, V. (1967). *Zeely.* New York: Macmillan/Aladdin Books.

Jones, C. (1997). *The lion and the mouse.* Boston: Houghton Mifflin.

(1995) *King Midas and the golden touch.* New York: Macmillan/McGraw Hill, Rabbit Ears Productions.

Lamb, C., and Lamb, M. (1988). *Tales from Shakespeare* (retold; illus. E. S. G. Elliott). New York: Crown Publishing.

Lincoln, P. (1987). *An actor's life for me!* New York: Viking Press.

Lord, B. (1984). *In the year of the boar and Jackie Robinson.* New York: NY: HarperTrophy.

Lowry, L. (1998). *Number the stars.* New York: Bantam Doubleday Dell Books.

MacDonald, M. R. (1986). *Twenty tellable tales: Audience participation folktales for the beginning storyteller.* Bronx, NY: H. W. Wilson.

MacDonald, M. R. (1990). *The skit book: 101 skits from kids* (illus. M.-L. Scull). Hamden, CT: Linnet Books.

Matsutani, M. (1968). *The crane maiden.* New York: Parent's Magazine Press.

McGovern, A. (1977). *Half a kingdom.* New York: Scholastic.

Paterson, K. (1996). *The great Gilly Hopkins.* Oxford: Heinemann New Winds.

Paulsen, G. (1984). *Tracker.* New York: Puffin.

Pryor, N. (1994). *Putting on a play.* A Wayland Book. New York: Thomson Learning.

Scholastic (1994). *Plays around the year: More than 20 thematic plays for the classroom* (Grades 1–3). New York: Scholastic Professional Books.

Scieszka, J. (1996). *The true story of the three little pigs.* New York: Puffin.

Sendak, M. (1991). *Where the wild things are.* New York: HarperCollins.

Snyder, Z. K. (1991). *Libby on Wednesday.* New York: Dell.

Storr, F. (1895, 1914). *Canterbury chimes: Chaucer tales retold for children.* London: Kegan Paul.

Stoutenburg, A. (1976). *American tall tales* (illus. R. M. Powers). New York: Puffin.

Taylor, M. (1987). *The friendship* and *The gold cadillac.* New York: Bantam Books.

Vuong L. D. (1993). *Six legends of Vietnam* (illus. V.-D. Mai). New York: HarperCollins.

Willard, N. (1989). *East of the sun and west of the moon* (illus. Barry Moser). New York: Harcourt Brace Jovanovich.

Wilson, L. (1993). *Daily life in a Victorian house.* New York: Puffin.

Yolen, J. (1993). *The emperor and the kite.* New York: Macmillan/McGraw-Hill.

◆ Additional Resources

Note: Asterisks indicate resources that are cited in the chapter.

Videotapes, Films, and Catalogs

*Heinemann Books
361 Hanover Street
Portsmouth, NH 03801
800-793-2154

*Paul Bunyan
Story Lane Theater
Rabbit Ears Productions
Simon & Schuster
Children's Press Division
866 Third Ave.
New York, NY 10022

*Shakespeare: The Animated Tales
(1992)
Knowledge Unlimited
P.O. Box 52
Madison, WI 53701-0052
(includes *A Midsummer Night's Dream, Hamlet, Macbeth,* and *Romeo and Juliet*)

*Shakespeare's Children (1997)
University of California Extension
Center for Media and Independent Learning
2000 Center Street, Fourth Floor
Berkeley, CA 94704
510-642-0460

Games and Props

Center Stage: Creative Dramatics Supplement
Dale Seymour Publications
P.O. Box 10888
Palo Alto, CA 94303
(dramatizing Aesop's fables)

Kids on Stage
Music for Little People
Department FGR
P.O. Box 1720
Lawndale, CA 90260
800-727-2233
(charades game for kids, primary grades)

Masks
Dover Children's Book Catalog
31 East Second Street
Mineola, NY 11501

The Play's the Thing
Teacher's Discovery
2741 Paldan Dr.
Auburn Hills, MI 48326
(introduction to Shakespeare board
game of three popular plays: *Romeo
and Juliet, Hamlet,* and *Julius
Caesar.*)

Quest
Putnam & Grosset Group
1 Grosset Drive
Kirkwood, NY 13795
(role-playing adventures)

Tragedy Set
Teacher's Discovery
2741 Paldan Dr.
Auburn Hills, MI 48326
(features *King Lear, Othello,* and
Macbeth)

Computer Software and Technology

Play Write
IBM Educational Systems
800-627-0920

Puppet Maker
IBM Educational Systems
800-627-0920

Internet Address

Play Scripts

Gopher
Name: English Server
Address: english-server.hss.cmu.edu
Choose: Drama
(plays, reviews, and drama-related
materials)

Vignette: Siskel and Ebert

In Mrs. Liang's sixth-grade class, children create a mock version of At the Movies, *a popular TV show in which two well-known personalities, Siskel and Ebert, review some of the latest films. Just weeks before, the class identified* The Lion King *to review. Now the actors Gene Siskel (S) and Roger Ebert (E) take their places on the set. The director shouts "Take One."*

S: Welcome to At the Movies. *Today we are reviewing a hot new Disney film that is already topping the box office charts. It's called* The Lion King *and it's about a lion cub named Simba, who avenges his father's death to claim his rightful title as Lion King. Here's a clip of the story.*

(sequentially show pictures from a Lion King coloring book or flap book)

E: *What superb animation, Gene, and I have to admit that I found myself humming Hakuna Matata as I left the theater. Let's listen.*

[plays music]

S: *I agree. The music was really catchy. One problem I had with the film, though, was that the characters seemed a bit "stereotypic." Scar was obviously the bad guy since everything associated with him was dark, dead, and ugly. Take a look at what I mean.*

[shows a hand-drawn picture]

E: *You are right about this. But there are plenty of good supporting characters.*

S: *There sure are. Rafiki and Pumbaa were terrific and I liked listening to the live voices of such Hollywood greats as Jeremy Irons, James Earl Jones, Matthew Broderick, and Whoopi Goldberg. I give it two thumbs up!*

E: *I am with you on this one, Roger. Disney has once again outdone itself with this marvelous animation. I give it two thumbs up! [See Figure 6–1.]*

2 THUMBS UP: A winner. One of the best movies I've ever seen. Go see it!

1 THUMB UP: OK. it's not one of the best films I've ever seen, but it's good.

1 THUMB DOWN: Yawn. I thought it was a bore. I hope there isn't a sequel.

2 THUMBS DOWN: YUK. Don't waste your time.

Figure 6–1 *Movie Ratings*

Siskel and Ebert now ask the judges in the balcony seats to hold up their cards:

[The camera zooms in on the audience]

Each member of the class chooses a placard (with words such as ordinary, boring, thrilling, action-packed, suspenseful*). All together they hold them up to the camera.*

[The camera pans the hand-held signs]

S: Well, you've heard what the audience thinks. That's it for now. Until the next time, save us the aisle seats!

[The filming ends. CUT!]

This activity in Mrs. Liang's class is a good example of film literacy, the art of producing and responding to nonprint media. In this instance, children began with a popular film, viewing and responding to it in much the same way as they might have responded to a book. They ended with the production of a TV show in which they used many of the literacy practices advocated throughout the book. Although the vignette of the Siskel and Ebert production reveals only the tip of the iceberg, behind the scenes, children engaged in many literacy tasks. They watched the film together and then held film workshops to discuss interpretations and write responses. Then they listened to videoclips of the TV program, Siskel and Ebert, to identify the routines and the formulaic expressions used in this media genre. Sprinkling such phrases into their scripts as "Save us the aisle seats" and "The film is topping the box office charts" helps identify the genre much as "once upon a time" marks a fairytale. Next, they separated into production teams to collaborate on different parts of the show. Some wrote the script, others worked on the set and made the pictures and evaluation props, and still others held auditions for those who wanted to play Siskel and Ebert or run the camcorder. All the children were involved in one or more of the essential parts of putting this production together.

"Cinema has been called the total art" (Green, 1994, p. 161) because it is a composite of many literacies inspired by a communal goal and accomplished through the collaborative efforts of many people. In the classroom, popular films represent a way to bridge school and home experiences by bringing familiar cultural worlds to children and overlaying them with thoughtful and critical perspectives. Because many children may have already seen these films, they are able to view them a second time with a more detailed analytic and critical response. If you choose to include instructional films, Cox (1996) lists some superb choices to get you started. Weston Woods Productions also has excellent videos on the best in children's literature (see "Additional Resources").

Since we have already explored the many literacy forms that give rise to film (e.g., visuals, music, motion, and drama) here we concentrate on a few of film's signature components, such as camera point of view, use of special lighting and effects, animation, and marketing strategies. When we revisit elements of storytelling, drama, and reportage (e.g., character, setting, conflict, or flashback), we will do so from the filmmaker's unique perspective or from the standpoint of critical language. As children define, redefine, and add new elements specific to the study of film and media literacy, they practice rethinking and shifting literacy strategies to meet new tasks at hand. In dialogue with others, they practice critical thinking and response techniques, rendering thoughtful views on the content and sociopolitical implications of popular films. Film and media are powerful forces in today's society. Children must come to understand how the media influences and shapes beliefs, understandings, and desires if they are to "resist the forces that press people into passivity and bland acquiescence" (Greene, 1991, p. 27). Children who are aware of sociopolitical issues, represented in films, bring another whole new dimension to the practice of literary response and expression. Our youth, with their enduring interest in computers, videos, movies, and other forms of popular culture, invite us to support and maximize their creative potential and critical awareness.

Since technical advances combine film, video, and other media, in this chapter we consider film to include visuals produced on camcorders and videocassettes as well as 8-mm projectors. Furthermore, because the world of electronics and technology claims an increasingly large part of children's lives, in the last section of the chapter we address the allied arts of television, video, and computer technology. Although this chapter deals with film and other media, you will not need elaborate equipment or technical training to practice or use the literacy processes and products discussed here. Learning to operate media equipment and new technologies is best left to team efforts with a media specialist and precocious children.

Let's begin with ways of inventing ideas for the production of a film. Then we can discuss techniques for critically viewing and responding to film.

INQUIRY STRAND: INVENTING IDEAS

Inventing ideas through kinetic sight-and-sound media (Shelton, 1993) is yet another aesthetic choice for sorting out values and practicing reasoned discrimination. Posing questions about the artistic integrity and significance of a film requires a certain detachment that comes from understanding some of the elements that viewers consider in making informed judgments. We begin this strand therefore with an introduction to film design, using elements such as *imaging, on-site locations, characters, film scores,* and *special effects* as a way to spark inquiry. Then we show how children construct and respond to films from many different perspectives. Each literacy task, worthy of doing in its own right, is used to foster ideas through unique inquiry appropriate to film.

Film Design

As in all texts, print or nonprint, the product guides the process strategies and resources that people choose. Throughout this section, we show how film design influences our creative and critical thinking approaches.

Imaging
Imaging is the act of forming ideas and translating them into objects and symbols that communicate messages to an audience. Some screenwriters generate ideas for a film with a verbal premise such as "What if it were your vacation and everything that could go wrong did go wrong? Or what if you lost your favorite pet and you discovered that your best friend took it?" Many writers, however, are motivated by sensory and associative details and connections. *Connections* is the operative word here. For instance, a

filmmaker observing the leaves on a windy fall day might think about the passing of time, a mood of loneliness, or a foreboding sign. Film is first and foremost a *visual* medium that allows the filmmaker to make connections with objects and events through images. Children who learn imaging add a qualitative dimension to gathering ideas that involves juxtaposing sensations, colors, contrasts, and other visual and sensory features.

The teacher will want children to observe and make visual connections just as filmmakers do. Three important techniques for juxtaposing images include *visual metaphors, visual symbols,* and *visual irony* (Whittock, 1990). For example, to show visual metaphor, a filmmaker might place the scene of a medieval feast next to a scene of pigs in a pen to suggest that medieval guests lacked etiquette because they ate with their hands. To show symbols of good and evil visually, the filmmaker might place doves and buzzards side by side on a fence. Visual irony, or linking opposites, is clearly apparent in the *Godfather* film, where murders take place at the same time that a church baptism is celebrated. Children can take these otherwise difficult concepts of metaphor, symbolism, and irony and make them concrete and understandable through a hands-on activity. Have them find ordinary magazine pictures that show visual connections and meanings. For instance, a picture of a child outdoors with a kite next to a picture of birds flying can become a visual metaphor for freedom or flight. Placing a picture of a mountain next to a mansion can stand for a concept such as size or wealth. A picture of a beast next to a beautiful girl, as in *Beauty and the Beast,* can visually show the irony between two otherwise unlikely matched characters. Have the children cut and paste these pictures onto cards and play match games. As they become aware of the film editor's job of assembling, cutting, and organizing picture frames to create visual meanings, they become more discerning when they watch a film or read books that use some of these same devices created with words.

Location Scouting

Places convey meanings and children need to develop a keen sense of settings, not only for film but for storywriting, poetry, and other literary genres. Film literacy allows children to review the concept of "setting" in a new way. Although they may have learned to read contextual and environmental print to decode meanings, now they are being asked to use environments, objects, and locations to encode and build meanings. On-location scouting is an occasion to observe real settings for shooting films. Have children scout locations in the school and snap photos of the cafeteria, the library, the playground, the gym, the hallway, and the classroom. As the children are visiting these locations the teacher calls their attention to the visual impact (a cluttered closet or stark hallway), emotional moods (quiet library or noisy playground), or symbolic messages (tables representing the cafeteria; a chalkboard representing the classroom). Next, they categorize their photos according to a set of probing questions; for example: Where is a good place to show a responsible school child studying for a test? (e.g., the library?) Where might you experience an invigorating and lively mood? (the cafeteria? the playground?) Where could you set up a picnic scene? (on the school grounds?)

At home, children rummage through old family photos and bring them to class. The teacher can talk about locations in the background. Where were these pictures taken? What happens in this particular place? Why did it happen there? They can also find magazine pictures or travel brochures for imaging locations. For example, a vacant lot with a dilapidated house might be an ideal place for filming a horror story. Or a skyline of snow-capped mountains and wide-open fields might provide the perfect background for a nature film. Children's picture books are also useful. *Away From Home* (Lobel, 1994) takes children on an alphabetical journey to the far corners of the world, while *O Canada* (Harrison, 1993) paints pictures that take the reader on a journey to the lands of our northern neighbors. Jorgensen (1993) suggests involving children in "milieu" drawings in which they sketch locations that are the backdrop of historical stories. By conferring with children on the accuracy of these drawings, the teacher emphasizes the importance of authenticity.

Video clips of actual films are another way to introduce sense of place through a medium other than a book, picture, drawing, or photo. The film *Alaska* underscores the importance of depicting adventure through location. Show children a few clips of the film, and have them make notes as shown in Figure 6–2 (front and back of a note card). As children view films or TV shows at home, they can keep notes of settings and the messages they convey (e.g., mountains and cacti for a Western film, or back alleys with garbage cans to show crime scenes).

(Front of card)   (Back of card)

Setting or Location	Film Messages
Sapphire blue skies; waterfalls; mountains	Adventure film; wide-open vista; freedom
Dangerous cliffs	Source of conflict
Cabin, living room with fireplace and blankets	Contrast to rugged outdoors; family solidarity
Alaska	State where the temperature is cold and there is lots of snow

Figure 6–2 *Location Note Card*

Character "Backstory"

What is the look, the talk, the walk, and the personality of the main character in your film? Who are the other characters, and what are their ages, habits, goals? In the theater chapter, these were some of the questions that teachers posed to help children act out personalities and behaviors. In film, performers come to know and identify with the characters they play through a backstory, a composite or personal account of a character, and the detailed information about the experiences that help shape his or her personality. Many performers get into the minds and habits of their characters by visiting places where their characters might reside and work. Sometimes they are able to live out, first hand, some of the characters' events and actions. Children should backstory characters to gain deeper understandings of the role they are to play. Children can backtrack a real person (parents, friends, neighbors) for a 24-hour period to follow their daily habits and behaviors. When they are finished, they share with the class the special details and insights they discovered through observing, living, or working with the person.

Backstory

Charles Witherspoon III

lives at Sussex Manor

is 10 years old

is a vegetarian

hates wearing a hat

enjoys playing soccer

scratches his head a lot

owns a cat named Sox

Children can compile their lists and then mix and match traits and habits to create character types for film stories. Matching characters to particular "types" that are suitable for a role is another important part of backstorying a character. Several character types are shown in Table 6–1.

Children write note-card entries and keep scrapbook pictures of character types. They look for the character's facial features, dress, and body posture and include photos and sketches of how these character's appearances and personalities change as they grow and mature over time. Some of the characters come from magazines or favorite books. Some they draw. When ready to produce a film, children search their files and

TABLE 6–1   Character Types

Round characters	Multidimensional personalities with layers of personality that unravel along the way; the character changes in some way over the course of the film; the character is someone you know and like (e.g., *The Little Princess*)
Flat characters	Two-dimensional predictable characters who lack complexity; they are good or evil (e.g., wicked stepsisters or fairy godmother in *Cinderella*)
Stock characters	One-dimensional characters who have very little to add to the storyline but have the caricature you are looking for; fill-ins (e.g., the burglars or the puppies in *101 Dalmations*)
Foils	Characters used for contrast; a minor character that brings out the personality traits of the major character; a character that has physical or personality features opposite the protagonist (e.g., *Beauty and the Beast*)
Static characters	Characters that do not develop or mature in any way; they do not grow emotionally or intellectually over the course of the film (e.g., Ernest P. Worrell in *Ernest Goes to Africa*)
Pivotal characters	Characters who cause reactions in the main character; a good supporting actor or actress (e.g., the bungling burglars in *Home Alone*)
Archetype	A character who is a universal representation of human behavior or experience (e.g., the orphan pets in search of their owners in *The Adventures of Milo and Otis*)

typecast personalities that will fit the storyline and genre. If it's a comedy, the children might look for static characters with funny expressions or physical qualities. If it's a crowd scene in a dramatic film, a group of pictures like the barnyard animals of *Homeward Bound: The Incredible Journey* might work. If it's a science fiction film, look for an adorable alien such as *E.T.* Children go back and forth discussing the storyline as the characters are reviewed and arranged. After the ideal prototype is identified for a particular scene or scenes, the children run ads describing the physical and personal attributes required. The other children skim through their files to see which characters will fit the part and answer the ad. The next step is to hold auditions for their characters to determine if a particular character matches the one specified in the ad. Each child presents his or her character and describes their attributes. A vote is taken for the final choice.

Film Scores
Film offers an excellent way to see relationships and connections between the emotional tone of a film and the music that helps give rise to it. Sometimes the musical rhythm matches the characters' actions or

general sentiment of the film. In some cases it provides tension and suspense or perhaps complements the film's plot or subject matter. Copland (1988) provides at least five reasons why music is integral to the film's story line. These are:

- ◆ It creates a more convincing atmosphere of time and place.
- ◆ It can play on the emotions of the spectators, shifting from a mood of sadness to humor in the blink of an eye.
- ◆ It serves as a kind of neutral background filler.
- ◆ It helps build a sense of continuity, tying scenes together.
- ◆ It can help the story conclude with a grand finale.

To realize the impact of music on a story, children listen to a film soundtrack to discuss how the music carries storyline through volume, movement, pace, timbre, and melody. Ask them to draw pictures inspired by the music. It might be a scene that comes to mind, or a character doing or feeling something. Then show the film clip in which the music occurs and discuss its impact on the scene. How does the music complement the scene?

Aware of the power of music for evoking messages and feelings in film, children add music to story readings, poetry, and other dramatic performances. Use the musical elements (discussed in Chapter 3) to determine whether the music adds or detracts from the written material.

The Beat

The *beat*, or subtext of an action segment, is shorthand for the intention that an action should convey. In every scene the director imposes a concept beyond what the script lines indicate. Giving the beat a name in the form of a short sentence or phrase, the director can call out a beat and the actor will know exactly how to interpret it (Boggs, 1996). When children practice the same beat across different scenes, they learn to empathize by experiencing similar feelings and actions in different settings. They also learn the relationship between an action and its emotional or aesthetic effect. Table 6-2 shows three different scenes that follow the same beat.

Children can make a list of beats and subtexts to go with them. Start by having them recall a time when they felt a certain way. Have them describe the emotional experience and show it through action. Now associate this action sequence with a phrase or sentence that will help them recall their actions and state of mind. By tying several different events to the same beat, children come to understand that although circumstances might differ, the results may have similar effects.

Promotional Campaigns

The financial success of a film is an essential goal of filmmakers. Most blockbuster movies are connected to well-thought-out promotional cam-

TABLE 6–2   The Beat

Beat name: "We'll always have Paris."

You use this phrase to play different scenes across different performances in a similar way. This beat refers to sad endings but pleasant memories.

◆ *Subtext:* You and your family are leaving the community to move to a place across the ocean. You are saying goodbye to your best friend. Both of you are very sad. Let your friend know that you will always remember him and the things you have done together. Play this goodbye scene in a melancholy but uplifting manner.

◆ *Subtext:* You must find a new home for your pet because you are going away to school and will no longer have time for him. You want to be fair to your pet and find him a home where he will be loved and will get lots of attention. Show us the goodbye scene knowing you are doing the right thing.

◆ *Subtext:* You have just lost a basketball game that would qualify you for a chance to play in the finals. Your team has won many championships in the past, but you wanted this game to set a record. Play the losing scene in a way that shows you are a good sport and can take the loss since you have had the experience of sweet success.

paigns. For example, following the release of a Disney film, every discount and department store around the country begins to stock huge supplies of stuffed animals, action figures, coloring books, games, and CDs. McDonald's distributes souvenirs and gimmicks with their Happy Meals. In short, advertisers know that to make a film profitable, they can market auxiliary products associated with it.

Children who plan promotional campaigns will learn to recognize the power of marketing. Have them select a storybook they would like to see made into a movie. They can brainstorm ideas for developing some of the products that will coincide with the book.

◆ What are the products associated with this book? (a musical cassette, a puppet, a bookmark, buttons and pins?)

◆ Who will you target as the consumer? (other children?)

◆ How will the product be showcased or packaged to get the consumer's attention? (slick, attractive packaging, interviews and book tours, CDs sold with the book?)

◆ What techniques will be used to persuade the audience that they desire this product? (a TV commercial, a poster, an announcement or display?)

◆ Where will the product be sold? distributed? advertised? (the school newspaper, a school catalog, in the library, in store windows?)

Following this brainstorming, children can work in groups to create some of the products and implement some of the marketing strategies.

Movie Viewing

Several educators have made a strong case for the use of film in the literacy classroom (Baines and Dial, 1995; Cox, 1983, 1985; Gallagher, 1988; Jurkiewicz, 1990). They believe that it not only encourages reading but also allows children to practice the art of watching and responding to film. Films offer a valuable form of lived experience where ideas are constructed moment to moment as actions move before your eyes (Langdorf, 1991). Since teachers are often pressed for time, and films, on average, take a couple of hours to view, they can show films during rainy-day recesses, Friday afternoons, or days before a holiday frenzy. Viewing a video for homework can offer children a welcome change from the traditional assignments. If once a month, there were at least three copies to send home with different children on a one-day rotating basis, it would take about a week for a class of 20 to view the same film. The teacher might collect these multiple copies by borrowing one from the public library, renting a video from the video-store, borrowing one from a child who already owns the video, or using a personal copy that is purchased.

Wholistic Response

After children view a film for the first time, they should engage in a wholistic response to give their overall impressions. Like a literary response, a wholistic film response gives children a chance to interact and interpret the experienced event. Children's observations may be broad and diverse at first, with reactions rooted in both affective and cognitive perceptions. Simple likes and dislikes or undifferentiated feelings and ideas provoked by the film may be the focus of the initial discussion. Some of the issues and types of response that can be elicited for a wholistic impression are noted in Table 6–3.

Analytic/Evaluative Response

Film experts suggest that wholistic responses be followed up with a more analytic response dealing with detailed aspects of content, technical qualities, format, and acting (Boggs, 1996; Langdorf, 1991; Valasek, 1992). For example, during class time, the teacher uses photo sequences of the film (from coloring books; children's books) or shows selected film clips to engage children in analytic/evaluative response (see Table 6–4). Such a response allows children to attend to the details of the film with more critical detachment and analysis. It also helps internalize a set of standards to fully appreciate and enhance film experiences.

These same criteria can be used for evaluating and judging the merit of the film. Children can nominate films for academy awards: For example, one student nominates *Pocahontas* for best animated film, another nominates *James and the Giant Peach*. Based on their evaluations, children try to persuade a panel of judges to select their nominees. Awarding Oscars in

TABLE 6–3   Wholistic Response

◆ *Personal response.* This is a subjective, personal reaction. Did you like the film, and why? If not, why not? How would you describe this film? Would you see it again? If so, why? If not, why not? If there was a sequel to this film, what might it be? How might your mood have affected your response to the movie? What expectations did you bring to the film? Where did these expectations come from? How did the audience around you affect your enjoyment of the film? Was the soundtrack audible? If the film reminded you of an experience you had, did this experience hinder or enhance your viewing of the film?

◆ *Aesthetic/evocative response.* This response involves your overall impression of the cinematic qualities, such as the image in motion, the visual features, the aural perceptions and technical qualities, all wrapped up in one. How did the film create a unique look, feel, style, or atmosphere? What mood was set? How would you describe the feelings you had as you watched this film? How did the movie tap into your imagination? How would you describe the aesthetics of the film? How did the film appeal to your five senses?

◆ *Affective response.* This is a subjective/intuitive reaction to the film. It describes how the film affected you emotionally. Did it make you cry? laugh? Why? How did this film strengthen your convictions or question them?

◆ *Interpretive response.* This response involves the negotiation of meaning between your experience and the experiences projected on screen. What did you see as the film's unifying statement or message? Did you find yourself predicting the outcomes? What did you predict? Do you think the film was trying to teach you something? make you feel a certain way? have a different opinion about something? Why?

◆ *Evaluative response.* This has to do with the judgments made about the quality of the film experience. Did you feel it was a good movie? Why? How did you feel about the acting? How would you rate this film in comparison to others you have seen? How did the film hold your attention? What did you think about the film's technical qualities? What did you think about the special effects?

the various categories motivates children and fosters a genuine appreciation of their strengths as critics.

Another way to use the evaluative criteria is to discuss movie ratings. There has been much controversy regarding the issue of screening appropriate and inappropriate material for children's viewings. Children can discuss the Motion Picture Association of America (MPAA) ratings for movies as noted in Table 6–5. Children may want to create their own ratings using language they all understand. For example, see Table 6–6.

Reading movie reviews in newspapers and magazines helps children monitor the criteria used to judge films. Children can discuss how the review affects their desire to see a film. By following reviews on a regular basis, they will discover a critic whose point of view matches their own. Who are the reviewers? What is their expertise? In what papers or periodicals do they write?

TABLE 6–4   Analytic/Evaluative Response

Content

◆ Was it a compelling story? Would you consider it original? Unique? Why?

◆ What was the unifying idea of the film?

◆ What was the hook that drew you in?

◆ What was the implicit meaning or subtext?

◆ Were you satisfied with the story's organization? Why?

◆ Was the dialogue effective? If yes, what made it so? If not, why not?

◆ From whose point of view was the story told? How would you characterize the perspective? too narrow? too broad? biased?

◆ Was the story edited properly to cut out unnecessary or unwanted parts? Which parts might you have tossed out? Were there any parts you would add in?

◆ What showed that the story was fair and authentic in its portrayal of characters and events?

Technical production

◆ Were the sound and picture clear? Was there a good soundtrack? If not, why not?

◆ How did the lighting affect interpretation?

◆ Was the music appealing or distracting? Did it complement the film or call attention to itself? How?

◆ How did the music or other sound effects carry meaning?

◆ How did the camera angles create the desired effects and bring a perspective to the story?

◆ How did the camera shots and angles emphasize certain points? (close-ups, long shots)

◆ Describe the special effects. How authentic were they? How do special effects arouse emotional responses?

◆ Was the choice for color or black and white an appropriate one? Why?

Format

◆ Was the film the best way to portray this idea? If not, what would you suggest?

◆ Was the length appropriate? Would you make it longer? shorter? How?

◆ How did every scene contribute to the overall effect of the film?

◆ What special formats were used (*flashback*—shot or sequence depicting action that will occur before the film's beginning; *montage*—fast cuts of events out of sequence; dream scene)

Acting

◆ Did you care about the characters? Which ones? Why?

◆ What would have made you care more?

◆ Which characters were portrayed as oversimplified or standardized representations of a race or ethnic group? Was this portrayal appropriate?

◆ Did you detect gender stereotyping? If so, where?

◆ How well do the characters deliver their lines? How could you tell?

TABLE 6–5   MPAA Ratings

G	General audiences; all ages admitted.
PG	Parental guidance suggested; some material may not be suitable for children.
PG-13	Parents strongly cautioned; some material may be inappropriate for children under 13.
R	Restricted: children under 17 require accompanying parent or adult guardian.
NC-17	No children under 17 admitted.

TABLE 6–6   Childrens' Movie Ratings

F	Fun for children of all ages
K-3	Content matter appropriate for children in primary grades
S-6	Scary film; children under 6 might have nightmares
B-13	Rated by 13-year-olds as boring

Critical Response

Critical response is questioning the hidden values and meanings in film that reproduce social attitudes or account for "taken-for-granted" norms and behaviors. In other words, this kind of response focuses on identifying social and political metamessages and developing habits of perceptive watching and questioning. Questions such as those shown in Table 6–7 frame ways to respond critically to film. However, critical response also means being able to apply these questions to salient social issues like that of power and culture, gender, contemporary values, and stereotypes. Later, in the story strand of this chapter, we show how to identify and question these issues by critically responding to a number of specific film genres.

LANGUAGING STRAND: THE LANGUAGE OF VISUALS

Film has a language and grammar of its own, born of sound, color, camera angles, lighting, and many other symbols. Thinking about elements of film design as a special language of visuals increases awareness of their communicative influence on the viewer. Hoban (1975) states that films include 70 to 80 percent visuals (meaning only 20 to 30 percent words and music). In this section we consider the importance of visual communicative symbols that speak to children without words.

TABLE 6–7   Critical Response

Validity of Information

◆ Was the information accurate? How did you know?

◆ Is there any evidence for what you see? Where might you go to find out?

◆ Whose point of view is projected in this film? Are there others?

◆ Is the information believable? What made it so?

◆ What does the film assume that the viewer already knows?

◆ What other information do we need?

◆ Are there alternatives for the information?

◆ What film images were put together to make you infer a particular meaning? Were you led to interpret events in a certain way. How?

Gender and diversity

◆ How are boys and girls portrayed in the film? What jobs do each do? Who has a bigger part? How do you know? What characters do they play? What admirable characteristics do each have? Are these traits equal in value?

◆ How does the film show the relationship between girls and boys? (as friends? adversaries? nuisances? equals?)

Power

◆ What audience do you think this film targets? Why do you think this audience was targeted?

◆ How would you describe the characters in the film who are most powerful? (those who are intelligent, have the money, have authority?)

◆ What is the meaning of power in this film?

◆ How does the film portray the victims?

◆ How are ethnic groups portrayed? How has the film avoided stereotypes?

Invented realities

◆ How does this film reflect real life?

◆ How does this film reproduce values and social customs?

◆ What is not shown in the picture you see? What choices about subject matter might the filmmaker have made before you saw this?

Values clarification

◆ How does the film reproduce values and beliefs?

◆ What about this film shows good and evil?

◆ How do you feel about the character's actions in this film?

Spotlighting the Message

Lighting has a language of its own. The type of lighting (strobe lights, spotlights, or candlelight) and the direction of the lighting (overhead, side, back, or front) produce different interpretations and images of characters, settings, and moods. For example, the cinematographer who is in charge of creating the "look" of the film might use backlighting to create a romantic moment. Backlighting is light that comes from behind an object and produces a halolike effect. Often referred to as *Rembrandt lighting,* it resembles the lighting in the portraits of the painter Rembrandt Van Rijn. Children can become aware of the "meanings" of lighting as outlined in Table 6–8.

Because the study of light is integral to science, children might experiment with these forms of lighting and write down discovered effects. In language arts class, they can link these effects to meaningful elements of setting, character, or story messages by asking the following questions:

◆ What lighting would you use if you wanted to show a dim-light street? a sunset?

◆ What lighting might you use if you wanted to show someone who was sinister?

◆ How can a dramatic effect be produced using striking contrasts?

◆ Can area lighting enlarge a space?

Call attention to lighting when using pictures and illustrations from children's books like that of Chris Van Allsburg's (1985) three-dimensional pictures filled with shading and shadows. Ask children about the impressions the light makes on their interpretations and feelings about the story.

TABLE 6–8   Lighting

Lighting	Effects
Natural light (like fire, sunlight, candles)	Creates shadows, quiet moods, time of day (daybreak; dusk)
Artificial light (lamps, street lights)	Can create romance, routine events
Spotlights (large bulbs)	Can focus on a character or object, draws eyes to the center of what is to be illuminated
Area lighting	Illuminates everything in view, all at once; the viewer can focus on whatever he or she chooses
Backlighting	Creates reflections and silhouettes, shadows, fireside glow, halo, faces bathed in sunlight

- Why might an illustrator use light (to give an illusion of depth or reality; create a mood, get your attention)?
- Why does the light in a picture come from a certain direction? How does the angle provide a point of view?
- What do you think is the source of the light?
- How can light send a message in a way that print cannot?

Camera Talk

The camera is a point of view and tells us what we will see and how we will see it (Berger, 1972; Boggs, 1996). Cinematographers who have their own special way of seeing a subject cogently articulate their viewpoints through camera angles, size of subject, and light filters. They use the camera to call attention to a character or to illustrate the magnitude of an event; their camera tells you what is significant or insignificant in the total image, what to perceive and what to make sense of, all in a matter of a few seconds. Visual experts, such as the cinematographer, know just where and how to frame ideas to influence others' perspective. Children should become aware of the camera's many functions, as it affects the way we are positioned to see and gather meaning from the film.

- Focuses *perceptions* and shapes *interpretations*. Not unlike shared readings, where an adult helps the child focus on certain aspects of print, or authors who by their special use of words place readers in a particular position to interpret stories, film uses the camera to do the very same thing. For example, high-angled camera shots make a character seem small and insignificant, long shots suggest distant social relationships, and extreme close-ups demand your emotional attention.
- Creates illusions of *time.* All print material includes a sense of time. Often, this time factor is signaled through words such as "a long time ago" or "after a while" or "weeks later." The camera, too, provides markers of time through transitions such as fade in, fade out, dissolve, or cut to. It can compress time by joining two separate shots: the first showing someone in ragged clothes entering a department store and the next shot showing the same person leaving the store in grand attire. Time is also compressed through visual montage to show the passing of time, multiple realities, and instantaneous transformations. Finally, the camera expands time by inserting shots into the main action to extend length or create suspense, as in horror films.
- Creates illusions of *space*. Space on the printed page is controlled by formatting or number of words. In film it is controlled by camera position. For example, tilting is a vertical movement that makes things look tall and long. Panning, moving the camera laterally from

right to left, gives a sense of wide-open spaces and spectacular vistas. Cameras positioned "straight on" give the effect of harsh or distorted images. Zooming in and out, moving close, then far away, creates a condensation or magnification of space in a split second.

◆ <u>Provides *perspective* and *point of view*</u>. All writing that works develops a point of view. So does film. If the camera goes behind a character at eye level, it can make a viewer literally and figuratively share a character's perspective. An objective camera is one much like a third-person omniscient narrator in a novel. Viewers can become observers or experience what the actor feels by alternating between subjective and objective points of view, a common technique used for flow. With these and other techniques, the camera brings different viewpoints, moods, and aesthetic moments to viewers.

Have children experiment with some of these effects without a camera, as shown in Table 6–9.

Video Camcorder School Squires (1992) shows some of these effects through pictures. Children can also consult this book if they wish to try

TABLE 6–9   Camera Effects

Camera shots focus perceptions and shape interpretations.

◆ Make a product ad and use color to draw attention to it.
◆ Draw a picture using distortions (enlargements, caricatures, angles, and curves) to focus attention on it.

Camera shots create illusions of time.

◆ Videotape a commercial that uses fast-cuts. Discuss how the speed affects your sense of time and meaning.
◆ Show through pictures the passing of time (e.g., a photo that compares the green leaves of summer with colored leaves of fall, a photo that shows someone in his youth and old age; a photo of the lake when the sun rises and then sets.)

Camera shots create illusions of space.

◆ Using postcards, compare a close-up view of the Grand Canyon with a panoramic, distant view. How is space distributed?
◆ Show a photograph of yourself in close-up and distant views. How do the images differ?

Camera shots provide perspective and point of view.

◆ Show a photograph taken from two different angles. What is seen or not seen in each?
◆ Stand in two different places in the classroom and describe what you see from each vantage point. How are they different? What is in front of you? behind you? What is in your peripheral vision?

out the camcorder to experiment with these techniques and their messages. For instance, they can capture the growth of a plant, life cycle of a butterfly, or changes in the landscape of their hometown. They can shoot pictures of toys and still life, peers playing outdoors, or a bird perched on a branch.

Storyboards

A good visual organizer for film is the storyboard, a pictorial outline that sequences drawings or photographs to show how the basic action shots will look on screen. The pictures can be hand-drawn, computer drawn, cut out from magazines, or assembled out of stickers, as in Figure 6–3. Constructing a storyboard helps children encode a story visually by directing attention to action, movement, images, and placement. Two children's books that provide good pictorial models of storyboards are *Flicks* (de Paola, 1979) and *From Pictures to Words* (Stevens, 1995). These storyboards, mapped onto a drawing board and divided into rectangles, show sketches of story elements in graphic form.

Storyboards are useful for many language arts purposes. They can serve as a form of rough draft for writing or as a visual stimuli for sequencing story ideas and demonstrating comprehension during reading. They might also be used as a prop for storytelling events. The storyboard is quite versatile and fun to create.

Special Effects

Special effects are the visual spectacles in film, the large-scale, flashy, original or unusual events. Today, the blockbuster film is measured, for good or ill, by its potential for rendering bigger and better effects. Special effects are very popular with children because they are exciting, eyecatching, and compelling. Here is a good opportunity to show children that "the medium is (sometimes) the message." Have them accentuate storytelling and other classroom speech events with special effects. For example, read a scary story by candlelight or flashlight. Burst a balloon to suggest the crack of thunder.

Children can discuss special effects in popular films they may have seen. What do they think about the huge dinosaurs of *Jurassic Park* and *The Lost World*, made using digital graphics and computer animation; the miniaturized characters in *Honey I Shrunk the Kids;* or the sheer wizardry of disappearances in *Casper*? Children interested in how these special effects are created can be encouraged to read trade books such as *The Art of Star Wars Galaxy* (Gerani, 1995) or *The Art of the Empire Strikes Back* (Bulluck, 1995).

Film Animation

Animation is the process in which inanimate objects or individual drawings are photographed frame by frame to create an illusion of movement.

Figure 6–3 *Storyboard*

Animation in film is like the "show don't tell" of good storywriting. It provides a visual way to show movements and action. The animation process need not be elaborate. Here we consider three simple versions of animation: flapbook, live action, and computer animation. For more details, children can read *Make Your Own Animated Movies and Videotapes* (Anderson, 1991) or the history of film animation in the children's book *Animated Films* (Nottridge, 1992a).

Flapbook

A motion picture is really a series of still pictures that are shown to the viewer in rapid order, giving the illusion that there is movement. Flapbooks are an easy way to illustrate this phonemenon. All you need is three

Figure 6–3 *(continued)*

or more sheets of paper. On each sheet of paper, draw a picture, altering it ever so slightly so that part of it changes position. Then stack the papers so that the pictures line up exactly and staple across the top. Cut the pages into three parts up to about 1/4 inch at the top. Then flip the pages rapidly with your thumb and watch still pictures turn into moving ones. Can you describe what you see? Is your character running, jumping, twisting, exercising?

Live-Action Animation

To make live-action animation, you need real objects and a camera. Position a drawn character or puppet, snap a picture, position it again, snap a picture, and on and on, until a sequence is born. Then put all the pictures together into a flapbook and the pictures will trick your eye into believing they are moving. This is called stop-motion animation and it is the technique used in the popular animated film *James and the Giant Peach.* Again, children can map words onto the actions they are creating to form a script that accompanies live-action animation.

Computer Animation Software

The computer offers a wonderful way for children to produce their own moving stories. Computer software such as *HyperStudio* from Roger Wagner Publishing and *Amazing Animation CD* from Claris allows children to create multimedia presentations with animation, sound, and special effects. Action sequences of characters superimposed on various backgrounds are organized through a series of buttons. Some software programs even offer what is known as flyby animation, where you position a figure in an initial frame and a final frame, and then the computer creates in succession all the frames in between. If children are interested in experimenting with these techniques, have the media specialist work with them to practice spatial concepts and imaging.

Film Editing

Deciding what to select, delete, arrange, and juxtapose is one of the most important parts of filmmaking. Editing is rearranging material already shot into a desired running order. It is similar to the revision stage of writing, where the writer cuts and pastes to shape and organize information for an audience. Film editing provides a unique opportunity to teach children about ways of sequencing ideas in nonprint media. Although some children might want to work with the media specialist using film editing equipment, others can use photographs and pictures to practice techniques for sequencing both artistically and grammatically. One type of sequence used in film and artistic expression is the *flashback.* Flashbacks are often used to show how a person's previous experiences affect his or her present motives or personality. They take us back in time to fill in a missing piece of the story through memories, dreams, or some other altered state. Because flashback occurs during a film's regular running time, they must be distinguished by music, lighting, or special effects. Flashbacks as well as flash forwards (future events) create perceived shifts in time and space.

Another editing technique that condenses time or summarizes events in a few scattershots is the montage. Picture frames are juxtaposed to produce a single flash of meaning or rapid passing of time. A good example of this is to sequence four different pictures of a tree as it appears in spring, summer, fall, and winter to show the span of one year.

Another way of sequencing film suggests parallelism rather than typical sequential order. *Cross-cutting,* or editing together shots of two or more actions occurring simultaneously, can be characterized by paralleling two

TABLE 6–10 Transitions

Cut to:	switch from one shot to another.
Fade:	gradual darkening of the film to blackness before a new scene opens.
Dissolve:	melting last scene into the first of another.
Wipe:	a line passes across the screen, eliminating the first image; as it passes through it introduces a new image.

images: for example, showing someone running a 3-mile race while another character is home sleeping.

One can also do something called *jump-cuts,* moving from one scene to another to show the passage of time, changes of action, or continuity of action. Table 6–10 is a short summary of a few transitions available on computer software programs, such as Microsoft's Power Point, that illustrate how editors might move from one image to the next.

Children can compare film transitions with those in storybooks; that is, how does the writer get from one point to another, one day to the next, one season to the next? Picture clues and formulaic phrases such as "after a short time" or "soon afterward," or "long, long ago" are typical ways of dealing with time changes in print.

STORY STRAND: FICTION FILMS

Films tell stories, much like books, but instead, use visuals and motion. Children who like to read books *and* watch films bring dual visibility to a story. For example, in the Chapter 1 medieval unit, children filmed the production of Robin Hood based on a book of Robin Hood adventures. Repeated exposure brought new interpretations and reinforced major themes. Teachers can organize a movie of the month club in which the children view a feature length film based on a book they are reading (e.g., *Matilda*).

In this section we focus primarily on a critical response to the many genres of popular films. We then compare books and book adaptations for film and outline steps for writing a fiction film.

Cinema Critiques

Teachers and parents are concerned about the power and influence of the media on children. It is therefore important to help children think critically about what they view. Here we consider children's typical genre films and how to help them question and reflect on what they see. We will use the categories in Table 6–7 as our framework to pose questions that address social and personal issues such as gender, diversity, power, values, and invented realities. Remember, these are just examples. You may want to brainstorm critical questions and categories of your own.

Disney's Animated Tales

One film genre that has become part of childhood lore is Walt Disney movies. Although the Disney tales have sometimes met with controversy, there is no denying that their popularity has had a far-reaching effect on children. Since these films are often overlaid with many social and moral messages, there is a strong argument for discussing these films in honest and thought-provoking ways. Some critical questions children can tackle include:

◆ Based on your experience, which events in Cinderella can really happen? (invented realities)

◆ Why are witches and villains unlikely to win in fairytales? (stereotypes)

◆ How do you feel about the Little Mermaid turning in her voice for legs to win the prince? Was that a good exchange? Would you do it? (gender issues)

◆ What makes Belle fall in love with a Beast? (values clarification)

Drama

Drama is a human story told by actors who impersonate characters. Favorite children's dramas seem to revolve around "animal stories" such as *The Adventures of Milo & Otis* (1989) or *Free Willy* (1993), "orphan stories" such as the four remakes of Hodgson Burnett's classic *The Secret Garden,* or "unique magical powers" such as *The Boy Who Could Fly* and *Matilda.* Certainly, many other themes comprise the category of drama, whether realistic or imaginary. Consider the following critical questions for children to consider in this category:

◆ How were these characters unlike other children? What made them special? (diversity)

◆ Which characters, if any, broke away from traditional gender roles? In other words, did the boys and girls do similar things? (gender)

◆ How did you feel about the way these characters reacted to certain incidents? Did the character react in a way that you found admirable? Why or why not? How would you have reacted? (values clarification)

◆ What made the story believable? (invented realities)

◆ Would you trade places with any of the characters? Why? (invented realities)

Horror Films

The horror film is a popular genre whose success depends primarily on the creation of an emotional response in the audience. Because many parents and teachers find the graphic nature of some of the popular films unsuitable for children, you might want to substitute books such as *Movie Monsters (The Eerie Series)* (Aylesworth, 1975), which presents stories and photographs of such favorite horror stars as King Kong, Godzilla, Frankenstein, the Wolf Man, and Mr. Hyde. Books such as *Horror Movies* (Powers, 1989) and *Horror Films* (Nottridge, 1992b) are also excellent resources for showing pictures of major horror films of the past. Popular but controversial books such as R. L. Stine's *Goosebumps* series will capture children's attention and may provide just the stimulus for asking critical questions that fuel debate and many different points of view.

- How do you feel about the subject matter in the horror films? (values clarification)
- How does the horror film create suspense and fear? (stereotypes)
- What kind of character is the dreaded monster? Who is the victim? (stereotypes; power)
- Are the monsters usually male or female or both? (gender)
- What in horror films might you characterize as "violent" (values clarification)

Science Fiction Films

Sci-fi thrillers run the gamut from aliens attacking earth, to science experiments gone awry (e.g., *Jurassic Park*), to robots and space odysseys. According to Parenti (1992), the basic formula is this: A quiet peaceful community is besieged by some monstrous creature or force that threatens to invade or take over the world (p. 33). The setting is often a strange or imaginary world of the future. Technology or science is frequently intrinsic to the solution of the story's problem and is a major focus of these films. Reflections on ethics and future scientific advances are a part of the critical discussions of sci-fi films. Some questions include:

- How do you feel about science having the capacity to create monsters and other creatures? (values clarification)
- With advanced technologies, can you think of something scientists should not create? When are advances in science justified? (values clarification; power).
- Who are the scientists in these films? men or women? (gender issues)
- How does the film represent people from many cultures? (multicultural)
- Who has the power in these films, and is it limited to certain characters? Who are they? (power)

For an enjoyable activity, read about classic movies of this genre, as in the book *Science Fiction Movies* (Staskowski, 1992).

Adventure

Jumanjii, Superman, and *Raiders of the Lost Ark* are a few of the films that project bigger-than-life adventures. Oversized creatures, swashbuckling rogues, and superhuman characters doing outrageous and dazzling stunts have audiences hanging on the edge of their seats. Action-packed events and special effects hook the viewers and bring them into the story as if it were real. But adventures also create suspense and interest by showing "tests of courage." Often, a group of characters faced with a challenge is asked to show their courage for a greater good. The viewer learns who is stoic, who is the coward, or who will selfishly betray others for greed or profit. These themes can open important discussions about courage and heroism. Children can make the following critical inquiries:

◆ Who are the active, adventurous, and courageous characters? Are they girls as well as boys? (gender)

◆ In what ways are each courageous? (gender; values clarification)

◆ What makes this story believable? (invented realities)

◆ How would you describe the character's action? (values clarification)

◆ Who is a hero or heroine? (values clarification)

Mysteries

The mystery is a genre based on the adventures of sharp-witted sleuths and private detectives such as Sherlock Holmes, Miss Jane Marple, or Hercule Poirot. The main character is usually somewhat eccentric and must ferret out secrets to solve a crime. Children's mysteries such as *Harriet the Spy* are often of the "who-dun-it" variety, with a touch of humor sprinkled along the way. Mysteries offer good examples for examining motives and discussing the issues of violence and crime. A few critical questions for the mystery movie include:

◆ Was it a crime? How terrible was this crime? Why? (values clarification)

◆ Why do you believe the suspect was unjustly accused? (values clarification)

◆ Was the detective a male or female? (gender)

◆ What punishment does the criminal deserve? (values clarification)

◆ Who are the criminals? Describe them. (stereotypes)

◆ Could this crime really happen? (invented realities)

Comedy

Children enjoy films that make them laugh. They revel in the mishaps and entanglements of a character who doesn't learn from mistakes but repeats actions with the same consequences. Consider Ernest P. Worrell (e.g., *Ernest Goes to Camp, Ernest Saves Christmas, Ernest Goes to Jail,* and others), a static character whose behavior is the same in all his films. Children find humor in his silly actions and deeds, unintentional misjudgments, and the ability to get caught in someone else's nightmare. But what is comedy for one person may not necessarily be funny to others. Humor is universal, but the form it takes may be culturally specific. A few critical questions to ask about this genre include:

◆ What makes you laugh? (values clarification)

◆ When are laughs justifiable, and when are they gained at someone else's expense? (values clarification)

◆ What is amusing about the characters? (stereotype)

◆ What kinds of events seem to be universally funny? Will the humor be understood by people of many cultures? (diversity)

◆ What or who is usually the comic? the butt of a joke? (gender and age)

Historical Drama

The historical drama is a film genre characterized by sweeping historical themes, heroic actions, spectacular sets, period costumes, and a large cast. Although these films often take cinematic liberties with history, they create a sense of former times, whether it is the Civil War in *Gone with the Wind* or the depression era in *Grapes of Wrath*. Hollywood's historical events approximate history but are not necessarily a recording of it. Since the images that children receive through films are a powerful influence on what they believe the past was like, they should discuss historical fiction from a critical standpoint:

◆ From whose point of view is the history written? Do you agree with character portrayals? (diversity)

◆ How are all histories selective in terms of what is presented and how? (power)

◆ How might you find out if this is a biased vision of the past? (values clarification)

◆ How does a filmmaker manipulate facts and evidence to create a good story? Is fabrication necessary for getting at a larger truth? (invented realities)

◆ How accurate are the details of the period (clothing, setting, dialogue)? (invented realities)

Filming Books

Books and films are different art forms that tell stories in different ways. Interrelationships exist but they are not the same experience at all. A film is not a replication of the written text, even though in some cases the

TABLE 6–11   Popular Books Adapted for Film

Film	Book by:
Adventures of Pinocchio, The (New Line/Savoy)	Carlo Collodi
Harriet the Spy (Paramount/Nickelodeon)	Louise Fitzhugh
Hunchback of Notre Dame, The (Disney)	Victor Hugo
James and the Giant Peach	Roald Dahl
Jumanjii	Chris Van Allsburg
Little Princess, A	Frances Hodgson Burnett
Matilda	Roald Dahl
Roxanne	Cyrano de Bergerac

messages may be faithful to the book. Novels construct narrative through the written word; the reader's imagination supplies the visual imagery. Film, on the other hand, constructs narrative by juxtaposing visual images (Allan, 1993, p. 153). Children should have an opportunity to compare many of their popular books with their film adaptation. See Table 6–11 for a few of them.

Several educators have offered ideas for using films and books together to explore connections (Baines, 1996; Shaw, 1991a, b; Shull, 1989; Street, 1983). They believe that film can encourage reading, and vice versa. Some of the following questions will help children compare the two:

◆ How are the characters the same? different?

◆ How has the film updated material in the book?

◆ How has the film changed the point of view?

◆ How did the film create a new emphasis for the story?

◆ How did the filmmaker organize the film for a new audience?

◆ How is the chronology of events presented for each?

◆ What scenes from the book are not in the film, and vice versa?

◆ How are scenes from the book altered?

◆ How are the endings the same? different?

Nonfiction is another important source of comparison between film and text. *Apollo 13* is a good example. While this film offers a glimpse into the fateful space mission and crisis of April 1970, it is done in a way that combines real events with entertainment. A reading of actual reports of this incident in newspapers and periodicals will illustrate the distinctions.

Stories about Film and Performers

There are a number of children's books that have been made into film, many of which have already been mentioned. Some tell about the making of a film, such as *Movie Monsters* (*The Eerie Series*) (Aylesworth, 1975), which offers a behind-the-scenes view of the best horror movies. *Flicks* by Tomie de Paolo is a wordless picture book showing several short films in storyboard format. *Ida Makes a Movie* (Choras, 1974) illustrates how a young girl learns aspects of the camera and film, lighting, and acting. Children can also read about the history of film animation in *Animated Films* (Nottridge, 1992a), *Science Fiction Movies* (Stakowski, 1992), or *Movies: The World on Film* (Hitzeroth and Heerboth, 1992), which gives a brief history of the movies and their effect on society.

Finally, to get an overview of the filmmaking process, have children read trade books such as *Lights! Camera! Action!: How a Movie Is Made,* (Gibbons, 1989), *That's a Wrap: How Movies Are Made,* (Dowd, 1991) or *How Movies Are Made* (Cherrell, 1989).

Screenwriting

Children can work on screenplays as part of story writing. They prepare scenes in draft form so that as the visual, aural, and kinetic features blend into the mix, they can modify and adapt the words. The fluidity with which the writing is done underscores the symbiotic relationship that exists between the verbal and nonprint media. Here are a few guidelines to follow using a script called *Lost in the Country*.

Lost in The Country

Screenplay by

A Sixth-Grade Class

Step 1: Develop a Treatment

A *treatment* is a prose description that tells the reader what the audience will see on the screen. It is a summary, usually written in the present tense, and told with lots of action. A set location list, along with the names of the cast, is also provided (Figure 6–4).

Summary

Lost in the Country is the story of a hamster named Homer who is caught in a series of adventures. Homer is the pet hamster of Molly Featherbottom. One day, Molly's mother asks her to pick up a few items at the country store. Molly decides to take Homer along with her. While she is at the counter paying the grocer for the items, Homer escapes from her pocket. The adventures begin as Homer tries to find his way back home to Molly. In the face of danger and loneliness, he finds some new friends ready and willing to help.

Figure 6–4 *Set, Location, and Cast*

INTERIORS:
Molly's house,
    kitchen   Day/night
Country store   Day/night

EXTERIORS:
Field
    Barn   Day
    Brook   Night

CAST

Homer . . . . .Johnnie Smith

Molly . . . . .Kate Jenkins

Grocer . . . . .Sam Lucas

Mrs. Featherbottom . . . . .Sally Spinelli

Mrs. Lillybe . . . . .Janice Finegold

Animals . . . . .Class

Step 2: Find a Hook

In any good film, there is a *hook*, something that holds the audience's attention. For example, the hook in *Lost in the Country* is a hamster separated from his owner, Molly. Faced with loneliness and near-miss escapes, he embarks on a series of adventures. The filmmaker presents Homer as a lovable and endearing pet that the audience comes to care about and love. His adventures have them worrying about what will happen to him and if he will be found.

Step 3: Know Your Point of Attack

Know your *point of attack,* that is, the point at which you will begin the action on screen. You needn't give a descriptive history of the character's life or the story's events. Start with the action. For example, the sixth-graders begin the story with Molly hammering a "lost pet" sign on a street pole. For now they want the audience to question what has happened. Since the story will be told from Homer's point of view, they plan to use flashback in relaying Homer's misfortune at the country store. The class feels that beginning the story with a little suspense engages the audience.

Step 4: Develop Rising Action

Rising action shows the progressive complications arising in the story. In the adventures of Homer, the situation worsens before it gets better. Someone finds a hamster and phones Molly, but as it turns out, it is not Homer. The weather gets cold and threatens Homer's survival. As one problem is solved, another one arises to complicate the character's action. Each incident becomes more and more extreme.

Step 5: Know Your Subtext

Write the *subtext* in the margins of your movie script. What do the words really mean in terms of intentions: "Your hamster is lost?" a friend asks. (Does this mean the friend is questioning if it is true? uncertain whether the hamster is lost or stolen? implying that a cat has eaten him?) How should you play this scene? What exactly is the intent of this line?

Step 6: Write Dialogue and Stage Directions

A movie script is a unique kind of text in that it must be short on words and long on sound and action. Shelton (1993) offers three tips to the screenwriter: (1) Write for the ear, not the eye; (2) do not write perfect grammar and syntax in writing dialogue; and (3) achieve continuity and coherence by visual, aural, and kinesthetic features along with words. Remember, dialogue is natural conversation artificially prepared for the film. The sentences are typically short and informal. Seven to ten written pages usually equal 1/2 hour of film (Levy, 1994).

Figure 6–5 is a short sample of how to format a script. For easy reference, the dialogue is written vertically, with the actors' character names above the sentences. Below these are parenthetical statements describing actions and other nonverbal messages. The script should include the directions abbreviated and placed in brackets. In all CAPS, tell whether the scene is IN (indoors) or OUT (outdoors); time of day (morning, night, twilight); the location (INTERIOR, like the kitchen); when the music begins, continues, or stops; SFX (sound effects); and when each scene changes (e.g., CUT TO, FADE IN, FADE OUT). Reading a script is very different from reading a story. Words of a script are not necessarily meant to be savored but are meant to be a blueprint from which the voice takes its direction.

Step 7: Check Audience Reactions

Audience reactions to a film are a major focus of the filmmaker. Some filmmakers try out different endings of a film before its completion and release. During a premiere, they check to be sure that the audience responds favorably to the conclusion, since it can affect the entire pleasure of the film (Boggs, 1996). Thus, before finalizing the script, children may want to try out different endings with audiences and have them choose the one they favor.

INFORMATION STRAND: THE MEDIUM IS THE MESSAGE

In a media-driven culture, new technologies change the societal norm of what it means to be literate. As we enter the twenty-first century, TV, video, cameras, and computers merge into newly integrated technologies that join sound, voice, motion, and pictures. Recognizing that youth are bombarded with millions of visual images every day, schools have an obligation

Prologue

FADE IN

Molly

1. [OUT. MORN. NEAR HOME]

> I'll just put up this sign. I know Homer will be home soon.
> Oh Homer, come back to me (Cries) MUSIC SEGUE

FADE OUT

ACT ONE

FADE IN

2. [INT. COUNTRY STORE.DAY]

(Molly is in the store; Homer slips out of Molly's pocket while she is getting change; she pays and leaves the store)

HOMER
Yikes, where am I? I think I hit my head. How long have I been here?
(looking around the floor)

GROCER
Thank you, Mrs. Lillybe
I hope you enjoy those jellies.

HOMER
(realizing Molly is gone, races and jumps into a sack of flour)
(SFX: Screech)
I'll just hide out here till dark

CUT TO:

3. [INT. MOLLY'S HOME. NIGHT]

MOLLY
(is at the dining room table moving food
around on her plate; unable to eat)
Oh, what will Homer have to eat tonight?
I can't bear it
(a tear falls down her cheek)
(SFX: The phone rings)

MRS. FEATHERBOTTOM

Figure 6–5 *Sample Script Format*

to teach them how to think critically about ideas in a nonprint, nonbook culture. The popular media are good starting points because they represent a common experience base shared among children (Cox, 1996). For purposes of discussion, this section is divided by media type, even though it is difficult to draw a line where one begins and the other ends. Although these alternative media consume a large portion of children's time, a full discussion of their impact is beyond the scope of this book. The language arts teacher, interested in these technologies, will want to explore them in further depth.

Television

Studies prior to the 1980s often criticized the television (TV) medium as a passive and ineffectual one in language learning (Clark and Clark, 1977; Nelson, 1973). Recent work, however, is challenging traditional assumptions and considering TV as interactive (Desmond, 1997; Postman and Powers, 1992). Here we consider a few simple ways that TV can be used as a language arts tool.

TV Talk

TV offers many occasions for children to study how language is used. For example, the interview, the news report, the melodrama, the game show, and the ubiquitous TV commercial are speech events that have characteristics instantaneously recognizable to the viewer. As explained in the Siskel and Ebert production in the opening vignette, certain stock phrases and routines identify the TV program. The teacher may want to introduce various speech events and their conventions using TV. Let's take the commercial, for example.

Children should have an opportunity to talk about TV commercials and more important, to produce some commercials themselves to learn firsthand the "tricks of the trade." (In Table 6–12, consider how to discuss and create two kinds of commercials: the image commercial and the information commercial.)

Smart producers know that product recognition and constructed desire for it are essential to the success of an ad. Because TV is such an influential medium, the schools should not only use it to teach but should also teach "how it uses us" (Rushkoff, 1994). Smart audiences should therefore ask questions that will make them active participants with the media. Can they learn to recognize attention-attracting elements and other influences on the processing of information?

- How might you characterize the nature and tone of the language? (childlike, playful, serious, sarcastic?) Why was this tone selected?
- Does the commercial lead you to act or not act in a certain way?
- What is the age of the target audience? values? gender? economic status? How does it appeal to these targets?
- What effects do the music, pictures, and images have?
- What techniques does it use to get your attention? (fast cuts; non-sequential images; surreal images; fast-paced formats; discontinuous images)

TABLE 6–12   TV Advertisements

Create an *image advertisement,* one that associates symbols or impressions with a product you are trying to sell, such as the leprechaun on a cereal box called Lucky Charms. Convey moods, feelings, and attitudes primarily through images and their associations. Try out techniques that will grab an audience's attention and help them remember the product, such as keeping the viewer waiting and guessing before revealing the product, to create interest and suspense. Think through the following:

◆ Who is the audience you are targeting? (children, boys, girls, adults)? How can you appeal to them? (e.g., placing a game on the back of the cereal box)

◆ What symbols or pictures can you use to imply a relationship with the product? (e.g., lucky and leprechauns)

◆ What do you want the audience to look at first? How can you draw their attention there (music, color, humor, shock values, suspense?)

◆ Why should you buy this product? (because of the game on the box? because the cereal is good for you?)

Create an *information advertisement* or make an "infomercial." Use strategies to inculcate the product name, assert and imply attributes, and develop slogans that penetrate an audience's consciousness. Think through these questions:

◆ How can you use this advertisement to make the viewer question habits or beliefs?

◆ How can you make the viewer think in a certain way? value something?

◆ How can you show that the product has a credible source? Who might endorse your product?

◆ What connotations are evoked through the repeated use of certain words? What vocabulary words can you use to create an image?

◆ How can you make your product a common sense necessity? How can you motivate the viewer to buy your product? (you must have this)

◆ How can this product solve someone's problem?

◆ What shared social context or relationship is assumed?

◆ What is your expectation based on the cues of the commercial?

TV as Storyteller

Critics of TV argue that it fosters an unthinking, passive receptivity (Parenti, 1992) better substituted for by other family activity. This is certainly reflected in many of the children's books about TV [e.g., *TV Monster* (Barden, 1989), *The Berenstain Bears and Too Much TV* (Berenstain and Berenstain, 1989), *Mouse TV* (Novak, 1994), and *The Day the TV Blew Up* (West, 1988)]. Yet proponents of TV see it as a learning tool that works in tandem with books (Desmond, 1997; Neuman, 1995). According to Marc Brown (1997), the author of the popular *Arthur* books, which have recently been made into a TV series, the visual and media representation of literature can enliven and enrich reading. He states that when children see a book dramatized on television, they are more likely to go out and buy the book. As catalysts for one another, books and TV spark children's interests and expose them to different forms of their favorite stories. Assuming this claim is true, the teacher can encourage children to think of TV and books as complementary media that broaden channels of communication. Children can compare and contrast books with TV counterparts looking for different symbols for constructing and processing meaning (Neuman, 1995), different ways of pacing and treating subject matter (Singer and Singer, 1983), and different interpretations made by readers (Meringoff et al., 1983).

Video as Narrative

Videos provide a visual and aural vehicle for telling storied lives. Because of their appeal to the senses (including movement), they are powerful methods of delivering entertainment and information. The teacher can find videos on children's literature such as Beverly Cleary's *Ramona* series or the *Reading Rainbow Series*. Because videocassettes are inexpensive and accessible, children can easily make their own storytelling dramas. If the teacher has access to a camcorder, the children should read books or dramatize them on video and then make them available at learning centers.

Computers

The computer's tremendous capacity to facilitate communication and provide information combines graphics, photography, sound, video, and animation. It unites art and technology in ways that translate into many new interactive encounters for children. Through the World Wide Web (WWW) children are linked from site to site with access to any number of experts and databases. In a matter of seconds, they can view pictures, read written information, and even watch movies. The computer offers many ways to teach traditional language arts and "the arts." Some possibilities for the literacy classroom are discussed here.

Hypertext and Hypermedia

Reading and producing hypertext offers a way to explore various dimensions of a topic. Hypertext is a nonlinear means of information gathering that allows the user to make connections from a main text to multimedia sources such as pictures, graphics, sound effects, and motion. This concept of multiple linkages to multimedia is often referred to as hypermedia.

Designing a hypertext requires associative thinking and a novel way of composing. Hypertext might be likened to a set of note cards called a *stack*. Each card is a screen and the user can move from card to card by clicking on buttons. At the very minimum, the writer should understand the overall concept of linking chunks of media interactively. Conceptual links cued in the text with key words are interconnected to other conceptual ideas in an endless web of text structures and pictures. Children can practice the idea of linking without a computer. A brief example is offered on medieval times, a topic that introduced the book. The children write a linear summary with hot links underlined to direct the viewer to groups of ideas that are part of a conceptual whole. It looks something like this:

> During the <u>medieval period</u>, a way of life known as <u>feudalism</u> dominated Europe. Because invaders and thieves ravaged whole villages, the commoners would exchange labor for protection by lords. The lords lived in <u>castles</u>, which were more functional than opulent. Those who lived in the castles followed a set of rules or code of <u>chivalry</u>. One famous story about chivalry is that of King Arthur and the Knights of the Round Table.

The underlined words spin off into links that give more information about these ideas. Table 6–13 shows how links can be graphics, pictures, or more text.

An integrated medium of dynamic texts will mean new views of authorship and audience. One might consider hypertext as a multiauthored work, that is, the professional readings, photographs, art reproductions, and textual documents assembled for a particular database represent contributions of many authors. Because the student can stretch the limits of information and resources to create multidimensional works, they must address new issues of ownership and intellectual property.

In a related challenge, the composers of new databases must reenvision the role of audience. They must be sure that users of hypertext are afforded the ease of navigating between words, pictures, and graphics so as to provide an efficient means for exploring a topic. Too many links might result in an endless maze and cause users to lose sight of what they were learning. If the hypermedia is well constructed, however, users can extend their scope of information at the push of a button, free to choose whatever unique pathways they wish to explore.

TABLE 6–13 The Links

Medieval link: includes descriptions of the period between 1100 and 1300 in Europe.

Feudalism link: shows a tree diagram of hierarchical power in the feudal system: king, lord, bishops, vassals (knights), and serfs (farmers)

Castle link: shows pictures from Macaulay's cross section *Castle.*

Chivalry link: offers a short story summary about the legend of King Arthur and the Knights of the Round Table.

Electronic Storybooks

Electronic books pose an entire new genre of texts for children to read. New integrated CDs allow children to read story narrative and click a pointer on words or pictures in the frame. When this is done, the narrative is expanded with further explanations, a sound effect, rhyming definitions, boxed words, sing-alongs, translations into other languages, or animations. Some programs allow children to finish the story ending or play games. Interactive stories differ from traditional narratives in that they are nonlinear. They allow the reader to explore story space and worlds created by the author. CD-ROM packages such as the *Electronic Bookshelf* are examples. Children can compare these stories with traditional ones and then create their own stories modeled after the electronic storybook. Duplicate a one-page story for children and ask them to underline key words to use as spin-offs. On another sheet of paper, have them write a short paragraph or add pictures to go with the underlined words. After the children have created additional text and visuals, have them cut out their written work (and pictures) and mount it on poster board in the form of a web. The center of the web is the one-page story that has been underlined. The spokes lead to the spin-offs. Once displayed, others can read these story webs. Children will recognize differences depending on which words were underlined and how they were extended. This activity shows visually how people read a text and what they consider important.

Quicktime Movies

Quicktime movies are like electronic time capsules. They combine video and audio stored digitally so that you can actually play movies on the computer. As the name suggests, they are quick, usually no more than 30 seconds of video (which takes up about 2 megabytes of disk space). Quicktime movies already available on the computer are possible to download from the Web. A quicktime movie can be distributed on videotape, CD-ROM, or the WWW. Such format flexibility allows it to reach a wide range of audiences. Teachers may want to use quicktime movies as the basis for creating film trailers or advertisements of films. Children can write catchy and dramatic language to accompany a quicktime movie to excite the audience about the film and give them a sneak preview. They should talk about why certain segments of film are used for advertising purposes and what techniques are used to make viewers want to go see the movie.

◆ School–Community Links

Although most film viewing is done outside of school, taking a class to see images on screen, bigger than life, is an adventure unlike typical video or TV viewing. Also mutual viewing of a film gives children a common experience in which to hold discussions with an adult and peers. So that children might attend movies, the school can initiate a big brother–big sister arrangement to pair elementary children with high school students, college students, or adult volunteers. This will give all children a chance to see some of the popular children's films and create a special friendship with their chaperon.

But going to films is only a small part of reaching out to the community. You will want to invite the community into the school. If a college is nearby, students from the film school might visit the classroom to share their film projects. Another possibility is to have local video proprietors present reviews of the latest films, show a few clips to excite children's interest, or share viewing habits of children (Which is the most rented film? least? Which age enjoys which films? and so on). Children should also call on school experts such as the media resource person to help them with technical aspects of a film. If feasible, the media specialist might offer special workshops for parents and children on the uses of technology. Because technology is the wave of the future, children will want to stay in constant touch with new technological developments via e-mail and the Internet. Not only will they communicate across the country and world, but they will take advantage of the resources in their own communities. Finally, you will want to encourage children to have their own film festivals and jubilees to showcase home movies or amateur videos. Having a local newspaper sponsor the event, complete with announcements, awards (for best film) and published movie reviews, gets the community involved in creating memorable experiences for children.

◆ *Activities for Professional Development*

1. Start a movie group. Gather outside school to attend movies together or show videos at one another's homes. Talk about the movie. Use the response questions in this chapter to discuss the films. You might want to identify children's films for viewing, such as those listed in the Additional Resources section. Another good place to begin is to view films with themes that are about the arts, as discussed in this book (see Table 6–14).

2. Make a home movie to share with your class. All you will need is a camcorder and a willingness to share a part of yourself. Show your home and introduce your family. Take the viewers to see your garden, the birdbath, or the fish pond. Children will get an opportunity to know you better and you can talk with them about the process you went through as you made the film.

3. Work in small groups to prepare an activity associated with film design. For example:

◆ *Film scores.* Play a sound track from a popular movie and have others draw a scene that comes to mind.

TABLE 6–14   Films for Teachers

♦ *All the Mornings of the World* (1994): Master cellist Saint Colombe and his student Marin Marais (114 min)

♦ *Amadeus* (1984): the story of Amadeus Mozart (158 min)

♦ *Camille Claudel* (1989): the story of a French sculptor and her romance with Pierre Rodin (159 min)

♦ *Chaplin* (1992): the story of the silent film star Charlie Chaplin (135 min)

♦ *Farinelli* (1995): the story of an eighteenth-century Italian castrato singer (110 min)

♦ *Flashdance* (1983): a girl's dream to dance for a well-known ballet (96 min)

♦ *Immortal Beloved* (1994): the story of the composer Ludwig van Beethoven (203 min)

♦ *Impromptu* (1991): the story of Chopin and George Sands (108 min)

♦ *Intervista* (1987): documentary-style picture of the making of Fellini's films (108 min)

♦ *Mr. Holland's Opus* (1996): the story of a music teacher who loses his job after 30 years because funding for the arts has been eliminated (143 min)

♦ *Vincent and Theo* (1990): the story of Vincent van Gogh and his brother Theo (138 min)

♦ *Character study.* List memorable characters from films such as *Matilda* or *Forrest Gump* and write a backstory about the character.

♦ *Settings and locations.* Create a travel brochure for a picture that you have been given.

♦ *Special effects.* Read a children's book and surprise the audience with special effects (sounds, pictures, puppets, music, or other creative ideas).

♦ *Works Cited*

Professional References

Allan, C. (1993). Homeward bound: The incredible journey of mass culture. In L. Rollin, (Ed.), *The antic art: Enhancing children's literary experiences through film and video* (pp. 153–166). Fort Atkinson, WI: Highsmith Press.

Anderson, Y. (1991). *Make your own animated movies and videotapes.* Boston: Little, Brown.

Baines, L. (1996). From page to screen: When a novel is interpreted for film, what gets lost in the translation? *Journal of Adolescent and Adult Literacy, 39,* 612–622.

Baines, L., and Dial, M. (1995). Scripting screenplays: An idea for integrating writing, reading, thinking, and media literacy. *English Journal, 84,* 86–91.

Berger, J. (1972). *Ways of seeing.* London: BBC/Penguin.

Boggs, J. M. (1996). *The art of watching films,* 4th ed. Mountain View, CA: Mayfield Publishing.

Brown, M. (1997). Reflections: Arthur moves to TV and CD's. In J. Flood, S. B. Heath, and D. Lapp (Eds.), *Handbook of research on teaching: Literacy through the communicative and visual arts.* New York: Macmillan.

Clark, H., and Clark, E. (1977). *Psychology and language.* New York: Harcourt Brace Jovanovich.

Copland, A. (1988). *What to listen for in music.* New York: New American Library.

Cox, C. (1983). Young filmmakers speak the language of film. *Language Arts, 60* (3), 296–372.

Cox, C. (1985). Filmmaking as a composing process. *Language Arts, 12* (1), 60–69.

Cox, C. (1996). *Teaching language arts,* 2nd ed. Needham Heights, MA: Allyn and Bacon.

Desmond, R. (1997). TV viewing, reading and media literacy. In J. Flood, S. B. Heath, and D. Lapp (Eds.), *Handbook of research on teaching literacy through the communicative and visual arts* (pp. 23–30). New York: Macmillan.

Gallagher, B. (1988). Film study and the teaching of English. *English Journal, 77,* 58–61.

Greene, M. (1991) Texts and Margins. *Harvard Educational Review,* 61, 27–39.

Green, J. (1994). *Coming to your senses: Writing about the arts,* 3rd ed. New York: McGraw-Hill

Hoban, C. F. (1975). The state of the art of film in instruction: A second look. *Audiovisual Instruction, 20,* 30–34.

Jorgensen, K. L. (1993). *History workshop.* Portsmouth, NH: Heinemann.

Jurkiewicz, K. (1990). Using film in the humanities classroom: The case of Metropolis. *English Journal, 79,* 47–50.

Langdorf, L. (1991). The emperor has only clothes: Toward a hermeneutic of the video text. In A. Olson, C. Parr, and D. Parr (Eds.), *Video: Icons and values* (pp. 45–62). Albany, NY: State University of New York Press.

Meringoff, L., Vibbert, M., Char, C., Fernie, D., Banker, G. and Gardner, H. (1983). How is children's learning from television distinctive? Exploiting the medium methodologically. In J. Bryant and D. Anderson (Eds.), *Children's understanding of television: Research on attention and comprehension* (pp. 151–180). San Diego, CA: Academic Press.

Nelson, K. (1973). Structure and strategy in learning to talk. *Monographs of the Society for Research in Child Development, 58* (149).

Neuman, S. B. (1995). *Literacy in the television age: The myth of the TV effect.* Norwood, NJ: Ablex Publishing.

Parenti, M. (1992). *Make-believe media: The politics of entertainment.* New York: St. Martin's Press.

Postman, N., and Powers, S. (1992). *How to watch TV news.* New York: Penguin.

Rushkoff, D. (1994). *Media virus! Hidden agendas in popular culture.* New York: Ballantine.

Shaw, E. (1991a). Letters from Vietnam: A film/book combination for a nonfiction course. *English Journal, 80,* 25–27.

Shaw, E. (1991b). What film/book combination from the last decade do you recommend for classroom use? *English Journal, 80,* 82–87.

Shelton, S. M. (1993). Script design for information film and video. *Technical Communication,* 4th Quarter, 655–668.

Shull, E. (1989). The reader, the text, the poem—and the film. *English Journal, 78,* 53–57.

Singer, J. L., and Singer, D. (1983). Implications of childhood television viewing for cognition, imagination, and emotion. In J. Bryant and D. Anderson (Eds.), *Children's understanding of television: Research on attention and comprehension* (pp. 265–296). San Diego, CA: Academic Press.

Street, D. (1983). *Children's novels and the movies.* New York: Ungar.

Valasek, T. (1992). *Frameworks: An introduction to film studies.* Dubuque, IA: W. C. Brown.

Whittock, T. (1990). *Metaphor and film.* Cambridge: Cambridge University Press.

Children's References

Aylesworth, T. G. (1975) *Movie monsters (The Eerie Series).* New York: Reader's Digest Books.

Barden, R. (1989). *TV monster.* New York: Crown Publishing.

Berenstain, S., and Berenstain, J. (1989). *The Berenstain bears and too much TV.* New York: Random House.

Bulluck, V. (1995). *The art of The Empire Strikes Back.* London: Titan Books.

Cherrell, G. (1989). *How movies are made.* How it is made series. New York: Facts On File.

Chorao, K. (1974). *Ida makes a movie.* New York: Seabury.

de Paolo, T. (1979). *Flicks.* New York: Harcourt Brace Jovanovich.

Dowd, N. (1991). *That's a wrap: How movies are made.* New York: Simon & Schuster.

Gerani, G. (1995). *The art of Star Wars Galaxy.* London: Titan Books.

Gibbons, G. (1989). *Lights! Camera! Action! How a movie is made.* New York: HarperTrophy.

Harrison, T. (1993). *O Canada.* New York: Ticknor & Fields.

Hitzeroth, D., and Heerboth, S. (1992). *Movies: The world on film.* Encyclopedia of discovery and invention series. San Diego, CA: Lucent Books.

Lobel, A. (1994). *Away from home.* New York: Greenwillow Books.

Nottridge, R. (1992a). *Animated films.* Films series. New York: Macmillan.

Nottridge, R. (1992b). *Horror films.* Films series. New York: Macmillan.

Novak, M. (1994). *Mouse TV.* New York: Orchard Books.

Powers, T. (1989). *Horror movies.* Minneapolis, MN: Lerner Publications.

Squires, M. (1992). *Video camcorder school.* Pleasantville, NY: The Reader's Digest Association.

Staskowski, A. (1992). *Science fiction movies.* Minneapolis, MN: Lerner Publications.

Stevens, J. (1995). *From pictures to words.* New York: Holiday House.

Stine, R. L. (1997). *Goosebumps.* New York: Scholastic.

Van Allsburg, C. (1985) *The polar express.* New York: Scholastic.

West, D. (1988). *The day the TV blew up* (illus. G. Fiammenghi). Niles, IL: Albert and Whitman.

Additional Resources

Note: Asterisks indicate references that are cited in the chapter.

Videotape and Computer Catalogs

Anne of Green Gables (1985)
Silvan Films
Walt Disney Home Videos
P.O. Box 126
Brea, CA 92622

*Anne of Avonlea (1988)
 Walt Disney Home Videos
 P.O. Box 126
 Brea, CA 92622

Broderbund
P.O. Box 6125
Novato, CA 94948-6125

Corinth Videos
Justin Patrick Co.
34 Gansevoort Street
New York, NY 10014-1597

Educational Resources
1550 Executive Drive
P.O. Box 1900
Elgin, IL 60121-1900

MECC
6160 Summit Drive North
Minneapolis, MN 55430-4003

PBS Videos
1320 Braddock Place
Alexandria, VA 22314
800-344-3337

*Ramona
 Warner Home Video:
 4000 Warner Blvd.
 Burbank, CA 91522
 800-323-5275
 (Beverly Cleary, 3 tapes, 60 minutes
 each)

*Reading Rainbow TV Series (PBS)
 1320 Braddock Place
 Alexandria, VA 22314

*Reading Rainbow Video
 University of Nebraska
 P.O. Box 80669
 Lincoln, NE 68501-0069

Sunburst
101 Castleton Street
Pleasantville, NY 10570

*Weston Woods Productions
 West, CT 06883
 800-243-5020

Computer Software and Technology

*Amazing Animation CD
 Claris
 5201 Patrick Henry Drive
 Santa Clara, CA 95052

Cinemania 97
Microsoft
Ztek
P.O. Box 1055
Louisville, KY 40201

*Electronic Bookshelf
 5276 South Country Road
 700 West
 Frankfort, IN 46041-8113

Encarta
Microsoft
Classroom Connect
431 Madrid Ave.
Torrance, CA 90501

*HyperStudio
 Roger Wagner
 Educational Resources
 1550 Executive Drive
 P.O. Box 1900
 Elgin, IL 60121

My Multimedia Workshop
WINGS for Learning
1600 Green Hills Road
P.O. Box 660002
Scotts Valley CA 95067–0002
800-321-7511

Postscript: Putting It All Together

The postscript illustrates how to use multiple literacies as vehicles for studying content across the curriculum. The first unit, designed for second-graders, is part of the life sciences in which they study the wonders of nature, specifically birds. The second unit, designed with fourth-graders in mind, is part of a unit on the American frontier in which the children become acquainted with the spirit of colonial life and the expansion westward.

THE WONDERS OF NATURE: SCIENCE, GRADE 2

The living world of nature is a source of endless fascination to children and an important unit of study in the science curriculum. Here we use all of the literacies to develop a lesson on the study of birds. The activities are provided as examples of how you might incorporate the literacies into the content areas.

Art Literacy

Observation is an important inquiry strategy of artists and scientists. In this activity children birdwatch by placing a bird feeder outside the classroom window. On a daily basis, children watch the birds and complete an observation matrix such as the one shown in Table P-1.

TABLE P-1   Observation Matrix

Bird	Feature		
	Considered a Song Bird	Has Bright Colors	Lives in Our Area
Oriole	+	−	+
Cardinal	−	+	+
Pigeon	−	−	+
Nightingale	+	−	−
Canary	+	+	−

Source: Adapted from Manzo and Manzo (1995, p. 259).

1. Children set up the matrix. They decide on a topic (e.g., birds) and in the first column on their paper they list examples of birds they wish to observe (e.g., oriole, cardinal, pigeon, nightingale, and canary). Next, the teacher asks leading questions about birds that will help them select features to observe (e.g., those dealing with color, anatomy, species, behaviors, habitats). These features they list across the rows of the matrix (e.g., considered a song bird, has bright colors, lives in our area).

2. Children fill in the matrix using plus (+) or minus (−) signs to indicate whether a particular bird has or does not have each feature.

3. Children analyze and discuss the matrix. After the matrix is completed, the teacher leads a discussion based on the patterns of pluses and minuses. This matrix provides a good beginning for the K-W-L approach: What do I *know*, what do I *want* to know, and what have I *learned*?

Children draw, cut out pictures, or study artwork of birds to help convey the information in the matrix. Audubon's sketches of birds provide a good example of refined observational skills and the ability to communicate information through drawings. Children can also discuss birds in Japanese and Chinese art, such as the plump thrushes in *Birds in Bamboo Tree* or the hanging silk scroll in *Swallow and Lotus.* Often, this work combines calligraphy, poetry, and painting. Abstract sculpture such as Brancusi's *Bird in Space,* a slender bronze figure that resembles a feather, shows the concept of bird and the essence of flight, offering children a stimulus for translating scientific information into poetic form.

Music Literacy

Music literacy can also be a way for children to learn about birds. Try sharpening the children's ears by reading *The Loon: Voice of the Wilderness* (Billings, 1988), which tracks the strange and eerie sounds of this large bird.

- *The territorial yodel:*
  A-a-whoo-quee-quee-whe-oooo-que!
  A-a-whoo-quee-quee-whe-oooo-que!
- *The aggressive defense, referred to as the "tremolo"*
  Described as an unearthly, weird sound
- *The talk for greeting in voiced staccato hoots*
  Kuk, gek-Gek

When you are finished reading the story, prepare the class for a nature walk. The children listen to sounds (e.g., "cheep, cheep" for birds, or "tsh-ee-eee-e-ou" for leaves) and jot them down in a notebook as they are heard. When they return to the classroom, they post their sounds on a chart and expand the sounds and words with adjectives (e.g., shrieking, wailing) or similes (e.g., sounds like chattering, banging, gossiping, knocking against a rock).

In addition to the nature walk, have children listen to the mood CDs of tropical rain forests and wildlife sounds, then draw pictures or write about what they hear. National Geographic makes a wall clock that pictures different birds representing the hours of the day. On the hour, each bird sings its song three times, acquainting children with the sound each bird makes. Singing songs about birds (e.g., Kookaburra) and examining the lyrics provides insights into bird descriptions and behavior. Children can also combine music and art, like the example in Figure P-1 where Jane Yolen uses song birds as the source of a poem and the artist, Ted Lewin, draws songbirds to create a musical picture (Yolen, 1990). Note how the birds are placed on five lines as though they were notes on a musical staff. Adding Beethoven's *Sixth Symphony* (the *Pastoral*), which imitates the nightingale, the quail, and the cuckoo, gives birth to a combined visual, auditory, and linguistic performance.

Dance Literacy

Dance and movement literacy offers another communicative channel for learning about birds. Have children observe the courtship dances of birds, especially the red-crowned crane, which has one of the most beautiful dances in the bird kingdom. Reading *The Paper Crane* (Bang, 1987) and then demonstrating courtship movements of the crane—bows, stretches, and backward arches—evokes a broad display of interpretive freedom and spontaneity. To exploit the connection between birds and dance, children can use "bird" as a metaphor for movement. Close inspection suggests a hovering movement in which a bird flaps its wings very fast, so that it can stay up in the air without moving. In such ballets as *Swan Lake* and the *Firebird* (see Chapter 4), dancers show how to swoop, glide, flap, and hover to create the flight of birds. If children learn what movements consist of and how they are portrayed, they will be better able to express the essence of a bird in haiku poems and movement poetry (see Chapter 4). Through reading, children will learn that birds have symbolic meanings that they can draw on to express ideas (e.g., the crane is widely revered in the Orient as a symbol of fidelity in marriage, good luck, and long life; the hawk, often pictured sitting on the shoulder of a knight in Medieval drawings, can represent peace, royalty, and power).

Theater and Film Literacy

Creating a nonfiction film or documentary about birds provides an opportunity to practice both drama and reportage. Children can objectively record the life and habits of birds as they observe them at a birdfeeder. Have them use a camera (older children use a videocamera) to capture what they see. After they arrange the photographs on a storyboard, they write down key points to use as references in narrating their documentary.

SONG/BIRDS

Along the wires,
like scattered notes
on lines of music,
sit a row of birds.

Starlings are the half notes,
finches the quarters,
and hummingbirds,
as brief as grace notes,
hover on the edges
of the tune.

Figure P-1 *"Song/Birds"* From *Bird Watch* by Jane Yolen. Illustration adapted from Ted Lewin. Copyright © 1990 by Ted Lewin. Used by permission of Philomel Books, a division of Penguin Putnam Inc.

At this point the photographs are made into slides for a slide show or transferred from the storyboard to filmstrip leader with special markers (see Cox, 1996, for step-by-step procedures). From here, the children are ready to enact the documentary by narrating the information that they have gathered and displayed on the storyboard. PBS Videos and National Geographic provide several good examples of how to interrelate pictures or film footage with narration. Often the Discovery Channel, Learning Channel, or Public Broadcasting Channel will run programs that feature documentaries of the animal world.

THE AMERICAN FRONTIER: HISTORY, GRADE 4

One of the major themes of the social studies curriculum is to recognize and explore our historical roots and links to the past. This unit uses all of the literacies to enrich the study of the early pioneer settlers and the expansion westward.

Art Literacy

Early American artifacts, especially fabric and textiles, provide a set of images and symbols for communicating our history. The women and girls of colonial days, whose occupation it was to weave, quilt, spin wool, and embroider, contributed not only to the basic needs of the family but also to the shared stories of home life, religious beliefs, and values revealed in their work. Select one of these fabric arts to engage children in writing about colonial life. For instance, have children talk about images portrayed on embroidery samplers. Use several different colonial embroidery samplers, with different scenes, and have children write description, narrative, or character point of view for their particular sampler:

- *Description.* A family is all decked out in their Sunday best, riding to church in a horse and buggy. It is a sunny day and the birds fly among the oak trees. The church is in front of them, and standing outside is the preacher holding a prayer book.

- *Narrative.* One day my family and I took the horse and buggy to church. Mother said "Look at the beautiful trees and birds." I was too busy thinking about the afternoon picnic to notice. When I finally glanced up, I saw Preacher Smithson standing in front of the church with a prayerbook in hand.

- *Perspective taking.* I stood at the church door with my prayer book in hand and saw the Morrison family riding up in the horse-drawn carriage. I could always count on them to attend Sunday service. It was a beautiful day and the birds were everywhere. I whispered to myself a prayer of thanksgiving.

When all the narratives are written, have children examine all the different embroidery samples and narratives to piece together a story of colonial life and historical events. Sew them together like a quilt (see Chapter 2).

Music Literacy

As mentioned in the opening vignette of Chapter 3, singing songs of the Old West gives children an opportunity to learn about the life and times of the American frontier. *Songs of the Wild West* (Axelrod, 1991) includes many favorites, such as *Cowboy Jack, The Cowboy,* and *Git Along, Little Dogies,* whose lyrics help children get a sense of the moral obligations of the cowboy, the importance of freedom, and the cowboy's life of perseverance and little luxury. Have children write their own songs based on books such as *Buffalo Gals* (Miller,1995) and *The Story of Women Who Shaped the West* (Fox, 1991).

Dance Literacy

The American square dance offers valuable insights into pioneer life. The sequenced action movements of the square dance, developed from the country dances, round dances, and quadrilles of Europe, were brought to New England and reinvented as a uniquely American institution. When the pioneers moved westward, they took this form of entertainment with them. It was a way to pass the time, create a sense of community, and demonstrate the freedoms of the new frontier.

Locate square dance routines of the pioneers, such as *Lady'round the Lady, Birdie in the Cage,* and *Dive for the Oyster.* Research the occasions for dance and perform the dances (using a caller). The caller chooses the steps and leads the dancers through them by calling or singing instructions. Typically, in the square dance a caller announces the movements of the dance sequence: do-si-do, promenade, sashay, and curtsy. They can also be hand movements, such as a handshake hold and hands up. Make a dictionary of new words associated with dance. Have children read books about the topic, such as *Turkey in the Straw* (Hazen, 1993) and *Noah's Square Dance* (Walton, 1995). Before performing the dance, teach them basic steps such as those described in Table P-2. Also find music to accompany the dance, such as *Yellow Rose of Texas* or *English Country Dances for Children.*

Theater and Film Literacy

To learn about the daily life of girls during colonial times, have the children perform plays such as those produced by the Pleasant Company (1995): *Five Plays: The American Girls Collection. Tea for Felicity* is a play about colonial American life. Felicity is learning fine stitchery and the proper way to serve tea. This play in five acts includes a summary, roles

TABLE P-2 Folk Dance Steps

Dance Step	Directions
Do-si-do	Partners face each other; pass by the right shoulder; circle each other back to back and return to place.
Promenade	Side by side and facing right, partners cross hands and move counterclockwise around the ring.
Sashay	Face the center of the circle; boys move right and behind girls; girls move left and in front of boys.
Curtsy	A full bow from the waist.

Source: Plater, Speyrer and Speyrer, (1993).

for the stage crew, and ways to create simple stage sets, props, and costumes. Using a videocamera, the teacher can videotape the play for review and class enjoyment.

◆ Works Cited

Professional Reference

Cox, C. (1996). *Teaching language arts.* Needham Heights, MA: Allyn and Bacon.
Manzo, A., and Manzo, U. C. (1995). *Teaching children to be literate.* New York: Holt, Rinehart and Winston.

◆ Children's References

Axelrod, A. (1991). *Songs of the wild west* (arrange D. Fox). Metropolitan Museum of Art with the Buffalo Bill Historical Center. New York: Simon & Schuster.
Bang, M. (1987) *The paper crane.* New York: Mulberry Books.
Billings, C. W. (1988). *The loon: Voice of the wilderness.* New York: Dodd, Mead.
Fox, M. V. (1991). *The story of women who shaped the west.* Chicago: Children's Press.
Hazen, B. S. (1993). *Turkey in the straw.* New York: Dial Books.
Miller, M. B. (1995). *Buffalo gals: Women of the old west.* Minneapolis, MN: Lerner Publications.
Plater, O., Speyrer, C., and Speyrer, R. (1993). *Cajun dancing.* Gretna, LA: Pelican Publishing.
Pleasant Company (1995). *Five plays: The American girls collection.* Middleton, WI: Pleasant Company Publications.
Walton, R. (1995). *Noah's square dance.* New York: Lothrop, Lee & Shepard.
Yolen, J. (1990). *Birdwatch: A book of poetry* (illus. T. Lewin). New York: Philomel Books.

Appendix A: Multiple Intelligences

You may want to use this book to address Gardner's (1993) *multiple intelligences*, a theory that considers the diversity and plurality of talents and invites dialogue about creative "ways of knowing." Gardner's intelligences include:

- *Linguistic intelligence:* using language strategies and words to maximize experience.
- *Logical-mathematical intelligence:* drawing on reasonable arguments and numerical symbols.
- *Music intelligence:* perceiving rhythm and time with a melodic mind.
- *Spatial intelligence:* thinking in pictures and images with the mind's eye.
- *Kinesthetic intelligence:* using the body and physical self.
- *Interpersonal intelligence:* noticing others and connecting with the social world; understanding others' temperament, meanings, and perspectives.
- *Intrapersonal intelligence:* Developing self-awareness and recognizing the range of emotions, habits, and actions that guide one's behavior.

These intelligences represent alternative routes and communicative channels for displaying competence and expressing self and the world. Using Gardner's seven intelligences, it is easy to see how we might slot the multiple literacy tasks and inquiry strategies of this book into Gardner's framework. A few examples are listed in Table A-1.

TABLE A-1   Multiple Intelligences

Strategy or Literacy Form	Linguistic	Logical	Spatial	Kinesthetic	Music	Interpersonal	Intrapersonal
Creative visualization	×		×	×			
Sensory impressions			×	×	×		
Figurative language	×						×
Questioning	×	×				×	×
Writing a "rap"	×			×	×		×
Dancing a story			×	×	×	×	
Role-playing	×			×		×	×
Creating special effects			×	×	×		

◆ *Work Cited*

Gardner, H. (1993). *Frames of mind: The theory of multiple intelligences,* 10th anniv. ed. New York: Basic Books.

Appendix B: National Standards for Literacy and the Arts

You may want to use this book as a way to address the NCTE/IRA standards, particularly the newest added components: viewing and representing. Multiple literacies offer teachers many different ways to represent ideas and capitalize on visual learning. As you review these standards and those from the National Standards of "Arts" Education listed here, you will see how all of the expressive arts are part of the communicative repertoire students can acquire.

English/Language Arts

- Students read and study a wide range of texts, fiction and nonfiction, that build their understanding of the culture and history of the United States
- Students learn and apply a wide range of strategies for comprehending, interpreting, and evaluating texts, including drawing on their prior experience and knowledge, and on other texts
- Students learn to approach writing tasks systematically and to use elements of the writing process appropriately, adapting a variety of approaches
- Students learn to apply knowledge of text structure, rhetorical devices, figurative, and descriptive language, grammar, spelling, and punctuation when they create, critique, and discuss fictional and nonfictional texts
- Students learn to use a variety of technological resources to gather and synthesize information and to create and communicate new knowledge
- Students learn how to use language to define, investigate, and represent questions, issues, and problems, as well as how to find and use resources to advance their investigations
- Students use language independently for learning and for enjoyment
- Students develop an understanding of and respect for diversity in language use, patterns, and dialects across cultures, ethnic groups, geographic regions, and social contexts
- Students whose first language is other than English develop fluency and competency in the English language arts by using their first language as a foundation

◆ Students learn to participate as knowledgeable, reflective, constructive, and critical members of a variety of literacy communities

Visual Arts

◆ Understanding and applying media, techniques, and processes
◆ Using knowledge of structures and functions
◆ Choosing and evaluating a range of subject matter, symbols, and ideas
◆ Understanding the visual arts in relation to history and cultures
◆ Reflecting upon and assessing the characteristics and merits of their work and the work of others
◆ Making connections between visual arts and other disciplines

Music

◆ Singing, alone and with others, a varied repertoire of music
◆ Performing on instruments, alone and with others, a varied repertoire of music
◆ Improvising melodies, variations, and accompaniments
◆ Composing and arranging music within specified guidelines
◆ Reading and notating music
◆ Listening to, analyzing, and describing music
◆ Evaluating music and music performances
◆ Understanding relationships between music, the other arts, and disciplines outside the arts
◆ Understanding music in relation to history and culture

Dance

◆ Identifying and demonstrating movement elements and skills in performing dance
◆ Understanding choreographic principles, processes, and structures
◆ Understanding dance as a way to create and communicate meaning
◆ Applying and demonstrating critical and creative thinking skills in dance
◆ Demonstrating and understanding dance in various cultures and historical periods
◆ Making connections between dance and healthful living
◆ Making connections between dance and other disciplines

Theater (Including TV, Film, and Electronic Media)

◆ Script writing by the creation of improvisations and scripted scenes based on personal experience and heritage, imagination, literature, and history

- Acting by developing basic acting skills to portray characters who interact in improvised and scripted scenes
- Designing by developing environments for improvised and scripted scenes
- Directing by organizing rehearsals for improvised and scripted scenes
- Researching by using cultural and historical information to support improvised and scripted scenes
- Comparing and incorporating art forms by analyzing methods of presentation and audience response for theater, dramatic media (such as film, television, and electronic media), and other art forms
- Analyzing, evaluating, and constructing meanings from improvised and scripted scenes and from theater, film, television, and electronic media productions
- Understanding context by analyzing the role of theater, film, television, and electronic media in the community and in other cultures

Index